NEW MERMAIDS

General editors
William C. Carroll, Boston University
Brian Gibbons, University of Münster
Tiffany Stern, University College, University of Oxford

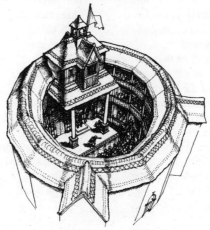

Reconstruction of an Elizabethan Theatre
by C. Walter Hodges

NEW MERMAIDS

The Alchemist
All for Love
Arden of Faversham
Arms and the Man
Bartholomew Fair
The Beaux' Stratagem
Bussy D'Ambois
The Changeling
A Chaste Maid in Cheapside
The Country Wife
The Critic
The Double-Dealer
Dr Faustus
The Duchesss of Malfi
The Dutch Courtesan
Eastward Ho!
Edward the Second
Elizabethan and Jacobean Tragedies
Epicoene or The Silent Woman
Every Man In His Humour
Five Restoration Comedies
An Ideal Husband
The Importance of Being Earnest
The Jew of Malta
The Knight of the Burning Pestle
Lady Windermere's Fan
London Assurance
Love for Love
Major Barbara
The Malcontent
The Man of Mode
Marriage A-la-Mode

Mrs Warren's Profession
A New Way to Pay Old Debts
The Old Wife's Tale
The Plain Dealer
The Playboy of the Western World
The Provoked Wife
Pygmalion
The Recruiting Officer
The Relapse
The Revenger's Tragedy
The Rivals
The Roaring Girl
The Rover
Saint Joan
The School for Scandal
She Stoops to Conquer
The Shoemaker's Holiday
The Spanish Tragedy
Tamburlaine
Three Late Medieval Morality Plays
    Mankind
    Everyman
    Mundus et Infans
'Tis Pity She's a Whore
Volpone
The Way of the World
The White Devil
The Witch
The Witch of Edmonton
A Woman Killed with Kindness
A Woman of No Importance
Women Beware Women

NEW MERMAIDS

JOHN WEBSTER

THE
WHITE DEVIL

Edited by Christina Luckyj

Professor of English, Dalhousie University

METHUEN DRAMA • LONDON

New Mermaids

1 3 5 7 9 10 8 6 4 2

Third edition with revised introduction published 2008

A & C Black Publishers Limited
38 Soho Square
London W1D 3HB
www.acblack.com

ISBN 978–0–7136–8137–6

© 2008 A & C Black Publishers Limited

First New Mermaid edition 1966
© 1966, 1978 Ernest Benn Limited

Second edition 1996
© 1996 A & C Black Publishers Limited

A CIP catalogue record for this book is available
from the British Library

This book is produced using paper made from
wood grown in managed, sustainable forests. It is natural,
renewable and recyclable. The logging and manufacturing
processes conform to the environmental regulations
of the country of origin.

Typeset by RefineCatch Ltd, Bungay, Suffolk

Printed in the UK by CPI Cox & Wyman, Reading, RG1 8EX

CONTENTS

ACKNOWLEDGEMENTS vi

ABBREVIATIONS viii

INTRODUCTION. ix

The Author. ix

Sources xi

The Play xiv

Tragic mode xiv

Flamineo xvi

Vittoria. xvii

Vittoria's arraignment xviii

Isabella and Zanche. xxii

The White Devil on the modern Stage xxiv

The White Devil at the Red Bull xxx

Note on the Text xxxiii

FURTHER READING. xxxv

THE WHITE DEVIL 1

Dramatis Personae 3

To the Reader 5

Text 7

ACKNOWLEDGEMENTS

I am deeply indebted to previous editors of *The White Devil*, especially to Elizabeth Brennan and John Russell Brown, who provided me with sound text and commentary to revise, augment and above all rely on. I am also extremely grateful to Anthony Hammond, D. C. Gunby and David Carnegie for generously allowing me to read their new Cambridge edition of Webster in proof. The present edition is deeply enriched by their painstaking scholarship. At New Mermaids, my immediate debts are to Professor Brian Gibbons for his encouragement and good sense, Anne Watts for her patience and efficiency, and Margaret Parker for her excellent copy-editing of this text. With the aid of a Research and Development Fund grant from my own university, I was able to employ three graduate research assistants: Tanya Caldwell, Dawn Henwood and Derrick Higginbotham, each of whom contributed something invaluable to the commentary. My colleagues Ronald Huebert and John Baxter supported my work. It is impossible to imagine my love of Webster without thinking of those who instilled and nurtured it: Alexander Leggatt and Sheldon Zitner. My deepest thanks go to my husband, Keith Lawson, who uncomplainingly tended babies and read drafts, sometimes at the same time. All errors are, of course, my own.

FOR KEITH

ABBREVIATIONS

Boklund   Gunnar Boklund, *The Sources of 'The White Devil'* (Cambridge, Mass.: Harvard University Press, 1957)

Brown   John Russell Brown, ed., *The White Devil* (The Revels Plays, London: Methuen, 1960)

Dent   R. W. Dent, *John Webster's Borrowing* (Berkeley and Los Angeles: University of California Press, 1960)

Lucas   F. L. Lucas, ed., *The Complete Works of John Webster* I (London: Chatto and Windus, 1927)

NCW   (The New Cambridge Webster) D. C. Gunby, David Carnegie and Anthony Hammond, eds., *The Works of John Webster* I (Cambridge: Cambridge University Press, 1995)

OED   J. A. Simpson and E. S. C. Weiner, general eds., *The Oxford English Dictionary*, 2nd ed. (Oxford: Clarendon, 1989)

Pettie   George Pettie, trans., *The Civile Conversation of M. Steeven Guazzo* (1581; London: Constable and New York: Alfred A. Knopf, 1925)

Shakespeare   *The Riverside Shakespeare*, ed. G. Blakemore Evans (Boston: Houghton Mifflin, 1974)

s.d.   stage direction

s.p.   speech prefix

Tilley   Morris Palmer Tilley, *A Dictionary of the Proverbs in England in the Sixteenth and Seventeenth Centuries* (Ann Arbor: University of Michigan Press, 1950)

Quotations are taken from the following New Mermaid texts: *A Chaste Maid in Cheapside*, ed. Alan Brissenden (1968); *Dr Faustus*, ed. Roma Gill (1989); *The Revenger's Tragedy*, ed. Brian Gibbons (1990); *The Duchess of Malfi*, ed. Elizabeth M. Brennan (1993).

INTRODUCTION

The Author

Unlike *The White Devil*'s bitter, impecunious Flamineo, John Webster came from the prosperous middle class. Born in 1578 or 1579 (about fifteen years after Shakespeare) to a wealthy coachmaker whose business – the making, hiring and selling of an increasingly fashionable mode of transport – elevated him to the 'status of a Renaissance Henry Ford or Walter Chrysler',[1] Webster grew up in the noisy, smelly, densely populated parish of St Sepulchre, near Smithfield, the hub of London's thriving manufacturing trade. Since his father supplied everything from carts for transporting whores and condemned criminals to vehicles for civic pageants and lavish coaches for the nobility, the young Webster might well have rubbed elbows with a wide spectrum of London society, including theatre professionals. As his father was a freeman of the Merchant Taylors' Company, Webster probably attended the famous Merchant Taylors' School (which boasted Thomas Kyd and Edmund Spenser among its former pupils). That school's rigorous and broad curriculum would have given him a foundation in the classics and an esteem for the vernacular championed by its first headmaster, Richard Mulcaster. Later, possibly after a brief stint as an actor,[2] Webster probably passed on to the New Inn and then to the Middle Temple, one of the Inns of Court, where his legal education became not only the inspiration for his many courtroom scenes but also a means of acquiring all the rhetorical skills, tastes and connections that were necessary to get ahead in Jacobean London.

Yet even if he did not share Flamineo's ruined fortunes, Webster may have adopted a similarly critical perspective of the authority of the king and court. Luke Wilson observes: 'As a London citizen with an Inns of Court education and family ties to the London business community, Webster lived in a milieu closely associated with both puritan and common law interests.' Such interests were increasingly at odds with James's autocratic style of monarchy as well as his ecclesiastical courts, perceived by Puritans as 'corrupt, reminiscent of Catholicism, and lacking

---

1   Charles R. Forker, *The Skull Beneath the Skin: The Achievement of John Webster* (Southern Illinois University Press, 1986), p. 4. I am indebted to Forker's book for its exhaustive study of Webster's life and work.

2   Forker discusses the 'extremely tenuous' evidence for Webster's involvement with Robert Browne's troupe of English actors in Germany in 1596 (*Skull*, p. 5).

jurisdictional authority'.[3] Indeed, Webster's allegiances may be reflected in his authorship of A Monumental Column, an elegy for the young Prince Henry (probably mirrored in Giovanni), who before his untimely death in 1612 was a focus 'for discontented men inclined towards a militantly Protestant and expansionist foreign policy'[4]. Webster's contributions to the second edition of Overbury's Characters (1614) certainly place him in the company of other 'literati members of the Protestant faction at court under the patronage of William Herbert, Earl of Pembroke'[5] – a faction highly critical of King James's pro-Spanish policies. And if The White Devil alludes at V.iv.36–40 to James's recent imprisonment of his cousin Arbella Stuart for marrying without his permission, an act 'understood by more than just playwrights, clerics and political theorists as an act of tyranny'[6], Webster's later portrait of the Duchess of Malfi could be seen as an even harsher indictment of royal male tyranny.[7] Such implicit critiques of authority – not uncommon during James's reign – were matched by Webster's ambitious career in the public theatre. After an apprenticeship as one of Philip Henslowe's journeyman dramatists, collaborating with others such as Thomas Dekker, Anthony Munday, Thomas Middleton, Henry Chettle, Thomas Heywood and Michael Drayton on the plays Caesar's Fall, Christmas Comes but Once a Year (both lost), and Lady Jane (which survives only in a condensed reconstruction as The Famous History of Sir Thomas Wyatt, 1607), Webster went on in 1604 to write an Induction and other additions for The Malcontent, by John Marston, fellow Middle Templar and 'a prominent member of the intellectual avant-garde',[8] for performance by the King's Men at the Globe. In 1604 and 1605 Webster collaborated with Dekker again on two racy citizen comedies, Westward Ho! and Northward Ho!, for the fashionable, private children's company, Paul's Boys. After these theatrical successes, Webster seems to have stopped writing for a time – whether because of the frequent

3   Luke Wilson, 'The White Devil and the Law,' in Early Modern English Drama, ed. Garrett A. Sullivan Jr., Patrick Cheney and Andrew Hadfield (Oxford: Oxford University Press, 2006), p. 231.

4   Alastair Bellany, The Politics of Court Scandal in Early Modern England: News Culture and the Overbury Affair (Cambridge: Cambridge University Press, 2002), p. 37.

5   Donald Beecher, ed., Characters (Ottawa: Dovehouse, 2003), p. 57.

6   Belinda Roberts Peters, Marriage in Seventeenth-Century English Political Thought (Houndmills: Palgrave Macmillan, 2004), p. 160.

7   Sara Jayne Steen uses contemporary attitudes to the Arbella Stuart affair to illuminate Webster's representation of the Duchess of Malfi, though she stops short of suggesting that the former directly influenced the latter. See 'The Crime of Marriage: Arbella Stuart and The Duchess of Malfi,' in Sixteenth-Century Journal 22.1 (1991): 61–76.

8   Forker, Skull, p. 75.

closure of the theatres due to plague, or his own hasty marriage in 1605/6 to Sara Peniall, who at the age of sixteen was seven months pregnant with the first of their several children. Not until 1612 did *The White Devil* appear, first performed at the Red Bull, where it failed to please. In the Preface to the published text, Webster strikes a pose of swaggering self-assurance: he not only scorns the 'ignorant asses' who failed to give his play its due, he also claims kinship with the learned dramatists Chapman and Johnson. During the year 1612, Webster wrote both *The Duchess of Malfi* for the King's Men and *A Monumental Column*, an elegy for the death of Prince Henry dedicated to the king's favourite, Sir Robert Carr. We can imagine that he felt he was transcending his origins as 'the Play-wright, Cart-wright'[9] of Cow Lane, West Smithfield. In fact, his confidence was unwarranted. Although he continued to write (thirty-two new characters for the sixth edition of Sir Thomas Overbury's *Characters* in 1615; *Guise*, a lost play, the date of which is unknown; *The Devil's Law-Case*, a tragicomedy, in 1617) and to collaborate (with Dekker, William Rowley and John Ford on *The Late Murder of the Son upon the Mother, or Keep the Widow Waking*, 1624, now lost; perhaps with Middleton on *Anything for a Quiet Life*, 1620/1, and *The Fair Maid of the Inn*, 1626; with Rowley and perhaps Heywood on *A Cure for a Cuckold*, 1624/5, and *Appius and Virginia*, 1627?), Webster never equalled the tragic mastery of his first two independent plays. He did, however, serve as official poet to the Merchant Taylors' Company in 1624, when he was commissioned to design the festivities for the investiture of Sir John Gore, a Merchant Taylor, as Lord Mayor of London; his *Monuments of Honour* was the most lavish and expensive pageant of the age. He probably died in the 1630s.

Sources

Webster had a restless and voracious intelligence: even more than his contemporaries, he mined the writings of other men for words, phrases and incidents which he then reshaped into his own art. He read widely in Renaissance literature (usually in English translation); *The White Devil* contains verbal borrowings from Montaigne (in Florio's translation), William Alexander's *The Alexandrean Tragedy* (1607), Stefano Guazzo's *Civil Conversation* (trans. George Pettie 1581), Nicolas de Montreux's *Honour's Academy* (trans. R. Tofte 1610), Richard Stanyhurst's *Description of Ireland* in Holinshed's *Chronicles* and Antonio de Guevara's *Dial of*

---

9 The satirical description of Webster is Henry Fitzgeffrey's from *Notes from Blackfriars, Satyres and Satyricall Epigrams* (1617), and is quoted in full in ibid., pp. 58–9.

Princes (trans. Thomas North 1557), to mention only a few. For incidents such as Brachiano's macabre death scene (V.iii.128–43), he was indebted to Erasmus' colloquy *Funus*; for the papal election in IV.iii, to H. Bignon's *A Treatise of the Election of Popes* (trans. 1605); for Cornelia's distraction after Marcello's death (V.ii.35–40; V.iv.71ff.), to Shakespeare's *King Lear* and *Hamlet*. Though a modern audience may recognize only the latter debt, originally a good deal of the play's intellectual pleasure may have depended on the audience's appreciation of Webster's ingenious adaptation of existing materials. His Preface indicates his desire to be read by the light of his fellow dramatists, and his play is marked by the sententiousness of Chapman, the biting satire of Marston, the shocking reversals of Beaumont and Fletcher, the citizen comedy of Dekker and the dark irony of Middleton, not to mention the moral intensity of Shakespeare. Thus to discover precise sources for Webster's drama is impossible, and perhaps undesirable, since its uniqueness lies in its fusion of disparate materials into a brilliant, eclectic whole.

It is, however, possible to locate sources for the story on which Webster bases *The White Devil*. Gunnar Boklund, in an exhaustive study of the play's sources,[10] has counted 109 manuscript versions and 6 published accounts of the notorious scandal, and identified two or three texts as the probable origins of Webster's play: first, *A Letter Lately Written from Rome, by an Italian Gentleman* (trans. Florio 1585); second, an Italian source (now lost) for a German newsletter written for the Fugger banking house (extant in manuscript); and third, another source more difficult to identify (perhaps Cesare Campana's *Delle Historie del Mondo*, 1596, and the early sixteenth-century Italian pamphlet *Il miserabil e compassionevol caso*). A conflation of these sources can give us some idea of what Webster probably believed of the affair (which is often quite distinct from historical fact).[11]

The story as Webster probably knew it began in 1580, when Paolo Giordano, Duke of Bracciano, husband (of twenty-two years) to Isabella de' Medici and father to Giovanni, met Vittoria Accoramboni, a beautiful gentlewoman married to a nephew of Cardinal Montalto. He fell in love with her, but she virtuously refused him. With the aid of her brother

---

10 *The Sources of 'The White Devil'* (Harvard University Press, 1957).

11 Historically, Isabella was strangled by her husband for carrying on an adulterous affair before he even set eyes on Vittoria. Later, after Bracciano had Vittoria's husband (Francesco Peretti) murdered, he twice married her secretly and subsequently left her at the Pope's command, the second time prompting her to attempt suicide. Bracciano died of natural causes in 1585. Lodovico Orsino took no personal part in the murders of Vittoria and her brother. Webster was probably ignorant of these facts.

Marcello, he then had her husband killed (at Monte Cavallo in Rome), but she again refused him. He then killed his own wife, and finally Vittoria submitted to him. His brother-in-law, Cardinal Medici, along with the Orsinis, entreated the Pope not to allow their kinsman to marry someone of so base a fortune. Cardinal Montalto desired to avenge his innocent nephew. Though Vittoria was apprehended on her way to Paolo Giordano's house in the country and confined in a nunnery, and later in Castel Sant'Angelo, Paolo Giordano set her free and married her. When Montalto was elected Pope Sixtus V, he advised Paolo Giordano to leave Rome. The couple went to Padua, where they kept a magnificent court. Two months later Paolo Giordano died, and there was suspicion of poison. His will left his young widow a large property. She was urged to put aside the will, but she refused. Fifty armed men then stormed her house at Padua and shot her brother Flaminio. A kinsman to her husband, Lodovico Orsini (who by age 34 had killed forty men, for which he had been forced to leave Rome), stabbed Vittoria at prayer. After this murder, his house was bombarded by cannon until he surrendered, dagger in hand. Once he had confessed that he had committed the deed at the command of great princes, he spoke only once more: 'sed manet altamente repostum' ('it shall be treasured up in the depths of my mind': cf. II.i.262). Afterwards he was privately strangled, while his accomplices were first riven asunder with red-hot tongs, then killed with a hammer and finally quartered.

This story, while it clearly contained enough lust and murder to fire Webster's imagination, was for dramatic purposes loose and sketchy. The changes Webster makes are designed to give his play dramatic momentum and structural unity: he develops characters like Lodovico and Francisco into full-scale, strongly motivated avengers present from the play's beginning. This also allows him to create patterns of parallel and contrast among different characters: Francisco is implicitly compared both with Brachiano, another murderous great man,[12] and with Flamineo, another Machiavellian schemer and social commentator, as the latter also stands in clear relation to Lodovico, his double (especially clear in III.iii). Analogies in turn suggest distinctions: while all are villains, they are driven by different impulses. Unlike the sources, where action

---

12 Francisco himself, when disguised as Mulinassar, draws attention to the analogy between himself and Brachiano: 'What difference is between the Duke and I?' he muses. 'No more than between two bricks; all made of one clay' (V.i.103–4). And, as Brachiano dominates the play's first half, stage-managing the action with the aid of Flamineo, so Francisco dominates the second half, with Flamineo as his constant companion.

originates simply in Paolo Giordano's vicious murders, in the play the interventions of family members (Cornelia, Francisco, Monticelso) actually seem to initiate events. Webster also chooses to problematize and complicate the simple story he inherits. Brachiano mistreats his saintly wife (characterless in Webster's source), then becomes merely a bystander at her murder. Thus Webster mitigates, even as he suggests, his villainy. Similarly, if the sources suggest Vittoria to be a woman of conventional, if flexible, virtue, the play daringly implicates her in adultery and murder while at the same time vindicating her – because she is a frustrated wife to a foolish, impotent husband, then an outraged victim of masculine hypocrisy in two trial scenes (III.ii and IV.ii) that are wholly Webster's invention. Finally, Webster conflates the two brothers from the sources, the evil Marcello and the innocent Flaminio, to create *The White Devil*'s Flamineo, whose incessant, sceptical commentary, brutal fratricide and dawning self-awareness are all Webster's inventions. Characters like Marcello, Cornelia and Giovanni (expanded from a mere hint in the sources to mete out final justice) are added to the play as exponents of an often tyrannical moral code.

The Play

Tragic mode

Webster's play does not fit easily into traditional tragic modes. At first glance, *The White Devil* appears to be a revenge tragedy, which pits justified revengers against their villainous enemies. These revengers, however, are deeply implicated in the corrupt world around them. Lodovico has already committed 'certain murders' (I.i.31) he considers 'flea-bitings' (I.i.32), and Monticelso vows to 'stake a brother's life' (II.i.388) to gain revenge – even before the murders of Camillo and Isabella are committed. After the murder of Isabella is discovered, Francisco summons the conventional props of the revenger only to dismiss them. Face to face with Isabella's ghost, he cries:

> Remove this object,
> Out of my brain with't: what have I to do
> With tombs, or death-beds, funerals, or tears,
> That have to meditate upon revenge?

(IV.i.111–14)

In fact, Francisco's revenge is fuelled by his 'wit' (IV.i.130); he parodies Brachiano by writing Vittoria a love letter and later arranges disguises which allow for elaborate verbal jokes (e.g. V.iii.38–9). As a revenger, he is close to the witty detachment of Vindice in *The Revenger's Tragedy* (1607). 'My tragedy must have some idle mirth in't' (IV.i.118), he declares. But, unlike Vindice, Francisco is not the hero of this play; neither his satiric perspective nor his rough justice can delimit the real heroes, who inhabit the world of *de casibus* rather than revenge tragedy.

De casibus tragedy in its simplest form is indebted to 'the medieval idea that tragedy is a fall from greatness resulting from the instability of all sublunary affairs'.[13] At the moment of death (which defines all Webster's characters), Brachiano attributes his fall, not to the 'unction . . . sent from the great Duke of Florence' (V.iii.28), but to his exalted position:

> O thou soft natural death, that art joint-twin
> To sweetest slumber: no rough-bearded comet
> Stares on thy mild departure: the dull owl
> Beats not against thy casement: the hoarse wolf
> Scents not thy carrion. Pity winds thy corse,
> Whilst horror waits on princes.
>
> (V.iii.30–5)

As Brachiano has reached the pinnacle of earthly success, with his marriage to Vittoria, he is flung down by Fortune, that 'right whore' (I.i.4). He can meditate on the instability of earthly power:

> I that have given life to offending slaves
> And wretched murderers, have I not power
> To lengthen mine own a twelvemonth?
>
> (V.iii.24–6)

Lee Bliss remarks: 'Far as his plays seem from the "old-fashioned" heroic tradition explored by Chapman and Shakespeare, Webster does in fact play out that dying mode'.[14] That 'dying mode' is, however, reshaped and revitalized by Webster's insistently social critique – a critique that is expressed largely through his other tragic characters, Flamineo and Vittoria.

---

13 Madeleine Doran, *Endeavors of Art: A Study of Form in Elizabethan Drama* (University of Wisconsin Press, 1954), p. 118.

14 Lee Bliss, *The World's Perspective: John Webster and the Jacobean Drama* (Harvester, 1983), p. 59.

Flamineo

Flamineo, a scurrilous pander and cynical malcontent, at first seems more suited to the role of comic manipulator than that of tragic hero. During the first four acts of *The White Devil*, his actions, including his murder of Camillo (in II.ii) are defined by his position as Brachiano's 'secretary'; in Act V, however, Flamineo begins to emerge as a tragic figure who can say 'at myself I will begin and end' (V.vi.254). The first sign of his new autonomy is his murder of his brother, Marcello, in an episode frequently condemned as superfluous by critics.[15] An outraged response to his family's moralistic attacks on his mistress, Zanche, Flamineo's fratricide finally stirs his 'compassion' (V.iv.109) for others and illuminates 'the maze of conscience' (V.iv.115) within himself. This glimpse of a complex interior life is more powerful for its understatement, and is followed by the appearance of Brachiano's ghost with its *memento mori* (V.iv.128). Flamineo's defiant cry 'I do dare my fate / To do its worst' (V.iv.136–7) links him with Shakespeare's tragic heroes: so Romeo, learning of the death of Juliet, cries 'Then I defy you, stars!' (V.i.24); so Hamlet, sensing his own death, says 'we defy augury' (V.ii.219). Like them, and like Brachiano, Flamineo conceives of himself as locked in a struggle, not with unworthy human opponents, but with Fate.

With Flamineo, however, Webster fuses the old-fashioned *de casibus* idea of tragedy (as human will confronting implacable destiny) with a more modern, Jacobean notion of human will confronting a corrupt society (a notion inherited from revenge tragedy). The two ideas are interlinked from the beginning of the play: Lodovico rails against both Fortune, that 'right whore' (I.i.4), and Fortune's worldly representatives, his 'great enemies' (I.i.7). Similarly, describing his act of murder as his 'misfortune' (V.ii.45), Flamineo recalls those Shakespearean heroes who feel themselves instruments of Fate even as they commit violent deeds: so Romeo, after killing Tybalt, cries, 'O, I am fortune's fool!' (III.i.136). Yet Flamineo's sense of suffering recalls Vindice's rather than Romeo's because it is rooted in a particular *economic* condition. As Flamineo cries to his mother in Act I:

---

15 See, for example, Harold Jenkins ('The Tragedy of Revenge in Shakespeare and Webster', *Shakespeare Survey* 14 (1961)), who deplores Webster's 'fatal tendency to complication' in *The White Devil* and contrasts it with *The Duchess of Malfi*, in which 'there is now no ghost, no mad wailing mother, no good brother to be killed by a bad' (p. 53). See also Larry S. Champion ('Webster's *The White Devil* and the Jacobean Tragic Perspective', *Texas Studies in Literature and Language* 16 (1974)), who contends that 'Marcello's murder and Cornelia's madness are never effectively integrated into the major action' (p. 457).

My father proved himself a gentleman,
Sold all's land, and like a fortunate fellow
Died ere the money was spent. You brought me up,
At Padua I confess, where I protest,
For want of means (the university judge me)
I have been fain to heel my tutor's stockings
At least seven years.

(I.ii.299–305)

In Renaissance Europe, downward social mobility and court sycophancy for well-born and educated young men like Flamineo bred dangerous discontent. For Webster Flamineo's struggle for 'preferment' is not vulgar social climbing but a desperate bid for a place in an increasingly corrupt and mobile society. 'We think caged birds sing, when indeed they cry' (V.iv.117), observes Flamineo of himself; the cage which he inhabits is at once the court and his own tortured mind. His final speech contains an indictment of 'great men' like Brachiano:

Let all that belong to great men remember th'old wives' tradition, to be like the lions i'th'Tower on Candlemas day, to mourn if the sun shine for fear of the pitiful remainder of winter to come.

(V.vi.261–4)

The lesson, characteristically (for Webster) couched in animal analogies, is one of bitter resignation – resignation not to cruel destiny, but to corrupt and powerful men.

Vittoria

The subtitle of the 1612 quarto of *The White Devil* is *The Tragedy of Paulo Giordano Ursini, Duke of Brachiano, with the Life and Death of Vittoria Corombona the famous Venetian Curtizan*; the ornamental title at the opening of Act I is *The Tragedy of Paulo Giordano Ursini Duke of Brachiano, and Vittoria Corombona*. While both titles may have been the work of the printer, their differing perspectives on Vittoria – as ancillary, or as central to the play's tragic vision – may reveal contemporary confusion about her role. Brachiano is the aristocratic, masculine hero of a familiar form of tragedy, and Flamineo straddles old and new, but Vittoria stands in uneasy relation to the traditional mode. With Brachiano, Webster is conservative, with Flamineo he is cautiously innovative; with Vittoria, however, Webster stands on the edge of a radical experiment. In *The White Devil*, as in Shakespeare's *Antony and Cleopatra*

(1606/7), the male hero dies first, and the female character survives to enact the play's tragic climax. Unlike Cleopatra, however, who dies crying 'O Antony!' (V.ii.312), Vittoria mentions Brachiano only when she is feigning martyrdom (V.vi.81–4) and implicitly accuses him with her last breath:

> O happy they that never saw the court,
> 'Nor ever knew great man but by report'.
>
> (V.vi.257–8)

Brachiano is the hero of his own tragedy, but he appears to be the villain in Vittoria's. He seduces her only to abandon her partway through her trial,[16] and later turns on her in private. If Flamineo is disadvantaged because of his class, Vittoria is doubly oppressed – both as a member of the fallen gentry and as a woman.

The White Devil was written at a time when controversy about the nature of woman had reached fever pitch. While attacks on women and defences of their virtue had been popular since antiquity, they proliferated during the Renaissance, when 'the English middle class had a distinct taste for this fare'.[17] Like many of his contemporaries (such as Tourneur), Webster writes some of the terms of the debate into his play: Vittoria is both a god and a wolf (IV.ii.87–8) to Brachiano. Unlike most contemporary dramatists and pamphleteers, however, Webster does not simply endorse misogyny, but probes its social and economic causes.

Vittoria's arraignment

Misogyny is a major force in *The White Devil*. From Lodovico's opening speech, in which he deflects blame from his 'great enemies' (I.i.7) onto a feminine Fortune, that 'right whore' (I.i.4), and a devouring she-wolf (I.i.8–9), to Flamineo's caution – 'Trust a woman? Never, never' (V.vi.157) – the men in the play constantly devalue woman as inherently

---

16 In a critical review of the 1991 National Theatre *White Devil*, Paul Taylor points out that 'Prowse does not make enough of her desertion by her adulterous paramour (played by Quilley as a shallow, childish sensualist). Because the vulnerability of her position here is underemphasised, her behaviour risks coming across as simple brazenness' (*Independent*, 20 June 1991).

17 Katherine Usher Henderson and Barbara F. McManus, eds., *Half Humankind: Contexts and Texts of the Controversy about Women in England, 1540–1640* (University of Illinois Press, 1985), p. 3. This book discusses the history and range of the controversy, and provides significant excerpts. For a more extended discussion, see Linda Woodbridge, *Women and the English Renaissance: Literature and the Nature of Womankind, 1540–1620* (University of Illinois Press, 1984).

evil and destructive to men. The antifeminist rhetoric clearly reaches its peak during the arraignment of Vittoria, when Monticelso invokes Eve as the cause of man's fall from grace, and suggests that 'Were there a second paradise to loose/This devil would betray it' (III.ii.70–1). The prosecutors are not without justification, moreover: Vittoria is implicated, however obliquely, in the murders of Camillo and Isabella when she recounts a dream in which – at least according to Flamineo – she instructs Brachiano to 'make away his Duchess and her husband' (I.ii.240). The arraignment has been interpreted in different ways: on the one hand celebrated as 'one of the great moments of the English stage',[18] on the other condemned by some critics as 'an artistic insincerity – a lie in the poet's heart',[19] an example of Webster's 'emphasis . . . on vivid sympathetic insights at the expense of ethical coherence',[20] or – more recently – as an illustration of the unstable and discontinuous position of women in early modern culture.[21]

The arraignment is carefully positioned in a series of more and less formal trial scenes (I.i, II.i, III.ii, IV.ii, V.vi) which illuminate it by parallel and contrast. Brachiano's informal trial is juxtaposed with Vittoria's much more formal one in III.ii to reveal not only a glaring double standard but also a significant relation between gender and genre. Whereas Francisco and Monticelso courteously invite Brachiano to sit (II.i.20; III.ii.4), they order Vittoria to 'stand to the table' (III.ii.8). And although we have seen Brachiano both arrange and oversee the murders of Camillo and Isabella (II.i.308–15; II.ii), it is Vittoria who is apprehended and tried – for her sexuality rather than for her uncertain role in the murders. Monticelso defines Brachiano's as a classic *de casibus* tragedy, lamenting his fall from 'High gifts of learning' and an 'awful throne' (II.i.30–1) to an 'insatiate bed' (II.i.32); he is an eagle 'that should gaze upon the sun' (II.i.49). By contrast, Vittoria can only 'fall' from appearance to reality: 'You see my lords what goodly fruit she seems', cries Monticelso. 'I will but touch her and you straight shall see/She'll fall to

---

18 Jack Landau, 'Elizabethan Art in a Mickey Spillane Setting', *Theatre Arts* 39 (1955); reprinted in R. V. Holdsworth, ed., *Webster: 'The White Devil' and 'The Duchess of Malfi': A Casebook* (Macmillan, 1975), p. 234.

19 Ian Jack, 'The Case of John Webster', *Scrutiny* 16 (1949); reprinted in *John Webster: A Critical Anthology*, ed. G. K. and S. K. Hunter (Penguin, 1969), p. 162.

20 Doran, *Endeavors of Art*, p. 355.

21 Catherine Belsey asserts that 'only Vittoria seems to have no place, intelligible to the audience as single and continuous, from which to speak, to be recognized' and perceives this as an illustration of the fact that 'in the family as in the state women had no single, unified, fixed position from which to speak' (*The Subject of Tragedy: Identity and Difference in Renaissance Drama* (Methuen, 1985), pp. 163, 160).

soot and ashes' (III.ii.63, 66–7). If Brachiano may 'to wilful shipwreck loose good fame' (II.i.41), Vittoria *is* a shipwreck 'in calmest weather' (III.ii.83). But Webster undermines the misogynist stereotypes by hinting at their social and economic base. Flamineo himself conflates woman's looseness with contemporary social unrest:

> These politic enclosures for paltry mutton makes more rebellion in the flesh than all the provocative electuaries doctors have uttered since last Jubilee.
>
> (I.ii.90–2)

Woman's 'lust', far from being innate, is a frustrated response to being oppressed that is analogous to the social rebellion produced by economic hardship. During the trial, the Cardinal significantly ties Vittoria's poverty to her sexuality when he describes her as 'a hard penny-worth, the ware being so light' (III.ii.242).

Throughout her trial, Vittoria 'personate[s] masculine virtue' (III.ii.136) so well that one is almost tempted to accept her account of the 'frosty answer' (III.ii.202) she gave to Brachiano's importunities. But the audience knows otherwise: Brachiano's initial gesture, spreading a gown on the floor (III.ii.3 s.d.), recalls their earlier embraces upon cushions (I.ii.197 s.d.), and Flamineo's shocked aside (III.ii.265) reminds us of his role as pander. In the next act, we hear Vittoria acknowledge herself as Brachiano's 'whore' (IV.ii.140) and cry bitterly:

> I do wish
> That I could make you full executor
> To all my sins–
>
> (IV.ii.119–21)

Thus Vittoria's 'masculine virtue' in the trial is effective but duplicitous. Most critics assume that this makes Vittoria the 'white devil' of the title, or reveals Webster's moral irresponsibility. It may equally, however, illuminate the impossible position of the female character in tragedy. To become authors of their own choices women must *act* in both senses of the word – take action and play a (male) role (as Vittoria and Isabella both do) – which can make them targets of misogyny.

Far from exposing Vittoria as a hypocrite or avoiding the problem altogether (as some critics suggest), the trial scene of *The White Devil* highlights the ambiguities of performance itself. Unlike the Duchess of Malfi, who accounts the world 'a tedious theatre' in which she plays a part against her will (IV.i.83–4), the women of *The White Devil* embrace theatricality, offering extraordinarily self-conscious performances. When, in the trial scene, Vittoria rejects the lawyer's use of Latin on the grounds that 'amongst this auditory / Which come to hear my cause, the half or more / May be ignorant in't' (III.ii.15–17), her remark is directed not only at the learned ambassadors but also at the Red Bull audience – as is Isabella's assertion that 'this divorce shall be as truly kept / As if in thronged court *a thousand ears* / Had heard it' (II.i.255–7, emphasis added). If they point beyond the staged law-court to the real space of the theatre, the women not only share a privileged relation to the theatre audience but expose all the on-stage characters as implicated in performance; Vittoria remarks, 'It doth not suit a reverend cardinal / To *play* the lawyer thus' (III.ii.60–1, emphasis added). In the Cardinal's view Vittoria is a 'counterfeit' jewel (l. 141) whose adulterous affair 'would be played o'th'stage, / But that vice many times finds such loud friends / That preachers are charmed silent' (ll. 249–51). From his predictable equation of illicit theatre with promiscuous sexuality, the Cardinal moves surprisingly to ally himself *with* the theatre, an instrument used by 'preachers' to expose 'vice.' He may promise to 'paint out' Vittoria's follies in 'more natural red and white' than that upon her cheeks (III.ii.51–3), but his comparison of her deceptive show to a whore's use of cosmetics adopts the same metaphor for his own rhetorical strategies.

For a character routinely accused of brazen theatricality, Vittoria herself is remarkably anti-theatrical. She begins the trial scene by pointedly invoking an 'auditory' (III.ii.15), thus taking the part of playwrights such as Webster who sought 'full and understanding' listeners rather than the gaping spectators of the common stages ('To the Reader' 6–7). By contrast, the Cardinal insistently foregrounds the visual, alternately inviting and rejecting 'ocular proof' of Vittoria's corruption. 'Observe this creature' (III.ii.57), 'look upon this creature' (l. 120), 'See my lords' (ll. 63, 129), he instructs the ambassadors (and the theatre audience). On one hand, the Cardinal continually draws attention to Vittoria's appearance. On the other hand, he insists that her appearance is no guide to her inner reality:

> You see my lords what goodly fruit she seems,
> Yet like those apples travellers report
> To grow where Sodom and Gomorrah stood:
> I will but touch her and you straight shall see
> She'll fall to soot and ashes.

(III.ii.63–7)

This kind of standard anti-feminist fare is reiterated in the Cardinal's description of a whore as 'Sweetmeats which rot the eater: in man's nostril / Poisoned perfumes' (ll. 81–2). The paradox is that what he seeks to prove by *sight* can never be *seen*, and must always therefore be subject to doubt. The final absurdity comes when he both invokes and dismisses his audience's visual sense: 'If the devil / Did ever take good shape behold his picture' (ll. 216–17). If the Cardinal depends both on the stability of outward signs and on their utter deceptiveness, Vittoria consistently emphasizes the latter. Contesting the Cardinal's reading of her heightened colour as the whore's overuse of cosmetics, for example, she corrects him: 'You raise a blood as noble in this cheek / As ever was your mother's' (53–5). 'The shameful blush,' David Bevington reminds us, 'may represent one of two opposite responses: dismay and confusion at an undeserved accusation or admission of guilt.'[22] By drawing attention to this ambiguous visual sign, Vittoria insists that it is as likely to manifest the confused dismay of a noblewoman as the cheap artifice of a whore. Later, the Cardinal draws attention to her sumptuous attire by charging: 'She comes not like a widow: she comes armed / With scorn and impudence. Is this a mourning habit?' (121–2). In reply, Vittoria points out: 'Had I foreknown his death as you suggest, / I would have bespoke my mourning' (123–4) – in her case, mourning attire would signify not grief but guilt.

If Vittoria challenges the intelligibility of performance, she also lays claim to inwardness, to 'thoughts' (l. 230) that cannot be represented. Webster, however, never makes it easy for his audience to sympathize with Vittoria. We are never given access to Vittoria's 'real', inner self, to her motives or feelings, as we are made privy to Brachiano's and Flamineo's. Is her dream intended to instigate murder? Does she love Brachiano or merely exploit him? Is she 'at . . . prayers' (V.vi.1) when the final scene opens and, if so, why? Vittoria is constantly withdrawn by Webster from our knowledge – most obviously at IV.ii.186, when she retires into a silence which may be quiet triumph, wordless contempt or mute devastation. By refusing to provide a full portrait of Vittoria, Webster challenges our conventional moral judgements and focuses attention on oppressive social forces which make her evasions necessary.

Isabella and Zanche

That Webster is interested in women as an exploited group with innate heroic potential is evident from his treatment of other women in the play. Isabella, for example, as Vittoria's rival and victim might be

22 *Action is Eloquence: Shakespeare's Language of Gesture* (Harvard University Press, 1984), p. 96.

expected to show up the latter's villainy; instead, Webster's artful dramatic construction places the two women in parallel relation. Because Webster chooses to suppress knowledge that Isabella has been murdered until after Vittoria's trial, Vittoria's victimization by masculine authority in III.ii is juxtaposed with Isabella's treatment by those who 'wrapped her in a cruel fold of lead' (III.ii.331). Vittoria's ambiguity – she engages in adultery in I.ii, yet hurls defiance at her accusers in III.ii – is mirrored in Isabella's, who is both a 'piteous' martyr (II.i.223) and a 'foolish, mad, / And jealous woman' (263–4). Though Isabella is supposedly playing a part in her rejection of Brachiano (II.i.224), like Vittoria she finds a convincing voice in the male role she adopts. Both women are identified with the dangerous female 'fury' (II.i.244; III.ii.278) in their rage. Isabella's lament could well speak for Vittoria:

> O that I were a man, or that I had power
> To execute my apprehended wishes,
>
> (II.i.242–3)

Vittoria is condemned by her mother, frustrated by her impotent husband, arraigned by hypocritical judges, accused and betrayed by her own lover, and finally murdered. Zanche, Vittoria's black servant, re-enacts her mistress's career in simplified form in the last act: she is put off by Flamineo, attacked by Cornelia and Marcello and finally killed. Vittoria and Zanche, tried together in III.ii, die side by side at the end. Webster finds in Vittoria an expression of the plight of her gender.

The White Devil first hints at the possibility of an alternative female heroism during the arraignment. Vittoria pointedly invokes matrillineage when she asserts her own high birth:

> You raise a blood as noble in this cheek
> As ever was your mother's.
>
> (III.ii.54–5)

When the trial ends, Vittoria identifies herself with the female emblem of blind Justice (III.ii.274) – an affirmative rival to the blind and fickle female Fortune often railed at by the men. The final scene begins with Flamineo giving full vent to his misogyny, as he successfully exposes the women's heroic vows of self-sacrifice (V.vi.80–97) as mere 'feminine arguments' (l. 67) which are abandoned as soon as they can 'tread upon' him (V.vi.116 s.d.). When the real murderers arrive Vittoria strikes the pose of masculine virtue so familiar from the trial scene:

> Yes, I shall welcome death
> As princes do some great ambassadors:
> I'll meet thy weapon halfway.

(V.vi.215–17)

When Lodovico expresses surprise at her lack of fear, however, Vittoria reformulates her heroism:

> O thou art deceived, I am too true a woman:
> Conceit can never kill me.

(V.vi.219–20)

Here Webster stakes everything on the abilities of the boy actor playing Vittoria, for she grounds her defiance, not in masculine heroism, but in female biology: 'conceit' contains a complex pun on 'conception'. Women's capacity to conceive life is extended by Flamineo when he says admiringly to Vittoria, in a reversal of his earlier misogyny:

> I love thee now. If woman do breed man
> She ought to teach him manhood:

(V.vi.238–9)

The White Devil on the modern stage

From a modern perspective, The White Devil may seem a strange and disorienting play composed of disparate elements. Its characters can speak with bold directness, prosy informality or formal sententiousness. Its scenes range from formal and ceremonial (like the papal election in IV.iii) to intense and intimate (like Brachiano's and Vittoria's quarrel in IV.ii); indeed, much of the play's power is derived from abrupt, ironic juxtaposition of private and public moments. Webster also uses many pre-Shakespearean stage conventions – such as the dumb shows of II.ii and the ghosts of IV.i and V.iv – alongside more innovative staging. Again, the mixture is purposeful since Webster often strives for a distancing effect only to engage his audience more fully in the surrounding drama.[23] Such stylistic eclecticism, however, poses problems for modern theatre professionals. As Peter Thomson points out, 'we must expect the "impure" confusion of convention and realism to reach the point of crisis

---

23 The best example of this is at II.ii.49–51, where Brachiano's confident detachment is suddenly undermined when the conjuror warns that they must escape from the 'armed men' of the dumb show, who are coming to Vittoria's house to arrest her.

for anyone who tries to act in his plays'.[24] Moreover, *The White Devil*, though set in sixteenth-century Italy, is peppered with allusions to contemporary England; Webster intended his play to involve his Jacobean audience. To be true to Webster, a modern director must approach the play not as a museum piece but as a drama to engage today's audiences directly. Though no single production of *The White Devil* has been entirely successful in doing so, four major British productions since 1969 have illuminated different aspects of this challenging play.

The curtain opened on the 1969 National Theatre *White Devil* at the Old Vic to reveal a massive wall of giant blocks of crumbling yellow stone, gliding apart to show ledges and alleyways along which brilliantly costumed actors scuttled like so many exotic insects. Designed by the Italian film director Fellini's frequent collaborator Piero Gherardi, this production appeared to adopt Rupert Brooke's description of Webster's drama as 'full of the feverish and ghastly turmoil of a nest of maggots'.[25] Geraldine McEwan as Vittoria first appeared in a towering wig and enormous, sweeping ruff, 'her frail body and naked back enveloped by a cobra-hood, her face evil with the mixed satiety and appetite, leer and snigger, coquetry and indecency, of the consummate whore'.[26] If Gherardi's designs dwarfed the actors and constricted their movement, Frank Dunlop's direction conspired to detach the audience from the play and reduce it to an exhibition of high camp. Vittoria, for example, who cast off her white cloak at the opening of the trial to reveal a red dress beneath, was simply a hypocritical whore in 'a world where selfishness and immediate satisfaction drench out tragedy and suffering'.[27] Although critical response was generally negative, the dumb shows were strikingly effective: Isabella's 'mimed death – the duchess sinking within her stiff, white, lacy draperies, convulsed silently and briefly like an insect trapped inside a muslin net – has a masque-like, formal beauty'.[28] The production, which conceived of Webster's characters as dehumanized creatures moving about in an abstract ballet of cruelty, here unexpectedly captured something of Webster's peculiar horror.

24 Peter Thomson, 'Webster and the Actor' in *John Webster*, ed. Brian Morris (Ernest Benn, 1970), p. 32.

25 From *John Webster and the Elizabethan Drama* (1916); reprinted in *John Webster: A Critical Anthology*, p. 94.

26 John Barber, 'Triumph for Designer in Jacobean Tragedy', *Daily Telegraph*, 14 November 1969.

27 Helen Dawson, '*The White Devil*: Old Vic', *Plays and Players* 17.4 (January 1970), 39.

28 Hilary Spurling, 'Devil Incarnate', *Spectator*, 22 November 1969, 722.

The production of *The White Devil* mounted by Michael Lindsay-Hogg seven years later at the same theatre was a direct response to – even a challenge to – the earlier one. Irving Wardle suggests that the 1969 production's mistake was 'to identify the characters as Them. This time, at least, they are supposed to be Us'.[29] Thus the simple set, equipped with a pair of swing-doors downstage, suggested the deserted foyer of a grand hotel, and the actors wore casual modern clothes, sometimes topped off with dressing gowns. The dramatist Edward Bond (author of *Saved* and *Lear*), who prepared the acting edition, turned Machiavellian acts of revenge into modern surgical operations. By emphasizing the play's brutal realism, however, the production exhibited 'puritanical disapproval' quite at odds with Webster's own 'complex and evasive' moral judgements.[30] Playing Webster's characters as seedy, jaded moderns or fantastic, fragile insects illuminated a double bind in staging *The White Devil*: emphasizing realism may mask the greatness of which Webster's characters are capable, while heightening their exoticism may remove them into a world estranged from our own.

The most significant difference between the two Old Vic productions lay in the interpretation of Vittoria. In contrast to Geraldine McEwan's coquettish whore, Glenda Jackson played her in 1976 as a bold feminist whose acute intelligence teaches her only the conditions of her own oppression.

> When she flinched with her whole body against Monticelso's abuse of the legal process, it was out of shocked recognition of his hatred of her sex; and when she majestically stood her ground, calmly showing him the degree to which he traduced his office as judge, she was defending more than her own self.[31]

This Vittoria was not only the Cardinal's victim but also Brachiano's and Flamineo's; in the final scene she exultantly trampled on the latter as 'the embodiment of all things male that she had come to loathe'.[32] Even if she could not 'reconcile the character's separate aspects',[33] this Vittoria could expose the conflicts in her situation as a woman.

29 Irving Wardle, '*The White Devil*: Old Vic', *The Times*, 13 July 1976.

30 Robert Cushman, *Observer*, London, 18 July 1976.

31 Richard Allen Cave, '*The White Devil*' and '*The Duchess of Malfi*': *Text and Performance* (Macmillan, 1988), p. 55. Cave's impressions of the 1976 production are far more positive in general than those of most of the reviewers.

32 Ibid., p. 56.

33 Wardle, *The Times*, 13 July 1976.

Philip Prowse, a designer-turned-director of the Glasgow Citizens' Theatre, who had directed *The Duchess of Malfi* for the National Theatre in 1985, returned to the National to direct *The White Devil* in 1991. So devoted to striking visual effects that he once notoriously remarked that 'the words of an author are no more important than the work of an usherette',[34] Prowse created a monumental set for the Olivier Theatre's vast acting space to suggest the claustrophobic grandeur of Renaissance Italy.

> Beneath a vast curved brick wall are huge tombs and altars, some topped by cobwebbed crosses, one by the shell of a model basilica . . . The effect is of a half-built crypt, or half-ruined mausoleum, a place to remind us of T. S. Eliot's view that Webster was 'much possessed by death and saw the skull beneath the skin'.[35]

Bells tolled, candles flickered and thunder rumbled as sinister, cowled monks and ghosts (including the murdered Camillo and Isabella) prowled the marble floor. This too was an extreme case of designer's theatre, which too often dwarfed the actors onstage. Paul Taylor remarks that 'the trouble with all this kitschy overkill is that it presents the decor of death while failing to impart any sense of its horrifying finality'.[36] Not only did this production thus diminish the real impact of the horror it wished to create, it also failed to capture the characters' exuberant appetites for life and sex.

Prowse opted to translate into theatrical and contemporary terms the play's social inequalities: he cast Vittoria and her family as black. 'The effect is electric', wrote one reviewer:

> When Vittoria is charged with the murder of her husband, it is a black family that is slumped in chains in the court alongside her. To the Cardinal and the Duke of Florence, Brachiano's liaison becomes a visible form of class treachery.[37]

Reviewers admired Josette Simon's Vittoria. 'She paints a compelling, languorously tragic portrait',[38] comments one reviewer:

---

34 Charles Spencer, *Daily Telegraph*, 20 June 1991.
35 Benedict Nightingale, *The Times*, 19 June 1991.
36 *Independent*, 20 June 1991.
37 Kirsty Milne, 'Rank Disorder', *New Statesman and Society*, June 1991.
38 Michael Coveney, *Observer*, 23 June 1991.

Josette Simon as Vittoria and Denis Quilley as Brachiano
in the Royal National Theatre production of 1991
(photo: Donald Cooper © Photostage)

She can shut her gilded eyelids and sensuously purr when male hands are on her. Yet whether she is facing accusing potentates, a suspicious lover, or even her murderer, there is something fine, proud and wonderfully defiant about her. She stands, looks, silently commands, and is herself: a gemlike flame in Prowse and Webster's funereal world.[39]

In contrast to Jackson's 1976 embittered Vittoria, Simon sought to reconcile the character's sensuality with her feminist defiance but did not conceal her guilt. Her subtle and complex performance clearly stood out in an otherwise heavy-handed production.

Five years later, in April 1996, the Royal Shakespeare Company combined an equally nuanced approach to Vittoria with a spare and intimate acting space at the Swan in Stratford-upon-Avon. Later transferred to the Pit at the Barbican, the company's first ever production of this play achieved widespread critical acclaim. Bathed in a single spotlight and framed by massive pillars, a square grating at centre stage focused the action visually and suggested a 'fatal pivot between this limbo and ultimate damnation,' figuring 'death, persecution and vulnerability' for the characters trapped within its perimeter.[40] Brachiano dropped his wedding ring through the grating and later died on it; Vittoria stood trial on it and later emerged through it as from a hellish confinement in the house of convertites. Freed from scenic clutter, the staging that allowed Webster's visual symmetries and power dynamics to emerge also highlighted his moral complexities. If, as one critic put it, 'Jane Gurnett's Vittoria is a strongly sexual figure who can hardly wait to unlace her blood red frock ... she greets the ravings of the Cardinal, Monticelso, with monumental dignity.' Webster's female characters thus offered a powerful collective critique of corrupt male power. Director Gale Edwards extended this 'contradiction of character' to others in the play: Isabella 'takes on the moral responsibility for Brachiano's rejection of her ... with a richly ambiguous mixture of altruism and anger' while Richard McCabe's 'excellent Flamineo is both the Jacobean intellectual malcontent and an incestuous pander who clearly wants to participate in Vittoria's couplings.'[41] Indeed, Flamineo was singled out as the moral

---

39 Benedict Nightingale, *The Times*, 19 June 1991.

40 Nick Tippler, 'Cunning with Pistols: Observations on Gale Edwards's 1996–7 RSC Production of John Webster's *The White Devil*,' in *Shakespeare and his Contemporaries in Performance*, ed. Edward Esche (Ashgate, 2000), p. 276, 281.

41 Michael Billington, 'Devilishly good,' *Guardian* 29-30 April 1996.

touchstone of the production for a cynical exuberance that only made his anguished remorse emerge more sharply. The sole objection to the production was its focus on sexual rather than social politics; John Peter observed that 'it is far from clear, in Edwards's production, that the two siblings and their mother are a socially ambitious family and that the Vittoria-Brachiano affair is both a matter of two murderous adulteries and a breach of social demarcation lines.' [42] In direct contrast to the 1991 National production, here Vittoria was white and Brachiano played by a black actor (Ray Fearon). While this casting choice may have downplayed Vittoria's social climbing, it heightened the director's interpretation of the play as 'a conflict between the established dynasties of Francisco and Monticelso, and Bracciano – the young pretender'.[43] While Edwards cut some moments of spectacle and rearranged the plot to heighten the victimization of Vittoria, this was clearly the most successful production of the play in the professional theatre to date.

The White Devil at the Red Bull

On a winter's day (probably in February) in 1612, *The White Devil* opened at the Red Bull Theatre on St John's Street in Clerkenwell, north of the city of London. The Red Bull and its neighbour, the Fortune, were citizen playhouses where the common fare tended to be 'heroic and spectacular'[44] in contrast to the subtler, romantic repertory of the rival Bankside theatres such as the Globe. Despite their heavier use of spectacle, however, Red Bull plays were performed on a stage structurally much like that of the Globe or the Swan.[45] Like the DeWitt drawing of the Swan, the Red Bull had a large, bare platform stage (about 12 metres across) with trap below and 'heavens' above (supported by posts and protecting the stage from the weather); actors entered through two doors from the tiring house, and possibly also through a central curtained 'discovery space';[46] and a balcony above the stage provided a limited area

---

42 John Peter, 'Two for the Road?' *Sunday Times* May 5 1996.

43 Tippler, p. 279.

44 Andrew Gurr, *The Shakespearean Stage, 1574–1642*, 2nd ed. (Cambridge University Press, 1980), p. 14.

45 George F. Reynolds, *The Staging of Elizabethan Plays at the Red Bull Theater 1605–1625* (Modern Language Association, 1940), p. 188.

46 Although no discovery space is shown in the DeWitt sketch, Gurr concludes that 'there was certainly some sort of enclosed space at the back of the stage, which could be pressed into use for the Globe plays' (*The Shakespearean Stage*, p. 137). Reynolds discusses the evidence for the Red Bull and concludes that 'a curtained space was available on the Red Bull stage' (*Staging of Elizabethan Plays*, p. 162), though he believes it may not have been a permanent feature.

for playing. The stage projected into the middle of the unroofed yard and was surrounded by tiers of galleries. Thus the two distinctive qualities of the Red Bull Theatre, like all Elizabethan theatres, were its simplicity and its close contact with the audience. With no painted scenery of an illusionistic kind, Elizabethan stagecraft emphasized the actors and their formal groupings, dramatic exits and entrances and visual contrasts and parallels; thronged about with spectators in broad daylight, the actors could either address them in asides or ignore them in a theatre which drew equally on the non-naturalistic staging of the morality play and the 'true imitation of life' (V.vi.302) commended by Webster.

Stage action ranges from Flamineo's private whisper in Branchiano's ear (I.ii.6) to the procession of the ambassadors (IV.iii.5–17), demanding close, intimate engagement or detached appreciation from the audience. The audience is often required to attend to more than one thing at a time: in II.i, for example, Francisco, Camillo and Marcello whisper together about their new commission while Flamineo and Brachiano hire Dr Julio as their assassin (ll. 282–318). Moreover, almost nothing in *The White Devil* happens without an onstage audience commenting on it. Occasionally this engagement becomes overt, as when Marcello directs the audience to 'Mark this strange encounter' (III.iii.60) or when Flamineo pre-empts criticism of his 'tale' by acknowledging that it 'may appear to some ridiculous/Thus to talk knave and madman' (IV.ii.234–5). Indeed, the Red Bull, a theatre in which (unlike the Globe) 'apprentices and small tradesmen ... might sit on the stage with the air of grandeur affected by the gallants who patronized the more stylish theatres',[47] may have encouraged an especially close actor-audience relationship.

The simplicity of the Elizabethan stage heightened its symbolic potential. The formal stage picture of I.ii, for example, with Brachiano and Vittoria framed by Flamineo on the one hand and Cornelia on the other, draws on (and complicates) the conventional pattern of the morality play, where Vice and Virtue solicit the human soul. Without the distraction of back-drops or sets, visual contrasts and parallels emerge with greater clarity: Brachiano and Vittoria probably kiss to seal their union (I.ii.197), while Brachiano and Isabella kiss to seal their divorce (II.i.252); Isabella kisses Brachiano's poisoned mouth in the portrait and dies (II.ii.23 s.d.), while Brachiano's beaver (mouthpiece) is poisoned to kill him (V.ii.75

---

47 Louis B. Wright, *Middle-Class Culture in Elizabethan England* (University of North Carolina Press, 1935), p. 611. Reynolds concurs that 'seats on the stage were counted among the regular sources of income' (*Staging of Elizabethan Plays*, pp. 8–9).

s.d.); Brachiano shows love for Vittoria by kissing her (IV.ii.188) and by not kissing her (V.iii.27).[48] As Antonelli and Gasparo frame Lodovico in I.i like a 'well . . . with two buckets' (I.i.29), so Francisco and Monticelso confront Brachiano in II.i, and the visual parallels suggest significant distinctions between a hardened villain and a passionate lover.

The actors would have provided a parade of lavish costumes.[49] Apparel is a visual sign of power in *The White Devil*, from the Cardinal's ecclesiastical scarlet to the ambassadors' magnificent robes as 'knights/Of several orders' (IV.iii.6–7). This is a world in which clothes do make the man, as Francisco points out with reference to Giovanni's suit of armour: 'a good habit makes a child a man,/Whereas a bad one makes a man a beast' (II.i.137–8). Flamineo expresses frustration at finding himself 'not a suit the richer' (I.ii.309) after his sojourn at court; Vittoria, on the other hand, as Brachiano's mistress can wear 'cloth of tissue' (II.i.55) and (probably) a sumptuous gown that advertises her 'scorn and impudence' (III.ii.122) at the trial. Yet the play is also constantly undermining appearances: Vittoria points out that charity is seldom found in scarlet (III.ii.71–2), while Flamineo notes that Camillo's outer garb of a 'politician' is really 'an ass in's foot-cloth' (I.ii.46–8). The proliferation of disguises in the final act further emphasizes the deceptiveness of appearances. Thus the play makes use of the company's large stock of lavish costumes to further its own biting satire.

Webster acknowledges in his preface to the reader that the Red Bull patrons did not provide a 'full and understanding auditory' for *The White Devil* at its first performance. One can only guess at the reasons. While Gurr blames the 'overcast wintry weather',[50] one may also imagine the cause to have been Webster's radical experimentation with gender and genre, as well as his unorthodox moral complexities. The Red Bull players were well known for a broad acting style (inherited from Edward Alleyn's playing of Marlowe).[51] The Red Bull was clearly the wrong theatre for a play as subtle and complex as *The White Devil*. Wisely, Webster

48 Peter Thomson explores kissing as a 'figure in action' in the play ('Webster and the Actor', pp. 39–41); David Gunby extends this analysis in his Critical Introduction to *The White Devil* (NCW, pp. 61–3).

49 Gurr points out that 'the impresarios and players invested much more money in apparel than in properties' (*The Shakespearean Stage*, p. 178); he prints a long list of sumptuous costumes from Henslowe's *Diary* for 1598. David Carnegie comments extensively on costume in the play in his Theatrical Introduction to the Cambridge edition (NCW, pp. 87–91).

50 Andrew Gurr, *Playgoing in Shakespeare's London* (Cambridge University Press, 1987) p. 36.

51 See Gurr, *The Shakespearean Stage*, pp. 110–11.

chose rival playhouses for the staging of *The Duchess of Malfi*; the Globe and its indoor venue, the Blackfriars. It has been noticed that studio theatre performance suits *The Duchess of Malfi*; certainly the intimate venue of the Royal Shakespeare Company's Swan Theatre (and later the Pit, Barbican) produced a critically acclaimed production of *The White Devil*.

Note on the Text

The White Devil was first printed in 1612 by Nicholas Okes, and is free from major textual obscurity. I have taken as my copy text the authoritative first quarto (British Museum shelfmark C.34. e.18). Press corrections have been supplied from John Russell Brown's list ('The Printing of John Webster's Plays (II)', *Studies in Bibliography* 8 (1956), 113–17); substantive press variants indicate that Webster himself may have been involved in proofreading and correcting. Recently, Anthony Hammond has distinguished three main compositors, whom he calls A, B and N, the latter (who set Blr–E4v) being the least experienced and most prone both to commit error and to follow his copy in matters of punctuation.[52]

The manuscript which Webster supplied to the printer was probably based on his 'foul papers' rather than on a text adapted for use in the theatre, judging from the irregular speech headings, misplaced entries and complete absence of act and scene divisions in the copy, as well as the truculent attitude he adopts in the preface towards the playhouse. As his afterword commending the players indicates, Webster was acutely sensitive to performance; indeed, he attempted to supplement the necessarily incomplete experience of a *reader* of the play by adding a number of stage directions to the second part of the text, perhaps while the first part was already being set by the printer. In the published text, these added stage directions occur in the margins after F3v. Since they are not different in kind from other stage directions, which the compositors usually squeezed into available text space, they are treated as accidental features of the printer's copy, and both marginal and other stage directions are incorporated into the text at appropriate points in the dialogue, though all changes to their position are recorded in the notes.

I have modernized spelling (unless the original spelling allowed for a play on words), eliminated both capitalized nouns and italicized proper names, regularized speech prefixes and expanded elisions such as final

---

52 Anthony Hammond, '*The White Devil* in Nicholas Okes's Shop', *Studies in Bibliography* 39 (1986), 135–76.

syllable apostrophes. Because there is reason to doubt compositorial consistency (Brown lxx), I have used quotation marks for all gnomic pointing in the copy (normally indicated by either italics or inverted commas). I have added the customary act and scene divisions in square brackets. In accordance with the policy of this series, I have followed the lineation of the copy text except when verse is obviously set as prose to save space, in which case the change is indicated in the notes. Blank verse lines are staggered when they are shared by two or more speakers. The light punctuation of Q has been followed wherever possible, though it has been necessary in some cases to add commas, semi-colons and dashes to capture, without arresting, Webster's fluid language.

FURTHER READING

Barker, Roberta. ' "Another Voyage": Death as Social Performance in John Webster's Major Tragedies', in *Early Theatre* 8.2 (2005), pp. 35–56

Behling, Laura L. ' "S/He Scandles Our Proceedings": The Anxiety of Alternative Sexualities in *The White Devil* and *The Duchess of Malfi*,' *English Language Notes* 33.4 (June 1996), pp. 24–43

Berry, Ralph. *The Art of John Webster* (Oxford: Clarendon, 1972)

Bliss, Lee. *The World's Perspective: John Webster and the Jacobean Drama* (Sussex: Harvester, 1983)

Boklund, Gunnar. *The Sources of 'The White Devil'* (Cambridge, Mass.: Harvard University Press, 1957)

Bovilsky, Lara. 'Black Beauties, White Devils: The English Italian in Milton and Webster', in *English Literary History* 70.3 (2003), pp. 625–651

Bradbrook, M. C. *John Webster: Citizen and Dramatist* (London: Weidenfeld and Nicolson, 1980)

Bromley, Laura G. 'The Rhetoric of Feminine Identity in *The White Devil*' in *In Another Country: Feminist Perspectives on Renaissance Drama*, ed. Dorothea Kehler and Susan Baker (Metuchen, N.J.: Scarecrow, 1991), pp. 50–70

Cave, Richard Allen. *'The White Devil' and 'The Duchess of Malfi': Text and Performance* (London: Macmillan, 1988)

Champion, Larry S. 'Webster's *The White Devil* and the Jacobean Tragic Perspective', *Texas Studies in Literature and Language* 16 (1974), pp. 447–62

Dollimore, Jonathan. *Radical Tragedy: Religion and Power in the Drama of Shakespeare and his Contemporaries* (Sussex: Harvester, 1984)

Ewbank, Inga-Stina. 'Webster's Realism, or, "A Cunning Piece Wrought Perspective" ' in *John Webster*, ed. Brian Morris (London: Ernest Benn, 1970), pp. 157–78

Finin-Farber, Kathryn R. 'Framing (the) Woman: *The White Devil* and the Deployment of Law,' in *Renaissance Drama* n.s. 25 (1994), pp. 219–45

Forker, Charles R. *The Skull Beneath the Skin: The Achievement of John Webster* (Carbondale: Southern Illinois University Press, 1986)

Goldberg, Dena. *Between Worlds: A Study of the Plays of John Webster* (Waterloo: Wilfrid Laurier University Press, 1987)

Goldberg, Dena ' "By Report": The Spectator as Voyeur in Webster's *The White Devil*', in *English Literary Renaissance* 17.1 (1987), pp. 67–84

Gunby, D. C., David Carnegie, and Anthony Hammond, eds. *The Works of John Webster* I (Cambridge: Cambridge University Press, 1995)

Habermann, Ina. 'She has that in her belly will dry up your ink': Femininity as Challenge in the 'Equitable Drama' of John Webster', in *Literature, Politics and Law in Renaissance England*, ed. Erica Sheen and Lorna Hutson (Basingstoke: Palgrave Macmillan, 2005), pp. 100–120

Hirsch, James. 'Vittoria's Secret: Teaching Webster's *The White Devil* as a Tragedy of Inscrutability,' in *Approaches to Teaching English Renaissance Drama*, ed. Karen Bamford and Alexander Leggatt (New York: Modern Language Association, 2002), pp. 73–9

Jenkins, Harold. 'The Tragedy of Revenge in Shakespeare and Webster', *Shakespeare Survey* 14 (1961), pp. 45–55

Jones, Ann Rosalind. 'Italians and Others: *The White Devil* (1612)' in *Staging the Renaissance: Reinterpretations of Elizabethan and Jacobean Drama* (New York: Routledge, 1991)

Luckyj, Christina. *A Winter's Snake: Dramatic Form in the Tragedies of John Webster* (Athens: University of Georgia Press, 1989)

Luckyj, Christina. 'Gender, Rhetoric and Performance in John Webster's *The White Devil*' in *Enacting Gender on the English Renaissance Stage*, ed. Viviana Comensoli and Anne Russell (Urbana: University of Illinois Press, 1998) pp. 190–207

McLeod, Susan H. *Dramatic Imagery in the Plays of John Webster*, Jacobean Drama Studies 68 (Salzburg: Universität Salzburg, 1977)

Mulryne, J. R. 'Webster and the Uses of Tragicomedy' in *John Webster*, ed. Brian Morris (London: Ernest Benn, 1970), pp. 133–55

Pearson, Jacqueline. *Tragedy and Tragicomedy in the Plays of John Webster* (Manchester: Manchester University Press, 1980)

Stevenson, Sheryl. ' "As Differing as Two Adamants": Sexual Difference in *The White Devil*' in *Sexuality and Politics in Renaissance Drama*, ed. Carole Levin and Karen Robertson (Lewiston: Edwin Mellen, 1991), pp. 159–74

Thomson, Peter. 'Webster and the Actor' in *John Webster*, ed. Brian Morris (London: Ernest Benn, 1970), pp. 23–44

Weil, Judith. '*The White Devil* and Old Wives' Tales', *Modern Language Review* 94.2 (April 1999), pp. 328–40

Wilson, Luke. '*The White Devil* and the Law,' in *Early Modern English Drama*, ed. Garrett A. Sullivan Jr., Patrick Cheney and Andrew Hadfield (Oxford: Oxford University Press, 2006), pp. 225–236

1612 title page:
non inferiora secutus 'Engaged in no less noble service' (Virgil, *Æneid*, vi, 170):
'The words should perhaps be rendered – "following no ignoble theme" or "a
theme not less noble than my rivals or predecessors have treated".'
(Lucas, *Webster*, i, 194)

THE
WHITE DIVEL,

OR,

The Tragedy of *Paulo Giordano*
Vrsini, Duke of *Brachiano*,

With

The Life and Death of Vittoria
Corombona the famous
Venetian Curtizan.

Acted by the Queenes Maiesties Seruants.

Written by IOHN WEBSTER.

Non inferiora secutus.

LONDON,
Printed by *N.O.* for *Thomas Archer*, and are to be sold
at his Shop in Popes head Pallace, neere the
Royall Exchange. 1612.

[DRAMATIS PERSONAE]

[MONTICELSO, a Cardinal; afterwards Pope PAUL IV

FRANCISCO DE' MEDICI, Duke of Florence; in the fifth act disguised
   for a Moor, under the name of MULINASSAR

BRACHIANO, otherwise PAULO GIORDANO URSINI, Duke of Brachiano;
   husband to Isabella and in love with Vittoria

GIOVANNI, his son, by Isabella

LODOVICO or LODOWICK, an Italian Count, but decayed

ANTONELLI and GASPARO, his friends, and dependents of the Duke of
   Florence

CAMILLO, husband to Vittoria

HORTENSIO, one of Brachiano's officers

MARCELLO, an attendant of the Duke of Florence, and brother to
   Vittoria

FLAMINEO, his brother; secretary to Brachiano

CARDINAL OF ARRAGON

DOCTOR JULIO, a conjuror

*CHRISTOPHERO, his assistant

*GUID-ANTONIO

*FERNESE

*JACQUES, a Moor, servant to Giovanni

ISABELLA, sister to Francisco de' Medici, and wife to Brachiano

VITTORIA COROMBONA, a Venetian Lady, first married to Camillo,
   afterwards to Brachiano

CORNELIA, mother to Vittoria, Flamineo and Marcello

ZANCHE, a Moor; servant to Vittoria

MATRON of the House of Convertites

CARLO

PEDRO

AMBASSADORS	CHANCELLOR
PHYSICIANS	REGISTER
COURTIERS	PAGE
LAWYERS	ARMOURER
OFFICERS	CONJUROR
ATTENDANTS	CONCLAVIST]

* non-speaking parts or 'ghost characters'

TO THE READER

In publishing this tragedy, I do but challenge to myself that liberty, which other men have ta'en before me; not that I affect praise by it, for, *nos haec novimus esse nihil,* only since it was acted, in so dull a time of winter, presented in so open and black a theatre, that it wanted (that which is the only grace and setting out of a tragedy)   5 a full and understanding auditory: and that since that time I have noted, most of the people that come to that play-house, resemble those ignorant asses (who visiting stationers' shops, their use is not to enquire for good books, but new books) I present it to the general view with this confidence: 10

> *Nec rhoncos metues, maligniorum,*
> *Nec scombris tunicas, dabis molestas.*

If it be objected this is no true dramatic poem, I shall easily confess it, – *non potes in nugas dicere plura meas: ipse ego quam dixi,* – willingly, and not ignorantly, in this kind have I faulted: for   15 should a man present to such an auditory, the most sententious tragedy that ever was written, observing all the critical laws, as height of style, and gravity of person; enrich it with the sententious *Chorus,* and as it were lifen death, in the passionate and weighty

---

1   *challenge* claim

3   *nos . . . nihil* 'We know these things are nothing' (Martial XIII, 2); Webster probably borrowed this quotation and that at ll. 14–15 from Dekker's preface to *Satiromastix* (1602).

4   *open . . . theatre* The Red Bull, the playhouse in which *The White Devil* was first performed in February or March 1612, was unroofed and thus open to the weather, which may have been quite 'black', or overcast on the occasion.

6   *understanding auditory* i.e. an appreciative audience (possibly in contrast to those simply 'standing under' the stage, in the yard); like his contemporaries, Webster commends the ear, not the eye (cf. his character of 'An Excellent Actor': 'Sit in a full theatre, and you will think you see so many lines drawn from the circumference of so many ears, while the actor is the centre.')

11–12   *Nec . . . molestas* 'You [the poet's book] will not fear the sneers of the malicious, nor supply wrappers for mackerel' (Martial IV, 86).

14–15   *non . . . dixi* 'You cannot say more against my trifles than I have said myself' (Martial XIII, 2).

15   *willingly . . . faulted* Thus Webster aligns his play not with the compressive simplicity of classical theatre but with the episodic multiplicity of native English drama.

18   *sententious* full of maxims and *sententiae,* as in the tragedies of Seneca

5

Nuntius: yet after all this divine rapture, *O dura messorum ilia*, the   20
breath that comes from the uncapable multitude is able to poison
it, and ere it be acted, let the author resolve to fix to every scene,
this of Horace,

> *Haec hodie porcis comedenda relinques.*

To those who report I was a long time in finishing this tragedy, I   25
confess I do not write with a goose-quill, winged with two feathers, and if they will needs make it my fault, I must answer them
with that of Euripides to Alcestides, a tragic writer: Alcestides
objecting that Euripides had only in three days composed three
verses, whereas himself had written three hundred: 'Thou tell'st   30
truth', (quoth he), 'but here's the difference: thine shall only be
read for three days, whereas mine shall continue three ages'.

Detraction is the sworn friend to ignorance: for mine own part
I have ever truly cherished my good opinion of other men's worthy
labours, especially of that full and heightened style of Master   35
Chapman, the laboured and understanding works of Master
Jonson: the no less worthy composures of the both worthily excellent Master Beaumont, and Master Fletcher: and lastly (without
wrong last to be named) the right happy and copious industry of
Master Shakespeare, Master Dekker, and Master Heywood, wishing   40
what I write may be read by their light: protesting, that, in the
strength of mine own judgement, I know them so worthy, that
though I rest silent in my own work, yet to most of theirs I dare
(without flattery) fix that of Martial:

> *non norunt, haec monumenta mori.*
>   45

19–20   *lifen . . . Nuntius* i.e. make death come alive in the report of the passionate and
            serious messenger
    20   *O . . . ilia* 'O strong stomachs of harvesters' (Horace, *Epodes* III, 4; alluding to
            peasants' love of garlic)
    24   *Haec . . . relinques* 'What you leave will go today to feed the pigs' (Horace, *Epistles* I,
            vii, 19)
  25–7   *I . . . feathers* Webster published nothing between 1605 and 1612, when *The White
            Devil* appeared; he may indeed have laboured over his first independent dramatic
            effort.
  28–32 In the original story (told by Valerius Maximus), the poet Alcestis writes a hundred
            verses in three days; Webster probably borrowed his version from L. Lloyd, *Linceus
            Spectacles* (1607).
    36   *understanding* intellectual
    45   *non . . . mori* 'These monuments do not know death' (Martial X, ii, 12; comparing
            literature with ruined tombs).

THE TRAGEDY OF PAULO GIORDANO URSINI DUKE OF BRACHIANO, AND VITTORIA COROMBONA

[ACT I, SCENE i]

Enter Count LODOVICO, ANTONELLI *and* GASPARO

LODOVICO
Banished?
ANTONELLI It grieved me much to hear the sentence.
LODOVICO
Ha, ha, O Democritus, thy gods
That govern the whole world: courtly reward,
And punishment. Fortune's a right whore:
If she give ought, she deals it in small parcels, 5
That she may take away all at one swoop.
This 'tis to have great enemies, God quite them.
Your wolf no longer seems to be a wolf
Than when she's hungry.
GASPARO You term those enemies
Are men of princely rank.
LODOVICO O I pray for them. 10
The violent thunder is adored by those
Are pashed in pieces by it.

---

0   s.d. The three men may enter and react together to a previous offstage sentence, or (probably more effective theatrically) Antonelli and Gasparo may enter to hand Lodovico his decree of banishment, visually re-enacting the confrontation between social forces and the anarchic individual. Not only does Webster choose to open and close the play with Lodovico, he also sets him up as an analogue to the desperate Brachiano of I.ii.

1–4   ed. (Banisht ... to / heare ... sentence / LODO ... Gods/That ... re- / ward ... whore Q – lineation altered to make room for ornamental first letter)

2   *Democritus, thy gods* Webster is here borrowing from Guevara's *Diall of Princes* (trans. North 1557), which attributes to Pliny and Democritus the view that 'there were two gods, which governed the universal world: . . . reward and punishment'.

5   *parcels* portions

6   *swoop* stroke

7   *quite* requite

12   *pashed* dashed

ANTONELLI   Come my lord,
You are justly doomed; look but a little back
Into your former life: you have in three years
Ruined the noblest earldom—

GASPARO   Your followers   15
Have swallowed you like mummia, and being sick
With such unnatural and horrid physic
Vomit you up i'th'kennel—

ANTONELLI   All the damnable degrees
Of drinkings have you staggered through. One citizen
Is lord of two fair manors, called you master   20
Only for caviar.

GASPARO   Those noblemen
Which were invited to your prodigal feasts,
Wherein the phoenix scarce could scape your throats,
Laugh at your misery, as fore-deeming you
An idle meteor which, drawn forth the earth,   25
Would be soon lost i'th'air.

ANTONELLI   Jest upon you
And say you were begotten in an earthquake,
You have ruined such fair lordships.

LODOVICO   Very good,
This well goes with two buckets, I must tend
The pouring out of either.

GASPARO   Worse than these,   30
You have acted certain murders here in Rome,
Bloody and full of horror.

16   *mummia* a medicine made from dead flesh, difficult to swallow but thought to
      produce excellent results
18   *kennel* gutter
19   *you* (you, you Q)
19–21 i.e. a citizen, though richer than you, was prepared to humble himself in order to
      get your gifts
23   *phoenix* legendary bird and rare delicacy. Since only one phoenix lived at one time,
      the new bird rose from the ashes of the old.
25   *idle* worthless
      meteor a luminous body seen temporarily in the sky and supposed to emerge from
      a lower region or corrupt source; an evil omen
29–30 *This . . . either* Lodovico uses the image of two buckets alternately drawing from a
      common well to caricature the alternation of Antonelli's and Gasparo's attacks as
      mechanical and composed of mere proverbs. The image may be reinforced visually,
      with Antonelli and Gasparo on either side of Lodovico (NCW I.ii.29–30 n.).
31   *acted* carried out

LODOVICO   'Las they were flea-bitings:
  Why took they not my head then?
GASPARO   O my lord
  The law doth sometimes mediate, thinks it good
  Not ever to steep violent sins in blood.   35
  This gentle penance may both end your crimes
  And in the example better these bad times.
LODOVICO
  So, but I wonder then some great men scape
  This banishment; there's Paulo Giordano Orsini,
  The Duke of Brachiano, now lives in Rome,   40
  And by close panderism seeks to prostitute
  The honour of Vittoria Corombona:
  Vittoria, she that might have got my pardon
  For one kiss to the Duke.
ANTONELLI   Have a full man within you.
  We see that trees bear no such pleasant fruit   45
  There where they grew first, as where they are new set.
  Perfumes, the more they are chafed, the more they render
  Their pleasing scents; and so affliction
  Expresseth virtue fully, whether true,
  Or else adulterate.
LODOVICO   Leave your painted comforts.   50
  I'll make Italian cut-works in their guts
  If ever I return.
GASPARO   O sir.
LODOVICO   I am patient.
  I have seen some ready to be executed
  Give pleasant looks, and money, and grown familiar
  With the knave hangman; so do I, I thank them,   55
  And would account them nobly merciful
  Would they dispatch me quickly.

36   *This gentle penance* i.e. banishment
41   *close* secret
44   *Have . . . you* i.e. be the complete and self-sufficient man
46   *they* ed. (the Q)
     new set transplanted
50   *painted* false, artificial
51   *Italian cut-works* openwork embroidery, an Italian fashion
55   *knave* menial servant; base rogue

ANTONELLI   Fare you well,
We shall find time I doubt not to repeal
Your banishment.   *Sennet [sounds]*
LODOVICO   I am ever bound to you:
This is the world's alms; pray make use of it;   60
Great men sell sheep, thus to be cut in pieces,
When first they have shorn them bare and sold their fleeces.

                                              Exeunt

[ACT I, SCENE ii]

Enter BRACHIANO, CAMILLO, FLAMINEO, VITTORIA
        COROMBONA [*and* ATTENDANTS *with torches*]

BRACHIANO
Your best of rest.
VITTORIA   Unto my lord the Duke
The best of welcome. More lights, attend the Duke.

                        [*Exeunt* VITTORIA *and* CAMILLO]

BRACHIANO
Flamineo.
FLAMINEO My lord.
BRACHIANO   Quite lost Flamineo.
FLAMINEO
Pursue your noble wishes, I am prompt
As lightning to your service, O my lord!   5
(*Whispers*) The fair Vittoria, my happy sister
Shall give you present audience. [*Aloud*] Gentlemen,

---

59   s.d. *Sennet* ed. (Enter Senate Q) a set of notes sounded on the trumpet to announce
     a ceremonial entrance (that of Vittoria, Brachiano and attendants in the following
     scene). The trumpeters may have appeared on the stage.
60   Previous editors have taken 'alms' to refer to the cynical adage that follows, but it is
     possible that Lodovico is giving Gasparo and Antonelli money to repeal his banish-
     ment, at the same time cynically referring to them as hangmen (l. 55).
     make use of it earn interest on it (NCW I.i.60 n.)

0–9 Vittoria passes over the stage in a blaze of light (cf. III.ii.294). In a typical stroke of
     dramaturgy, Webster first crowds and illuminates the stage only to empty and
     (imaginatively, in an outdoor theatre) darken it: a public, ceremonial world quickly
     gives way to the private intensity of Brachiano's illicit passion.
6   s.d. *(Whispers)* ed. (whisper r. margin opposite l. 7 in Q)

Let the caroche go on, and 'tis his pleasure
You put out all your torches and depart.

[*Exeunt* ATTENDANTS *with torches*]

BRACHIANO

Are we so happy?

FLAMINEO   Can't be otherwise?   10
Observed you not tonight, my honoured lord,
Which way so e'er you went she threw her eyes?
I have dealt already with her chamber-maid
Zanche the Moor, and she is wondrous proud
To be the agent for so high a spirit.   15

BRACHIANO

We are happy above thought, because 'bove merit.

FLAMINEO

'Bove merit! We may now talk freely: 'bove merit; what is't you
doubt? Her coyness, that's but the superficies of lust most women
have. Yet why should ladies blush to hear that named, which they
do not fear to handle? O they are politic; they know our desire is   20
increased by the difficulty of enjoying, whereas satiety is a blunt,
weary and drowsy passion. If the buttery-hatch at court stood
continually open there would be nothing so passionate crowding,
nor hot suit after the beverage.

BRACHIANO

O but her jealous husband—   25

FLAMINEO

Hang him, a gilder that hath his brains perished with quicksilver
is not more cold in the liver. The great barriers moulted not

___

8 *caroche* luxurious coach for town use
15 i.e. help you because of your outstanding desire and high rank
17 *talk freely* As Flamineo relaxes with Brachiano on a stage now cleared of observers,
    his speech acquires the metrical looseness of prose.
21 *whereas* ed. (where a Q)
22 *buttery-hatch* the half-door over which were served food and drink from the
    buttery
26–7 *gilder . . . liver* Gilders used a mixture of gold and mercury to gild objects, then later
    drew off the mercury with heat, thereby inhaling the fumes, causing mercury poi-
    soning; the symptoms include tremors, insanity and general torpor (or reduction
    in body heat). Flamineo compares Camillo to gilders because he is so lacking in
    passion. The liver was supposedly the seat of the passions.
27–8 *great barriers . . . hairs* During barriers, a martial tournament fought with short
    swords or pikes across a low railing (cf. V.iii), the feathers in the helmets of combat-
    ants would often be struck off. As the challengers at barriers lose feathers, so Camillo's
    sexual encounters have given him syphilis, which causes hair loss and impotence.

11

more feathers than he hath shed hairs by the confession of his
doctor. An Irish gamester that will play himself naked, and then
wage all downward, at hazard, is not more venturous. So unable   30
to please a woman that like a Dutch doublet all his back is
shrunk into his breeches.
Shroud you within this closet, good my lord;
Some trick now must be thought on to divide
My brother-in-law from his fair bed-fellow.   35

BRACHIANO

O should she fail to come!

FLAMINEO

I must not have your lordship thus unwisely amorous; I myself
have loved a lady and pursued her with a great deal of under-
age protestation, whom some three or four gallants that have
enjoyed would with all their hearts have been glad to have been   40
rid of. 'Tis just like a summer bird-cage in a garden: the birds
that are without, despair to get in, and the birds that are within
despair and are in a consumption for fear they shall never get
out: away, away my lord—

Enter CAMILLO [BRACHIANO *withdraws*]

See, here he comes; this fellow by his apparel   45
Some men would judge a politician,
But call his wit in question, you shall find it

29–30 *An Irish gamester ... venturous* According to Richard Stanyhurst's *Description of
       Irelande* in Holinshed's *Chronicles*, some 'wild Irish' would gamble away their
       clothes until they were stark naked, then pawn their fingernails, toenails and even
       their testicles, which they lost or redeemed at the courtesy of the winner. The sense
       here is that Camillo has pawned his virility.

31–2   *Dutch doublet ... breeches* Like a Dutch doublet, which was close fitting except for
       its large breeches, Camillo's 'back' (manhood) has withered or shrunk.

  33   *Shroud you ... closet* It is unlikely that Brachiano actually disappears from the audi-
       ence's view here (or at l. 44), since the effectiveness of Flamineo's cross-talk would be
       heightened by Brachiano's visibility. The actor may simply retreat to a different part of
       the stage, crouching, perhaps, behind an arras or door; later in the scene, Cornelia is
       likewise visible to the audience but invisible to the other characters. The stage direction
       for Brachiano's entrance at l. 179 thus registers his coming forward to centre stage.

38–9   *under-age protestation* inexperienced or immature declaration of love

45–6   *his apparel ... politician* Camillo appears dressed in the long robes of a counsellor
       of state or an old man (NCW I.ii.47 n.)

Merely an ass in's foot-cloth. [*To* CAMILLO] How now, brother,
What, travailing to bed to your kind wife?

CAMILLO

I assure you brother, no. My voyage lies   50
More northerly, in a far colder clime;
I do not well remember, I protest,
When I last lay with her.

FLAMINEO   Strange you should lose your count.

CAMILLO

We never lay together but ere morning
There grew a flaw between us.

FLAMINEO   'T had been your part   55
To have made up that flaw.

CAMILLO   True, but she loathes
I should be seen in't.

FLAMINEO   Why sir, what's the matter?

CAMILLO

The Duke your master visits me, I thank him,
And I perceive how like an earnest bowler
He very passionately leans that way   60
He should have his bowl run.

FLAMINEO   I hope you do not think–

CAMILLO

That noblemen bowl booty? 'Faith his cheek

---

48 *foot-cloth* a large and richly ornamented cloth laid over the back of a horse, hanging
     down to the ground on either side, considered a mark of dignity (here, adorning
     an ass)

48–9 ed. (cloath/How . . . wife? Q)

49 *travailing* archaic form of 'travelling', containing both the straightforward sense of
     'journeying' and the more sardonic sense of 'labouring, exerting yourself' (with
     another disparaging glance at Camillo's futile exertions as a lover)

52–3 ed. (I do not well . . . her/Strange Q)

53 *lose your count* a bawdy pun, again at Camillo's expense. 'Count' was a variant
     spelling of (and probably close in pronunciation to) 'cunt'.

55 *flaw* a sudden storm or squall (which would part two ships which 'lay together'
     after a 'voyage'), or, figuratively, a passionate outburst; also a breach or crack (with
     a bawdy allusion to the female genitals; cf. *A Chaste Maid in Cheapside* I.i.29)

56–7 ed. (Trew . . . in't/Why Q)

62 *bowl booty* a term from the game of bowls: to conspire with another player in order
     to victimize a third player; hence, to play the game falsely so as to gain a desired
     object. (Camillo suspects Brachiano and Flamineo are conspiring against him to
     win Vittoria.)

Hath a most excellent bias, it would fain
Jump with my mistress.

FLAMINEO   Will you be an ass
Despite your Aristotle, or a cuckold   65
Contrary to your ephemerides
Which shows you under what a smiling planet
You were first swaddled?

CAMILLO   Pew wew, sir tell not me
Of planets nor of ephemerides.
A man may be made cuckold in the day-time   70
When the stars' eyes are out.

FLAMINEO   Sir, God boy you,
I do commit you to your pitiful pillow
Stuffed with horn-shavings.

CAMILLO   Brother—

FLAMINEO   God refuse me
Might I advise you now your only course
Were to lock up your wife.

CAMILLO   'Twere very good.   75

FLAMINEO
Bar her the sight of revels.

CAMILLO   Excellent.

FLAMINEO
Let her not go to church, but like a hound
In leon at your heels.

CAMILLO   'Twere for her honour.

FLAMINEO
And so you should be certain in one fortnight,
Despite her chastity or innocence,   80

62–4   *his cheek . . . mistress* Camillo goes on to compare Brachiano's cheek (buttock) to
       the bowl itself, whose off-centre weighting (bias) causes it to run in an oblique line
       towards the 'mistress', the smaller white ball at which the bowls are aimed.

64   *jump with* lie with. When one bowl touches another one or the 'mistress', it is said
       to 'kiss' it. Camillo wants to suggest Brachiano's overtly sexual motives.

63–4   ed. (Hath . . . mistress/Will . . . asse Q)

65   *your* ed. (you Q) *Aristotle* philosophical learning

66   *ephemerides* astrological tables showing predicted positions of heavenly bodies on
       successive days

71   *God boy you* God be with you (ironically dismissive)

73   *horn-shavings* Horns were supposed to grow on the foreheads of men whose wives
       were unfaithful.

78   *leon* leash

To be cuckolded, which yet is in suspense:
This is my counsel and I ask no fee for't.

CAMILLO

Come, you know not where my nightcap wrings me.

FLAMINEO

Wear it o'th'old fashion, let your large ears come through, it
will be more easy; nay, I will be bitter: bar your wife of her   85
entertainment: women are more willingly and more gloriously
chaste, when they are least restrained of their liberty. It seems
you would be a fine capricious mathematically jealous cox-
comb, take the height of your own horns with a Jacob's staff
afore they are up. These politic enclosures for paltry mutton   90
makes more rebellion in the flesh than all the provocative
electuaries doctors have uttered since last Jubilee.

CAMILLO

This doth not physic me.

FLAMINEO

It seems you are jealous. I'll show you the error of it by a
familiar example: I have seen a pair of spectacles fashioned   95
with such perspective art that, lay down but one twelve pence
o'th'board, 'twill appear as if there were twenty; now should you
wear a pair of these spectacles, and see your wife tying her shoe,
you would imagine twenty hands were taking up of your wife's
clothes, and this would put you into a horrible causeless fury.   100

CAMILLO

The fault there, sir, is not in the eyesight—

---

83   *my nightcap ... me* i.e. my nightcap pinches me (because of the cuckold's horns
      sprouting from my forehead)
84   *large ears* ass's ears (cf. 1. 84)
89   *Jacob's staff* instrument used for measuring height or distance
90–1 *politic ... flesh* Flamineo's punning is based on 'mutton', slang for loose woman. As
      the enclosure of common land by rich men leads to peasant uprisings, so putting
      restraints on loose women leads to their sexual rebellion.
91–2 *provocative electuaries* aphrodisiacs
92   *uttered* issued, supplied
      Jubilee a year (first instituted by the Pope in 1300) of remission from sin by papal
      indulgence through various acts of piety. The 'last Jubilee' before the play's per-
      formance was 1600.
96   *perspective art* the skill of constructing a picture or figure so as to produce some
      fantastic optical effect. These spectacles were cut into facets so as to multiply the
      image twentyfold.
99   *wife's* ed. (wives Q)

15

FLAMINEO

True, but they that have the yellow jaundice, think all objects they look on to be yellow. Jealousy is worser, her fits present to a man, like so many bubbles in a basin of water, twenty several crabbed faces; many times makes his own shadow his cuckold-maker.   105

Enter [VITTORIA] COROM[BON]A

See she comes; what reason have you to be jealous of this creature? What an ignorant ass or flattering knave might he be counted, that should write sonnets to her eyes, or call her brow the snow of Ida, or ivory of Corinth, or compare her hair to the blackbird's bill, when 'tis liker the blackbird's feather. This is all: 110
be wise; I will make you friends and you shall go to bed together; marry look you, it shall not be your seeking, do you stand upon that by any means; walk you aloof, I would not have you seen in't. [*Aside*] Sister, my lord attends you in the banqueting-house – [*Aloud*] your husband is wondrous discontented.   115

VITTORIA

I did nothing to displease him, I carved to him at supper-time.

FLAMINEO

You need not have carved him in faith, they say he is a capon already. I must now seemingly fall out with you. [*Aloud*] Shall a

103   *worser* worse
105   s.d. ed. (Enter Coroma l. margin; asterisk after -maker Q)
109   *Ida* sacred mountain near Troy, usually associated with the green groves in which Paris lived as a shepherd
       ivory of Corinth Corinth was famous for excessive luxury.
110   *blackbird's bill . . . feather* The blackbird's bill is yellow, its feathers black; in sonneteering convention fair-haired women were considered more beautiful than dark-haired women.
111   *friends* lovers
113   *walk . . . aloof* Flamineo removes Camillo to a safe distance. He thus jokes privately with Vittoria at Camillo's expense, possibly in stage whispers (cf. I.ii.6).
115–44   I have added dashes to those already in the copy text in order to clarify Flamineo's cross-talk. Up to l. 130, Flamineo's jokes depend on remarks which Vittoria (and Brachiano) can hear and Camillo cannot; the double meaning of l. 132 depends on Camillo's ignorance of Flamineo's asides. After l. 132, since Flamineo has promised Vittoria's sexual favours to Brachiano and Camillo, his lines apply equally well to both men.
116   *carved* shown great courtesy; made seductive advances – 'by signalling with the fingers' (Lucas, p. 209)
117   *carved* castrated
       capon a castrated cock; a eunuch

gentleman so well descended as Camillo [*Aside*] a lousy slave
that within this twenty years rode with the black-guard in the   120
Duke's carriage 'mongst spits and dripping-pans–

CAMILLO

Now he begins to tickle her.

FLAMINEO

An excellent scholar – one that hath a head filled with calves'
brains without any sage in them – come crouching in the hams to
you for a night's lodging – that hath an itch in's hams, which like   125
the fire at the glass-house hath not gone out this seven years – Is
he not a courtly gentleman? – When he wears white satin one
would take him by his black muzzle to be no other creature than a
maggot – You are a goodly foil, I confess, well set out – but
covered with a false stone, yon counterfeit diamond.   130

CAMILLO

He will make her know what is in me.

FLAMINEO

Come, my lord attends you; thou shalt go to bed to my lord.

CAMILLO

Now he comes to't.

FLAMINEO

With a relish as curious as a vintner going to taste new wine, I
am opening your case hard.   135

CAMILLO

A virtuous brother o' my credit.

FLAMINEO

He will give thee a ring with a philosopher's stone in it.

---

120 *black-guard* lowest menial servants of a noble household; scullions and kitchen-
knaves
122 *tickle* excite agreeably, arouse
123–4 *calves' . . . them* Calves' brains unseasoned by the culinary herb sage are a metaphor
for the brains of a dolt unseasoned by wisdom.
124 *crouching . . . hams* in a servile, bowing position
125 *itch in's hams* irritation in the thighs and buttocks
126 *glass-house* the glass factory in which fires were always kept burning; in Webster
metaphorically associated with sexual organs
129 *foil* setting of a jewel
135 *case* legal case; and punning on the sense, the female genitals
137 *philosopher's stone* miraculous substance sought by alchemists which would turn
base metals into precious ones, cure disease and prolong life; here also a bawdy
reference to the testicle (stone)

CAMILLO

Indeed I am studying alchemy.

FLAMINEO

Thou shalt lie in a bed stuffed with turtles' feathers, swoon in
perfumed linen like the fellow was smothered in roses, so   140
perfect shall be thy happiness, that as men at sea think land and
trees and ships go that way they go, so both heaven and earth
shall seem to go your voyage. Shalt meet him, 'tis fixed, with
nails of diamonds to inevitable necessity.

VITTORIA

[*Aside*] How shall's rid him hence?   145

FLAMINEO

[*Aside*] I will put breese in's tail, set him gadding presently. [*To*
CAMILLO] I have almost wrought her to it, I find her coming,
but might I advise you now for this night I would not lie with
her, I would cross her humour to make her more humble.

CAMILLO

Shall I? Shall I?   150

FLAMINEO

It will show in you a supremacy of judgement.

CAMILLO

True, and a mind differing from the tumultuary opinion, for
quae negata grata.

FLAMINEO

Right, you are the adamant shall draw her to you, though you
keep distance off.   155

CAMILLO

A philosophical reason.

FLAMINEO

Walk by her o' the nobleman's fashion, and tell her you will lie
with her at the end of the progress.

---

139 *turtles'* turtle doves', emblems of fidelity in love
145 i.e. how shall we get rid of him?
146 *breese* gadflies
147 *coming* well inclined; sexually receptive
152 *tumultuary* irregular, confused
153 *quae negata grata* what is denied is desired
154 *adamant* magnet
156 *philosophical* wise; scientific
158 *progress* a state procession. Camillo might parade himself before Vittoria during
     these speeches (NCW I.ii.160 n.).

CAMILLO

Vittoria, I cannot be induced or as a man would say incited—

VITTORIA

To do what sir? 160

CAMILLO

To lie with you tonight; your silkworm useth to fast every third day, and the next following spins the better. Tomorrow at night I am for you.

VITTORIA

You'll spin a fair thread, trust to't.

FLAMINEO

But do you hear, I shall have you steal to her chamber about 165 midnight.

CAMILLO

Do you think so? Why look you brother, because you shall not think I'll gull you, take the key, lock me into the chamber, and say you shall be sure of me.

FLAMINEO

In truth I will, I'll be your jailer once; 170
But have you ne'er a false door?

CAMILLO

A pox on't, as I am a Christian tell me tomorrow how scurvily she takes my unkind parting.

FLAMINEO

I will.

CAMILLO

Didst thou not mark the jest of the silkworm? Good night; in 175 faith I will use this trick often.

FLAMINEO

Do, do, do.

Exit CAMILLO

So now you are safe. Ha ha ha, thou entanglest thyself in thine own work like a silkworm.

164   *thread* punning on the sense 'semen'
168   *gull* deceive
172   *scurvily* sourly
175   *mark* ed. (make Q)
179   s.d. ed. (*Enter Brachiano* Q). See l. 33n. above.

[BRACHIANO *comes forward*]

Come sister, darkness hides your blush; women are like cursed   180
dogs, civility keeps them tied all daytime, but they are let loose
at midnight; then they do most good or most mischief. My
lord, my lord—

BRACHIANO

Give credit: I could wish time would stand still
And never end this interview this hour,   185
But all delight doth itself soon'st devour.

> ZANCHE *brings out a carpet, spreads it and lays on it*
> *two fair cushions*

> *Enter* CORNELIA [*listening*]

Let me into your bosom, happy lady,
Pour out instead of eloquence my vows;
Loose me not madam, for if you forgo me
I am lost eternally.   190

VITTORIA

Sir in the way of pity I wish you heart-whole.

BRACHIANO

You are a sweet physician.

VITTORIA

Sure sir a loathed cruelty in ladies
Is as to doctors many funerals:
It takes away their credit.

180   *cursed* vicious; (often of women) shrewish
184   *Give credit* i.e. trust me (addressed either to Vittoria or to Flamineo)
186   s.d. The compositor squeezed this stage direction into the text space available
      beside Brachiano's speech. While we cannot therefore be certain of the exact posi-
      tion of the stage direction in the copy, Zanche's actions (and Cornelia's entrance)
      are especially significant if they occur as Brachiano addresses Vittoria. Brachiano's
      courtly vows are thus immediately counterbalanced by the overtly sexual nature of
      the lovers' encounter suggested by the placing of cushions and also by the presence
      of an outsider and critic (Comelia, perhaps wearing a crucifix). The staging recalls
      that of the morality play, with Vice (Flamineo and Zanche) and Virtue (Cornelia)
      present as observers, probably framing the lovers on either side.
189   *loose* release; lose (in modern sense)
189–90   ed. (one line in Q)
194–5   ed. (Is . . . credit / Excellent Q)

20

BRACHIANO   Excellent creature.   195
　We call the cruel fair, what name for you
　That are so merciful?   [*They embrace*]
ZANCHE   See now they close.
FLAMINEO
　Most happy union.
CORNELIA
　[*Aside*] My fears are fall'n upon me, O my heart!
　My son the pander: now I find our house   200
　Sinking to ruin. Earthquakes leave behind,
　Where they have tyrannized, iron, or lead, or stone,
　But, woe to ruin, violent lust leaves none.
BRACHIANO
　What value is this jewel?
VITTORIA   'Tis the ornament
　Of a weak fortune.   205
BRACHIANO
　In sooth I'll have it; nay I will but change
　My jewel for your jewel.
FLAMINEO   Excellent,
　His jewel for her jewel; well put in Duke.
BRACHIANO
　Nay let me see you wear it.
VITTORIA   Here sir.
BRACHIANO
　Nay lower, you shall wear my jewel lower.   210
FLAMINEO
　That's better; she must wear his jewel lower.

197　*close* come together
204　*jewel* Brachiano presumably fingers a gem worn by Vittoria, and then offers one of
　　his own, as in a formal betrothal ceremony in which tokens were exchanged before
　　witnesses; 'jewel' signifies both married chastity or 'maidenhead' and the sexual
　　organ – hence the subsequent word-play. Brachiano encourages Vittoria to pin his
　　jewel at the base of her dress's V-shaped bodice, over her pudendum (NCW
　　I.ii.205–12 n.).
208　*put in* make a claim; also with a sexual innuendo
209　*Here* ed. (Heare Q)

21

VITTORIA
　To pass away the time I'll tell your Grace
　A dream I had last night.
BRACHIANO　　　　　　　　Most wishedly.
VITTORIA
　A foolish idle dream:
　Methought I walked about the mid of night,　　　　　　　　215
　Into a church-yard, where a goodly yew-tree
　Spread her large root in ground; under that yew,
　As I sat sadly leaning on a grave,
　Checkered with cross-sticks, there came stealing in
　Your Duchess and my husband; one of them　　　　　　　220
　A pick-axe bore, th'other a rusty spade,
　And in rough terms they gan to challenge me,
　About this yew.
BRACHIANO　　　That tree.
VITTORIA　　　　　　　　This harmless yew.
　They told me my intent was to root up
　That well-grown yew, and plant i'th'stead of it　　　　　　225
　A withered blackthorn, and for that they vowed
　To bury me alive: my husband straight
　With pick-axe gan to dig, and your fell Duchess
　With shovel, like a fury, voided out
　The earth and scattered bones. Lord, how methought　　　230
　I trembled, and yet for all this terror
　I could not pray.
FLAMINEO　　　No, the devil was in your dream.
VITTORIA
　When to my rescue there arose, methought,
　A whirlwind which let fall a massy arm

214–37　By recounting her dream, Vittoria physically disengages herself from Brachiano's
　　　　sexual overtures, perhaps walking about the stage as she imaginatively re-enacts it
　　　　(NCW I.ii.216 n.). When she has finished, Brachiano reasserts control by renewing
　　　　his embrace.
　219　cross-sticks May mean any of the following: wooden crosses sticking out of graves;
　　　　the 'chequered pattern of light and shade' created by the overhanging branches of
　　　　the yew tree against the night sky (Brown, I.ii.236 n.); criss-crossed osiers protect-
　　　　ing the grave; devices used by witches to raise tempests.
　225　yew traditionally associated with death (cf. IV.iii.120), here an ambiguous symbol.
　　　　Isabella and Camillo would think of 'that well-grown yew' as Camillo himself, the
　　　　deserving husband, or perhaps as Brachiano, still uncorrupted; Vittoria's obvious
　　　　pun on 'you' and the end of the dream clearly suggest Brachiano as the yew.

From that strong plant, 235
And both were struck dead by that sacred yew
In that base shallow grave that was their due.

FLAMINEO

Excellent devil.
She hath taught him in a dream
To make away his Duchess and her husband. 240

BRACHIANO

Sweetly shall I interpret this your dream:
You are lodged within his arms who shall protect you
From all the fevers of a jealous husband,
From the poor envy of our phlegmatic Duchess;
I'll seat you above law and above scandal, 245
Give to your thoughts the invention of delight
And the fruition; nor shall government
Divide me from you longer than a care
To keep you great: you shall to me at once
Be dukedom, health, wife, children, friends, and all. 250

CORNELIA

[Approaching them] Woe to light hearts, they still fore-run
our fall.

FLAMINEO

What fury raised thee up? Away, away—

Exit ZANCHE

CORNELIA

What make you here, my lord, this dead of night?
Never dropped mildew on a flower here,
Till now.

FLAMINEO I pray will you go to bed then, 255
Lest you be blasted?

CORNELIA   O that this fair garden
Had with all poisoned herbs of Thessaly
At first been planted, made a nursery

---

247   *government* i.e. governing my dukedom
252   *fury* in classical mythology one of the avenging deities, dread goddesses with snakes
      twined in their hair
      s.d. Flamineo's direction to Zanche provides an early hint of their illicit relation-
      ship of which Cornelia later shows open disapproval (V.i.175).
254–5 ed. (one line in Q)
257   *with* ed. (not in Q)
      Thessaly the special home of witches and poisonous herbs

For witchcraft; rather than a burial plot
For both your honours.

VITTORIA [*Kneeling*]   Dearest mother hear me.   260

CORNELIA

O thou dost make my brow bend to the earth
Sooner than nature. See the curse of children.
In life they keep us frequently in tears,
And in the cold grave leave us in pale fears.

BRACHIANO

Come, come, I will not hear you.

VITTORIA   Dear my lord.   265

CORNELIA

Where is thy Duchess now, adulterous Duke?
Thou little dreamed'st this night she is come to Rome.

FLAMINEO

How? Come to Rome!

VITTORIA   The Duchess–

BRACHIANO   She had been better–

CORNELIA

The lives of princes should like dials move,
Whose regular example is so strong,   270
They make the times by them go right or wrong.

FLAMINEO

So, have you done?

CORNELIA   Unfortunate Camillo.

VITTORIA

I do protest if any chaste denial,
If anything but blood could have allayed
His long suit to me–

CORNELIA [*Kneeling*] I will join with thee,   275
To the most woeful end e'er mother kneeled,
If thou dishonour thus thy husband's bed,

---

259   *than* ed. (not in Q)

260   s.d. Vittoria probably kneels at this point, as she pleads with her mother, whose
'brow bend[s] to the earth'; at l. 275, Cornelia clearly indicates that she kneels to join
Vittoria. Vittoria's kneeling posture – a traditional show of respect for authority –
softens 'the curse of children' of which Cornelia accuses her daughter.

264   *leave* ed. (leaves Q)

274   *blood* her reciprocated sexual passion, life itself (Vittoria's own death or Brachiano's
suicide) or bloodshed (crimes which Brachiano is prepared to commit to win her)

24

> Be thy life short as are the funeral tears
> In great men's.

BRACHIANO   Fie, fie, the woman's mad.

CORNELIA
> Be thy act Judas-like, betray in kissing;   280
> May'st thou be envied during his short breath,
> And pitied like a wretch after his death.

VITTORIA
> O me accursed.   *Exit*

FLAMINEO
> Are you out of your wits? My lord,
> I'll fetch her back again!

BRACHIANO   No, I'll to bed.   285
> Send Doctor Julio to me presently.
> Uncharitable woman, thy rash tongue
> Hath raised a fearful and prodigious storm.
> Be thou the cause of all ensuing harm.   *Exit*

FLAMINEO
> Now, you that stand so much upon your honour,   290
> Is this a fitting time o' night, think you,
> To send a duke home without e'er a man?
> I would fain know where lies the mass of wealth
> Which you have hoarded for my maintenance,
> That I may bear my beard out of the level   295
> Of my lord's stirrup.

CORNELIA   What? Because we are poor,
> Shall we be vicious?

FLAMINEO   Pray what means have you
> To keep me from the galleys, or the gallows?
> My father proved himself a gentleman,
> Sold all's land, and like a fortunate fellow   300

---

282   *his* ed. (this Q)

283   s.d. *Exit* ed. (Exit Victoria Q)

284   *Are . . . wits?* The copy text does not reveal whether Flamineo's insolent question is addressed to Brachiano or Cornelia. While Flamineo is clearly furious with his mother for spoiling the lovers' meeting, he may also be angry with Brachiano for not actively preventing Vittoria's departure. The choice is left to the actor.

289   s.d. *Exit* ed. (Exit Brachiano Q)

295–6   *bear . . . stirrup* be in a higher position than unmounted foot attendant to my lord; hence, rise above my subservient position

299–300 *gentleman . . . land* alluding ironically to a contemporary social evil

Died ere the money was spent. You brought me up,
At Padua I confess, where I protest,
For want of means (the university judge me)
I have been fain to heel my tutor's stockings
At least seven years. Conspiring with a beard   305
Made me a graduate, then to this Duke's service;
I visited the court, whence I returned—
More courteous, more lecherous by far,
But not a suit the richer – and shall I,
Having a path so open and so free   310
To my preferment, still retain your milk
In my pale forehead? No, this face of mine
I'll arm and fortify with lusty wine
'Gainst shame and blushing.

CORNELIA
O that I ne'er had borne thee!

FLAMINEO   So would I.   315
I would the common'st courtezan in Rome
Had been my mother rather than thyself.
Nature is very pitiful to whores
To give them but few children, yet those children
Plurality of fathers; they are sure   320
They shall not want. Go, go,
Complain unto my great lord cardinal,
Yet may be he will justify the act.
Lycurgus wondered much, men would provide
Good stallions for their mares, and yet would suffer   325
Their fair wives to be barren.

CORNELIA
Misery of miseries.   *Exit*

FLAMINEO
The Duchess come to court, I like not that;
We are engaged to mischief and must on.

305–6 *Conspiring . . . graduate* Flamineo earned his degree, probably by simply reaching physical (rather than intellectual) maturity or possibly by conspiring with an older man.

308 *courteous* with manners befitting the court of a prince

324–6 *Lycurgus . . . barren* According to Plutarch, Lycurgus advocated that men should share their wives with other 'worthy' men, not to fulfil the needs of barren women, but to provide the state with citizens from the best possible stock.

327 s.d. *Exit* ed. (Exit Cornelia Q)

As rivers, to find out the ocean   330
Flow with crook bendings beneath forced banks,
Or as we see, to aspire some mountain's top
The way ascends not straight but imitates
The subtle foldings of a winter's snake,
So, who knows policy and her true aspect,   335
Shall find her ways winding and indirect.   *Exit*

[ACT II, SCENE i]

Enter FRANCISCO DE' MEDICI, *Cardinal* MONTICELSO,
MARCELLO, ISABELLA, *young* GIOVANNI, *with little*
JACQUES *the Moor*

FRANCISCO
Have you not seen your husband since you arrived?
ISABELLA
Not yet sir.
FRANCISCO   Surely he is wondrous kind;
If I had such a dove-house as Camillo's
I would set fire on't, were't but to destroy
The pole-cats that haunt to't – [*To* GIOVANNI] my sweet cousin–   5

---

331   *crook* crooked
      forced artificially made
334   *winter's snake* probably the mythical *amphisbaena*, symbol of the devil, whose two
      heads allowed elaborate serpentine movement and which, unlike most snakes,
      deliberately sought cold temperatures

  0   s.d.1 MONTICELSO ed. (Mountcelso Q)
      s.d.3 *little* JACQUES the Moor A mysterious ghost character with no speaking part,
      perhaps (as most editors think) a trace in the manuscript of an idea that was subse-
      quently undeveloped or discarded by Webster; but Webster may have intended
      the presence of the silent young Moor among the company to hint at the sinister
      potential of apparently virtuous characters such as Monticelso and Francisco.
      Aaron, also a Moor, appears but does not speak in the first scene of Shakespeare's
      Titus Andronicus; his brooding presence casts a shadow over the apparently
      virtuous Tamora (later revealed as Aaron's mistress) as she pleads for her son's life.
  3   *such a* ed. (a such Q)
      dove-house a house for doves; here referring ironically to Vittoria, since the dove
      was traditionally a symbol of peace and innocence
  5   *pole-cats* small, foul-smelling predatory mammals; a term of abuse for a vile person
      or a prostitute

GIOVANNI
Lord uncle, you did promise me a horse
And armour.

FRANCISCO   That I did my pretty cousin;
Marcello see it fitted.

MARCELLO   My lord the Duke is here.

FRANCISCO
Sister away, you must not yet be seen.

ISABELLA
I do beseech you entreat him mildly,   10
Let not your rough tongue
Set us at louder variance; all my wrongs
Are freely pardoned, and I do not doubt
As men to try the precious unicorn's horn
Make of the powder a preservative circle   15
And in it put a spider, so these arms
Shall charm his poison, force it to obeying
And keep him chaste from an infected straying.

FRANCISCO
I wish it may. Be gone.

                                              Exit [ISABELLA]

                   Enter BRACHIANO *and* FLAMINEO

                   Void the chamber;
      [*Exeunt* FLAMINEO, MARCELLO, GIOVANNI *and* JACQUES]
You are welcome, will you sit? [BRACHIANO *sits*] I pray my lord   20
Be you my orator, my heart's too full;
I'll second you anon.

MONTICELSO   Ere I begin
Let me entreat your grace forego all passion
Which may be raised by my free discourse.

14–16   *unicorn's horn . . . spider* In this test a spider was encircled by an extremely rare and
        expensive powder believed to come from the mythological unicorn's horn, which
        was thought to be an antidote to poison; if the horn were genuine, the spider would
        remain inside the circle.

  19   *Void the chamber* A bold stroke of staging on Webster's part: no sooner is the stage
        crowded with actors than it is suddenly cleared at Francisco's command. The stage
        picture – in which two men chastise a third for unseemly behaviour – replicates I.i,
        in which Gasparo and Antonelli reprimand Lodovico.

BRACHIANO

    As silent as i'th'church – you may proceed.   25

MONTICELSO

    It is a wonder to your noble friends

    That you have as 'twere entered the world

    With a free sceptre in your able hand,

    And have to th'use of nature well applied

    High gifts of learning, should in your prime age   30

    Neglect your awful throne, for the soft down

    Of an insatiate bed. O my lord,

    The drunkard after all his lavish cups

    Is dry, and then is sober; so at length

    When you awake from this lascivious dream,   35

    Repentance then will follow, like the sting

    Placed in the adder's tail: wretched are princes

    When fortune blasteth but a petty flower

    Of their unwiedly crowns; or ravisheth

    But one pearl from their sceptre; but alas!   40

    When they to wilful shipwreck loose good fame

    All princely titles perish with their name.

BRACHIANO

    You have said, my lord,–

MONTICELSO   Enough to give you taste

    How far I am from flattering your greatness?

BRACHIANO

    Now you that are his second, what say you?   45

    Do not like young hawks fetch a course about;

    Your game flies fair and for you.

FRANCISCO   Do not fear it:

    I'll answer you in your own hawking phrase;

    Some eagles that should gaze upon the sun

---

  31 *awful* awe-inspiring

36–7 *sting . . . tail* While the adder inflicts injury primarily with its mouth or fangs, the hindpart of its tail was also supposed to be able to sting. Monticelso may be implying that, while Brachiano's affair now primarily injures his public reputation, he will later badly regret it himself.

38–9 *fortune . . . crowns* Not a mixed metaphor but a cunning play on words: 'flower' could mean a jewel in a crown; 'crown' could mean a garland of flowers.

  42 *name* good name, reputation

  46 *fetch a course about* change direction, turn tail (as young hawks are supposed to do when directed to fly at old game)

Seldom soar high, but take their lustful ease,   50
Since they from dunghill birds their prey can seize.
You know Vittoria.
BRACHIANO   Yes.
FRANCISCO   You shift your shirt there
When you retire from tennis.
BRACHIANO   Happily.
FRANCISCO
Her husband is lord of a poor fortune
Yet she wears cloth of tissue.
BRACHIANO   What of this?   55
Will you urge that, my good lord cardinal,
As part of her confession at next shrift,
And know from whence it sails?
FRANCISCO   She is your strumpet.
BRACHIANO
Uncivil sir there's hemlock in thy breath
And that black slander; were she a whore of mine   60
All thy loud cannons and thy borrowed Switzers,
Thy galleys nor thy sworn confederates
Durst not supplant her.
FRANCISCO   Let's not talk on thunder.
Thou hast a wife, our sister; would I had given
Both her white hands to death, bound and locked fast   65
In her last winding-sheet, when I gave thee
But one.
BRACHIANO Thou hadst given a soul to God then.

---

51 *prey* ed. (pery Q)
    dunghill birds birds (such as ravens, kites and common barnyard fowl) whose prey
    is offal, contrasted to eagles, by popular belief the only bird able to look directly at
    the sun. Francisco is comparing Brachiano to an eagle sluggish enough to seize the
    contemptible, corrupt prey (Vittoria) of an inferior bird (Camillo).
52 *shift* change
53 *Happily* Perhaps
55 *cloth of tissue* a rich kind of cloth, often interwoven with gold or silver, that sump-
    tuary laws restricted to women of high birth (NCW II.i.55 n.)
59 *hemlock* poison
61 *borrowed Switzers* Swiss mercenary soldiers
67 *Thou ... then* Brachiano is acknowledging Isabella's fitness for the spiritual life.
    Does he mean this as a genuine compliment, or as an ironic comment on her unfit-
    ness for the real world? The ambiguity aptly prepares an audience for a character
    whose saintly self-sacrifice leads her to deliver vicious harangues.

FRANCISCO   True:
  Thy ghostly father with all's absolution
  Shall ne'er do so by thee.
BRACHIANO   Spit thy poison.
FRANCISCO
  I shall not need, lust carries her sharp whip   70
  At her own girdle; look to't, for our anger
  Is making thunder-bolts.
BRACHIANO   Thunder? In faith,
  They are but crackers.
FRANCISCO   We'll end this with the cannon.
BRACHIANO
  Thou'lt get nought by it but iron in thy wounds,
  And gunpowder in thy nostrils.
FRANCISCO   Better that   75
  Than change perfumes for plasters.
BRACHIANO   Pity on thee,
  'Twere good you'ld show your slaves or men condemned
  Your new-ploughed forehead. Defiance! And I'll meet thee,
  Even in a thicket of thy ablest men.
MONTICELSO
  My lords, you shall not word it any further   80
  Without a milder limit.
FRANCISCO   Willingly.
BRACHIANO
  Have you proclaimed a triumph that you bait
  A lion thus?
MONTICELSO My lord.
BRACHIANO   I am tame, I am tame sir.

---

  68 *ghostly* spiritual
  73 *crackers* explosive fireworks (as in modern sense); also, boasts or lies
  76 *change ... plasters* i.e. exchange the sweet smells of sensual indulgence for its
      consequences, the bandages to treat venereal disease
  78 *new-ploughed* deeply furrowed (with anger)
      forehead ... thee ed. (fore-head defiance, and I'le meete thee Q) Repunctuation is
      necessary to make sense of the text. 'Defiance!' is a plausible trumpet call to mark
      Brachiano's shift from contempt for Francisco to self-assertion.
  80 *word it* argue, dispute
  82 *triumph* a public festivity during which, in ancient Rome, lions might be 'baited', or
      taunted to fight
  82–3 ed. (baite a/Lyon thus Q)

FRANCISCO

We send unto the Duke for conference
'Bout levies 'gainst the pirates. My lord Duke   85
Is not at home. We come ourself in person,
Still my lord Duke is busied; but we fear
When Tiber to each prowling passenger
Discovers flocks of wild ducks, then my lord
'Bout moulting time, I mean we shall be certain   90
To find you sure enough and speak with you.

BRACHIANO   Ha?

FRANCISCO

A mere tale of a tub, my words are idle,
But to express the sonnet by natural reason,
When stags grow melancholic you'll find the season.

Enter GIOVANNI [*in armour*]

MONTICELSO

No more my lord; here comes a champion   95
Shall end the difference between you both,
Your son the prince Giovanni. See my lords
What hopes you store in him; this is a casket
For both your crowns, and should be held like dear.
Now is he apt for knowledge; therefore know   100

---

88   *prowling* ed. (proling Q)
     prowling passenger peregrine falcon in search of prey
89   *wild ducks* prey for the falcon; prostitutes
90   *moulting time* when birds shed their plumage; when people lose their hair (as a result
     of venereal disease; cf. I.ii.27–9); i.e. when his hair begins to fall out, Brachiano will
     discover Vittoria is a prostitute – another dig at Vittoria's reputation (cf. l. 76)
92   *tale of a tub* proverbial, a cock and bull story; and punning on the sweating tub
     used in treatment of venereal disease
93   *express . . . reason* i.e. explain this little poem by common sense
94   *stags* male deer; cuckolds (like Brachiano if he discovers Vittoria is a prostitute)
     stags . . . melancholic After stags mated, they were supposed to retreat into solitary
     ditches to lie alone.
     season fit occasion or opportunity (to meet with us)
     s.d. ed. (to r. of l. 93 in Q)
95   *champion* a valiant combatant. Giovanni is now outfitted in the suit of armour
     Francisco promised him at the beginning of the scene, a living emblem of
     the chivalric ideal Brachiano should strive for (identified in Webster's time with
     Prince Henry).

It is a more direct and even way
To train to virtue those of princely blood
By examples than by precepts: if by examples
Whom should he rather strive to imitate
Than his own father: be his pattern then,   105
Leave him a stock of virtue that may last,
Should fortune rend his sails and split his mast.

BRACHIANO
Your hand boy – [*Shaking his hand*] growing to a soldier?

GIOVANNI
Give me a pike.

                                 [*One hands him a pike*]

FRANCISCO
What, practising your pike so young, fair coz?   110

GIOVANNI
[*Tossing the pike*] Suppose me one of Homer's frogs, my lord,
Tossing my bullrush thus; pray sir tell me
Might not a child of good discretion
Be leader to an army?

FRANCISCO   Yes cousin, a young prince
Of good discretion might.

GIOVANNI   Say you so?   115
Indeed I have heard 'tis fit a general
Should not endanger his own person oft,
So that he make a noise when he's a horseback
Like a Dansk drummer. O 'tis excellent.
He need not fight; methinks his horse as well   120
Might lead an army for him. If I live
I'll charge the French foe, in the very front
Of all my troops, the foremost man.

---

106   *stock* line of descent; store, fund
108   *to a* ed. (to Q)
109   *pike* spear-like weapon used by foot soldiers; the penis
111   *Homer's frogs* from *The Battle of Frogs and Mice*, a burlesque epic attributed to
       Homer in which the frogs used bulrushes as pikes
113   *discretion* good judgement, prudence, circumspection, as in Falstaff's 'the better
       part of valour is discretion' (*1 Henry IV* V.iv.119–20). Giovanni's answer
       (ll. 116–17) suggests he takes Francisco to be playing on the latter meaning.
119   *Dansk* Danish (famous for martial music, including drums)

FRANCISCO   What, what!

GIOVANNI
    And will not bid my soldiers up and follow
    But bid them follow me.

BRACHIANO   Forward lapwing.   125
    He flies with the shell on's head.

FRANCISCO   Pretty cousin.

GIOVANNI
    The first year uncle that I go to war
    All prisoners that I take I will set free
    Without their ransom.

FRANCISCO   Ha, without their ransom?
    How then will you reward your soldiers   130
    That took those prisoners for you?

GIOVANNI   Thus my lord:
    I'll marry them to all the wealthy widows
    That falls that year.

FRANCISCO   Why then the next year following
    You'll have no men to go with you to war.

GIOVANNI
    Why then I'll press the women to the war,   135
    And then the men will follow.

MONTICELSO   Witty prince.

FRANCISCO
    See, a good habit makes a child a man,
    Whereas a bad one makes a man a beast:
    Come, you and I are friends.

BRACHIANO   Most wishedly,
    Like bones which broke in sunder and well set   140
    Knit the more strongly.

FRANCISCO [*Calling offstage*] Call Camillo hither.
    You have received the rumour, how Count Lodowick
    Is turned a pirate.

BRACHIANO   Yes.

FRANCISCO   We are now preparing
    Some ships to fetch him in.

---

125 *lapwing* proverbial type of precocity, supposed to run (if not to fly) immediately
     after hatching
137 *habit* garment (applied to Giovanni); custom, practice (applied to Brachiano)

[*Enter* ISABELLA]

                    Behold your Duchess;
We will now leave you and expect from you   145
Nothing but kind entreaty.
BRACHIANO   You have charmed me.
         Exeunt FR[ANCISCO], MON[TICELSO], GIOV[ANNI]
You are in health we see.
ISABELLA   And above health
To see my lord well.
BRACHIANO   So I wonder much,
What amorous whirlwind hurried you to Rome.
ISABELLA
Devotion, my lord.
BRACHIANO   Devotion?   150
Is your soul charged with any grievous sin?
ISABELLA
'Tis burdened with too many, and I think
The oft'ner that we cast our reckonings up,
Our sleeps will be the sounder.
BRACHIANO   Take your chamber!
ISABELLA
Nay my dear lord, I will not have you angry;   155
Doth not my absence from you two months
Merit one kiss?
BRACHIANO   I do not use to kiss.
If that will dispossess your jealousy,
I'll swear it to you.
ISABELLA   O my loved lord,
I do not come to chide; my jealousy,   160
I am to learn what that Italian means;
You are as welcome to these longing arms,
As I to you a virgin.   [*Attempts to embrace him*]

---

146 s.d. ed. (placed opposite ll. 144–5 in Q for lack of text space)
152–4 *'Tis ... sounder* The historical Isabella had a lover, but Webster was probably
      unaware of this (Boklund, p. 118); rather, Isabella's 'devotion' to Brachiano includes
      implicating herself in his transgressions (compare Desdemona's 'heaven forgive us'
      in *Othello* IV.ii.87).
161 *am to learn* am yet to learn (am ignorant of)
     Italian i.e. characteristically Italian emotion (jealousy)

BRACHIANO [*Turning away*] O your breath!
Out upon sweetmeats, and continued physic.
The plague is in them.
ISABELLA   You have oft for these two lips   165
Neglected cassia or the natural sweets
Of the spring violet; they are not yet much withered.
My lord I should be merry; these your frowns
Show in a helmet lovely, but on me,
In such a peaceful interview methinks   170
They are too too roughly knit.
BRACHIANO   O dissemblance.
Do you bandy factions 'gainst me? Have you learnt
The trick of impudent baseness to complain
Unto your kindred?
ISABELLA   Never my dear lord.
BRACHIANO
Must I be haunted out, or wasn't your trick   175
To meet some amorous gallant here in Rome
That must supply our discontinuance?
ISABELLA
I pray sir burst my heart, and in my death
Turn to your ancient pity, though not love.
BRACHIANO
Because your brother is the corpulent Duke,   180
– That is the great Duke – 'Sdeath I shall not shortly
Racket away five hundred crowns at tennis,
But it shall rest upon record: I scorn him
Like a shaved Polack: all his reverent wit
Lies in his wardrobe; he's a discreet fellow   185
When he's made up in his robes of state.
Your brother the great Duke, because h'as galleys,

166   *cassia* a kind of cinnamon; in poetic usage, a sweet-smelling herb or perfume
171   *too too* ed. (to too Q)
172   *bandy factions* i.e. form conspiracies
175   *haunted out* visited frequently (with perhaps also the sense of 'hunted out': chased away)
181–3 *'Sdeath . . . record* i.e. by God's death, soon I shall not be able to lose 500 crowns wagered at tennis without having it recorded as evidence (probably referring to Francisco's charge at ll. 52–3)
183–4 *I scorn . . . Polack* i.e. I scorn him as of no account. Poles, according to Fynes Morison, *Itinerary*, 1617, shaved all their heads except the forehead.

And now and then ransacks a Turkish fly-boat,
(Now all the hellish Furies take his soul),
First made this match – accursed be the priest   190
That sang the wedding mass, and even my issue.

ISABELLA
O too too far you have cursed.

BRACHIANO   Your hand I'll kiss:
This is the latest ceremony of my love,
Henceforth I'll never lie with thee, by this,
This wedding ring: I'll ne'er more lie with thee.   195
And this divorce shall be as truly kept
As if the judge had doomed it: fare you well,
Our sleeps are severed.

ISABELLA   Forbid it the sweet union
Of all things blessed; why, the saints in heaven
Will knit their brows at that.

BRACHIANO   Let not thy love   200
Make thee an unbeliever. This my vow
Shall never on my soul be satisfied
With my repentance: let thy brother rage
Beyond a horrid tempest or sea-fight,
My vow is fixed.

ISABELLA   O my winding sheet,   205
Now shall I need thee shortly; dear my lord,
Let me hear once more what I would not hear:
Never.

BRACHIANO Never!

ISABELLA
O my unkind lord, may your sins find mercy
As I upon a woeful widowed bed   210
Shall pray for you, if not to turn your eyes
Upon your wretched wife and hopeful son,
Yet that in time you'll fix them upon heaven.

---

188 *fly-boat* pinnace or fast sailing boat
192 *too too* ed. (to too Q)
193 *latest* last
193–8 *This . . . severed* Brachiano's ceremony of 'love' is a parody or inversion of the wed-
       ding rites, when vows and rings are exchanged. In Jacobean England, one spouse
       could divorce another from bed and board (*a mensa et thoro*), especially on
       grounds of adultery (of which Brachiano accuses Isabella at ll. 175–7). Such
       divorce did not, however, allow for remarriage.

BRACHIANO

No more; go, go, complain to the great Duke.

ISABELLA

No my dear lord, you shall have present witness   215
How I'll work peace between you; I will make
Myself the author of your cursed vow.
I have some cause to do it, you have none;
Conceal it I beseech you, for the weal
Of both your dukedoms, that you wrought the means   220
Of such a separation; let the fault
Remain with my supposed jealousy,
And think with what a piteous and rent heart
I shall perform this sad ensuing part.

Enter FRANCISCO, FLAMINEO, MONTICELSO, MARCELLO
[ISABELLA *weeps*]

BRACHIANO

Well, take your course – my honourable brother.   225

FRANCISCO

Sister – this is not well my lord – why, sister–
She merits not this welcome.

BRACHIANO   Welcome, say?
She hath given a sharp welcome.

FRANCISCO   Are you foolish?
Come dry your tears; is this a modest course,
To better what is nought, to rail and weep?   230
Grow to a reconcilement, or by heaven,
I'll ne'er more deal between you.

ISABELLA   Sir you shall not,
No though Vittoria upon that condition
Would become honest.

FRANCISCO   Was your husband loud,
Since we departed?

---

224   s.d. MONTICELSO ed. (Montcelso Q)
        Enter . . . MARCELLO ed. (Enter . . . MARCELLO, CAMILLO Q)
225   *take . . . course* Previous editors punctuate so that Brachiano addresses these words
        to Isabella. Without emendation, however, the line may be read as Brachiano's
        invitation to Francisco to proceed against Isabella.
230   *nought* wicked, immoral
234   *honest* chaste

ISABELLA   By my life sir no.   235
  I swear by that I do not care to loose.
  Are all these ruins of my former beauty
  Laid out for a whore's triumph?
FRANCISCO   Do you hear?
  Look upon other women, with what patience
  They suffer these slight wrongs, with what justice   240
  They study to requite them; take that course.
ISABELLA
  O that I were a man, or that I had power
  To execute my apprehended wishes,
  I would whip some with scorpions.
FRANCISCO   What? Turned fury?
ISABELLA
  To dig the strumpet's eyes out, let her lie   245
  Some twenty months a-dying, to cut off
  Her nose and lips, pull out her rotten teeth,
  Preserve her flesh like mummia, for trophies
  Of my just anger! Hell to my affliction
  Is mere snow-water. By your favour sir—   250
  Brother draw near, and my lord cardinal—
  Sir, let me borrow of you but one kiss.

                      [*Kisses* BRACHIANO]

  Henceforth I'll never lie with you, by this,
  This wedding-ring.
FRANCISCO   How? ne'er more lie with him!
ISABELLA
  And this divorce shall be as truly kept   255
  As if in thronged court a thousand ears

---

243   *apprehended* conceived, fully understood
244   *I . . . scorpions* Originally a biblical reference (to I Kings 12.11: 'my father hath chas-
     tised you with whips, but I will chastise you with scorpions'), the phrase denotes
     punishment by a whip made of knotted cords or steel spikes.
     Turned fury Cf. Flamineo's words to Cornelia at I.ii.252; a specific style of acting
     may have been required.
248   *mummia* Cf. I.i.16n.
251–62 *Brother . . . repentance* Unlike Brachiano, Isabella theatricalizes her 'divorce' by
     drawing attention to spectators/auditors both onstage and off. His appeal to the
     authority of a 'judge' (l. 197) becomes her evocation of 'a thousand ears' (the the-
     atre audience). Compare Vittoria's appeal to 'this auditory/Which come to hear my
     cause' at III.ii.15–16. Here Isabella is both parodying and outdoing Brachiano.

Had heard it, and a thousand lawyers' hands
Sealed to the separation.

BRACHIANO   Ne'er lie with me?

ISABELLA
Let not my former dotage
Make thee an unbeliever; this my vow   260
Shall never on my soul be satisfied
With my repentance: *manet alta mente repostum.*

FRANCISCO
Now by my birth you are a foolish, mad,
And jealous woman.

BRACHIANO   You see 'tis not my seeking.

FRANCISCO
Was this your circle of pure unicorn's horn,   265
You said should charm your lord? Now horns upon thee,
For jealousy deserves them; keep your vow
And take your chamber.

ISABELLA
No sir, I'll presently to Padua,
I will not stay a minute.

MONTICELSO   O good madam.   270

BRACHIANO
'Twere best to let her have her humour,
Some half-day's journey will bring down her stomach,
And then she'll turn in post.

FRANCISCO   To see her come
To my lord cardinal for a dispensation
Of her rash vow will beget excellent laughter.   275

262   *manet alta mente repostum* a common phrase originating in Virgil's description of
       Juno's smouldering resentments, 'It shall be treasured up in the depths of my mind'
       (*Aeneid* I, 26) and thus appropriate to Isabella. In the depths of Juno's mind lay
       hatred both for Paris, who scorned her beauty (in choosing Venus), and for the
       Trojan race, descendants of Jupiter's union with Electra, Juno's rival.
       repostum ed. (repositum Q)
266   *horns upon thee* normally, those which grow upon a cuckolded husband's forehead;
       here transferred to Isabella, whose jealousy in Francisco's view has now licensed
       Brachiano's adultery
268   *take . . . chamber* Cf. Brachiano's command at 1.154.
268–9 ed. (one line in Q)
272   *stomach* pride, obstinacy; vexation, pique (*OED*)
273   *turn in post* return post-haste

ISABELLA

[*Aside*] 'Unkindness do thy office, poor heart break,
Those are the killing griefs which dare not speak.'   *Exit*

Enter CAMILLO

MARCELLO

Camillo's come my lord.

FRANCISCO

Where's the commission?

MARCELLO

'Tis here.   280

FRANCISCO

Give me the signet.

FLAMINEO

[*To* BRACHIANO] My lord, do you mark their whispering; I will
compound a medicine out of their two heads, stronger than
garlic, deadlier than stibium; the cantharides which are scarce
seen to stick upon the flesh when they work to the heart, shall   285
not do it with more silence or invisible cunning.

Enter Doctor [JULIO]

BRACHIANO

About the murder.

FLAMINEO

They are sending him to Naples, but I'll send him to
Candy; [*Seeing the doctor*] here's another property too.

276–7   *Unkindness . . . speak* a common proverb, signalled in the text by inverted commas
at the left margin. Cf. Seneca, *Hippolytus, or Phaedra* 607: 'Curae leves loquuntur,
ingentes stupent.'

279–80 ed. (one line in Q)

282–322 At this point Webster shifts to a split stage, a characteristic technique (cf. *The
Duchess of Malfi* I.ii.75–133, III.iii), which allows him to highlight visual parallels
and contrasts between different groups.

284   *stibium* metallic antinomy, used as a poison
cantharides the dried beetle *cantharis vesicatoria*, or Spanish Fly, applied externally
to produce blisters as a counter-irritant (and taken internally as an aphrodisiac,
among other things), but poisonous if taken in excess

288–9 *to Candy* to Candia (now Crete), whose inhabitants were believed to live on
poisonous snakes – hence, to death

289   *property* stage accessory (for the 'play' Flamineo and Brachiano are writing);
instrument, tool
here's ed. (her's Q)

BRACHIANO

O the doctor.   290

FLAMINEO

A poor quack-salving knave, my lord, one that should have been
lashed for's lechery, but that he confessed a judgement, had an
execution laid upon him, and so put the whip to a *non plus*.

DOCTOR

And was cozened, my lord, by an arranter knave than myself,
and made pay all the colourable execution.   295

FLAMINEO

He will shoot pills into a man's guts, shall make them have more
ventages than a cornet or a lamprey; he will poison a kiss, and
was once minded, for his masterpiece, because Ireland breeds
no poison, to have prepared a deadly vapour in a Spaniard's fart
that should have poisoned all Dublin.   300

BRACHIANO

O Saint Anthony's fire!

DOCTOR

Your secretary is merry my lord.

291 *quack-salving* characteristic of a quack doctor
291–3 *should ... non plus* i.e. he should have been whipped for lechery, but that he
claimed to be under a previous sentence (for debt), was taken into custody, and in
this way rendered the whip ineffectual
294–5 *And ... execution* The doctor was then tricked by a greater rascal than himself
(who pretended to be the creditor to whom money was owed), and he was forced
to pay out everything required by the legal judgement.
295 *colourable execution* supposed judgement
296 *shoot pills* fire bullets in the form of pills
296–7 *more ... lamprey* more holes than a cornet (wind instrument) or a lamprey (fish
with numerous apertures on its head)
298–9 *Ireland ... poison* Ireland was supposed to be free of venomous beasts, because of
either the properties of the soil or the influence of St Patrick.
299–300 *deadly ... Dublin* A doubly xenophobic jest: a Spaniard, Don Diego, was notorious
for breaking wind in St Paul's some time before 1598; the Irish were supposed to
find such smells particularly offensive.
301 *Saint Anthony's fire* or *ignis sacer* (sacred fire), probably slang for breaking wind
(Dent, p. 96)
Anthony's ed. (Anthony Q)

FLAMINEO

O thou cursed antipathy to nature; look, his eye's bloodshed like
a needle a chirurgeon stitcheth a wound with. Let me embrace
thee toad, and love thee, [*Embraces him*] O thou abhominable   305
loathsome gargarism, that will fetch up lungs, lights, heart, and
liver by scruples.

BRACHIANO

No more; I must employ thee honest doctor,
You must to Padua and by the way
Use some of your skill for us.

DOCTOR   Sir I shall.   310

BRACHIANO

But for Camillo?

FLAMINEO

He dies this night by such a politic strain
Men shall suppose him by's own engine slain.
But for your Duchess' death—

DOCTOR   I'll make her sure.

BRACHIANO

Small mischiefs are by greater made secure.   315

FLAMINEO

Remember this you slave; when knaves come to preferment
they rise as gallowses are raised i'th'Low Countries, one upon
another's shoulders.

                Exeunt [BRACHIANO, FLAMINEO *and Doctor* JULIO]

MONTICELSO

[*Hands* CAMILLO *a paper*] Here is an emblem nephew, pray
    peruse it.
'Twas thrown in at your window.

303   *bloodshed* bloodshot
305   *abhominable* The common Renaissance spelling retains the false etymology of the
      word as from the Latin *ab homine*, away from man, inhuman, beastly.
306   *gargarism* gargle
      lights another word for lungs
307   *by scruples* in very small quantities
309–10 ed. (one line in Q)
312   *politic strain* cunning exigency; apparent accident
313   *engine* device, means
317–18 *they ... shoulders* improvised gallows, where one man hoists the other on his
      shoulders before stepping aside to leave the prisoner hanging
318   *another's* ed. (another Q)
319   *emblem* a picture expressing a moral fable or allegory, usually accompanied by a
      written gloss, extremely popular in Renaissance Europe

CAMILLO   At my window?   320
　　Here is a stag, my lord, hath shed his horns,
　　And for the loss of them the poor beast weeps:
　　The word *Inopem me copia fecit*.
MONTICELSO   That is:
　　Plenty of horns hath made him poor of horns.
CAMILLO
　　What should this mean?
MONTICELSO   I'll tell you: 'tis given out   325
　　You are a cuckold.
CAMILLO   Is it given out so?
　　I had rather such report as that my lord
　　Should keep within doors.
FRANCISCO   Have you any children?
CAMILLO
　　None my lord.
FRANCISCO   You are the happier:
　　I'll tell you a tale.
CAMILLO   Pray my lord.
FRANCISCO   An old tale.   330
　　Upon a time Phoebus the god of light,
　　Or him we call the sun, would need be married.
　　The gods gave their consent and Mercury
　　Was sent to voice it to the general world.
　　But what a piteous cry there straight arose   335
　　Amongst smiths, and feltmakers, brewers and cooks,

323　　*word* motto

　　Inopem . . . fecit 'My plenty makes me poor' (Narcissus complaining to his shadow
　　in Ovid, *Metamorphoses* III, 466). Like many of Webster's allegories, this one has
　　several possible applications, all hinging on the bawdy double meaning of 'horns' as
　　the sign for cuckold and penis, deprivation and potency, as well as their ambiguous
　　reference to Camillo and Brachiano. Thus the motto could mean that Camillo's
　　obvious status as a cuckold has made him impotent (like the weeping stag); or that
　　Brachiano's ample sexual satisfaction with Vittoria has left Camillo deprived; or
　　even that Brachiano's potency has left him sexually spent (cf. Lodge, *Wits Miserie*,
　　Works IV, ii, 321–4: 'his horns are not yet budded, because he moulted them verie
　　lately, in the lap of an Harlot', cited by Dent, p. 99).

330–51　This 'old tale' is borrowed from *The Fables of Esop in English* (1596 ed.). It appears
　　first to apply mockingly either to the foolish Camillo or to the 'fiery' Brachiano,
　　both of whom should be 'gelded', castrated; Francisco neatly twists it to apply to
　　Vittoria at the end.

Reapers and butter-women, amongst fishmongers
And thousand other trades, which are annoyed
By his excessive heat! 'Twas lamentable.
They came to Jupiter all in a sweat   340
And do forbid the bans. A great fat cook
Was made their speaker, who entreats of Jove
That Phoebus might be gelded, for if now
When there was but one sun, so many men
Were like to perish by his violent heat,   345
What should they do if he were married
And should beget more, and those children
Make fireworks like their father? So say I,
Only I will apply it to your wife:
Her issue, should not providence prevent it,   350
Would make both nature, time, and man repent it.

MONTICELSO
Look you cousin,
Go change the air for shame. See if your absence
Will blast your cornucopia. Marcello
Is chosen with you joint commissioner   355
For the relieving our Italian coast
From pirates.

MARCELLO   I am much honoured in't.

CAMILLO   But sir,
Ere I return the stag's horns may be sprouted
Greater than these are shed.

MONTICELSO   Do not fear it,
I'll be your ranger.

CAMILLO   You must watch i'th'nights,   360
Then's the most danger.

---

341   *bans* (banns) of marriage, called in church
348   *fireworks* fiery displays; products of fire or passion (more children); venereal disease; devils (NCW II.i.330–50 n.)
353   *Go ... air* go and leave this place
354   *cornucopia* normally a symbol of fertility, the 'horn of plenty', here ironically the 'plenty of horns' that are the cuckold's heraldry
358–9   *stag's ... shed* Are these 'stag's horns' Camillo's or Brachiano's? Since the stag sprouted horns in preparation for mating, Camillo may anticipate Brachiano's greater sexual vigour in his absence; but since the stag commonly represented the cuckold, Camillo may simply fear his shameful status will become more obvious.
360   *ranger* gamekeeper

FRANCISCO   Farewell good Marcello.
All the best fortunes of a soldier's wish
Bring you o'ship-board.

CAMILLO
Were I not best now I am turned soldier,
Ere that I leave my wife, sell all she hath   365
And then take leave of her?

MONTICELSO   I expect good from you,
Your parting is so merry.

CAMILLO
Merry my lord, o'th'captain's humour right;
I am resolved to be drunk this night.

Exit [*with* MARCELLO]

FRANCISCO
So, 'twas well fitted, now shall we discern   370
How his wished absence will give violent way
To Duke Brachiano's lust.

MONTICELSO   Why that was it;
To what scorned purpose else should we make choice
Of him for a sea-captain, and besides,
Count Lodowick which was rumoured for a pirate,   375
Is now in Padua.

FRANCISCO   Is't true?

MONTICELSO   Most certain.
I have letters from him, which are suppliant
To work his quick repeal from banishment;
He means to address himself for pension
Unto our sister Duchess.

FRANCISCO   O 'twas well.   380
We shall not want his absence past six days;
I fain would have the Duke Brachiano run
Into notorious scandal, for there's nought
In such cursed dotage to repair his name,
Only the deep sense of some deathless shame.   385

MONTICELSO
It may be objected I am dishonourable
To play thus with my kinsman, but I answer,

---

364   *Were I not best* i.e. would not the best thing for me be
380   *sister Duchess* Monticelso is Camillo's uncle, not Isabella's brother. 'Sister' may be a
       title of courtesy, or Webster may have confused Cardinal Monticelso with Cardinal
       de' Medici, Isabella's brother in life.

For my revenge I'd stake a brother's life
That being wronged durst not avenge himself.

FRANCISCO

Come to observe this strumpet.

MONTICELSO   Curse of greatness,   390
Sure he'll not leave her.

FRANCISCO   There's small pity in't.
Like mistletoe on sere elms spent by weather,
Let him cleave to her and both rot together.

Exeunt

[ACT II, SCENE ii]

Enter BRACHIANO *with one in the habit of a Conjuror*

BRACHIANO

Now sir I claim your promise; 'tis dead midnight,
The time prefixed to show me by your art
How the intended murder of Camillo
And our loathed Duchess grow to action.

CONJUROR

You have won me by your bounty to a deed   5
I do not often practise; some there are,
Which by sophistic tricks aspire that name
Which I would gladly lose, of nigromancer;
As some that use to juggle upon cards,
Seeming to conjure when indeed they cheat;   10
Others that raise up their confederate spirits
'Bout windmills, and endanger their own necks

---

392 *Like ... weather* Cf. III.i.47–8, where Flamineo alludes to the rare medicinal qualities of mistletoe, here ironically associated with Brachiano.

8 *lose* ed. (loose Q)
   nigromancer one who claims to carry on communication with the dead; wizard, conjuror (with a suggestion of the 'black art' contained in the prefix nigro-, from Latin *niger*, black)
9 *juggle* play tricks so as to cheat or deceive
12 *windmills* fanciful schemes or projects

For making of a squib; and some there are
Will keep a curtal to show juggling tricks
And give out 'tis a spirit: besides these   15
Such a whole ream of almanac-makers, figure-flingers,
Fellows indeed that only live by stealth,
Since they do merely lie about stol'n goods,
They'd make men think the devil were fast and loose,
With speaking fustian Latin. Pray sit down,   20
Put on this night-cap sir, 'tis charmed, and now
I'll show you by my strong-commanding art
The circumstance that breaks your Duchess' heart.

A DUMB SHOW

Enter suspiciously, DOCTOR JULIO *and* CHRISTOPHERO; *they
draw a curtain where* BRACHIANO's *picture is, they put on
spectacles of glass which cover their eyes and noses, and then burn
perfumes afore the picture and wash the lips of the picture; that*

13   *squib* explosive firework
13–15   *some ... spirit* one of many Renaissance references to Mr Banks, who travelled
         around England and the Continent with his performing horse, which was by 1595 a
         docked bay gelding, or curtal, named Morocco. Banks trained Morocco to perform
         some marvellous circus tricks, such as dancing, playing dead, counting money and
         responding to elaborate verbal instructions. Far from giving out that his horse was a
         spirit, however, Banks frequently defended himself against charges of witchcraft –
         apparently successfully, since despite Jonson's claim that he was burned at Rome as a
         witch (*Epigrams* no. 133), he retired to be a vintner in Cheapside.
16   *ream* realm (kingdom); large quantity (of paper)
      figure-flingers casters of horoscopes, pretenders to astrology
17–18   *live ... goods* possible reference to the casting of horoscopes to find stolen goods
19   *fast and loose* a proverbial phrase meaning shifty, unscrupulous: originally, a cheating
      game (in which a string which appeared to be easily made 'fast' or tight was in fact
      'loose', easily undone)
20   *fustian* inflated, made-up gibberish (cf. Francisco to the lawyer at III.ii.46)
23   *breaks ... heart* an echo of Isabella's own last words at II.i.276
23   s.d. *DUMB SHOW* The first dumb show anticipates Brachiano's own death by a
      poisoned beaver in V.iii (when he fears his kiss will poison Vittoria, l. 27). It also
      recapitulates allegorically the interview between Brachiano and Isabella in II.i, by
      restaging symbolically their kiss of divorce (l. 252). Both these elaborate dumb
      shows allow Webster to represent highly dramatic action while formalizing and dis-
      tancing its emotional impact (especially important in the case of Isabella's murder).
      Each dumb show was probably staged at either side of the full stage (not in a
      discovery space) to maximize the visual spectacle.
23   s.d.1 *suspiciously* in a manner deserving of suspicion
      CHRISTOPHERO like little Jacques the Moor (II.i.0 s.d.) and Guid-Antonio (below), a
      so-called 'ghost character' who appears briefly but delivers no lines. Usually explained

done, quenching the fire, and putting off their spectacles, they
depart laughing. Enter ISABELLA *in her nightgown as to*
bedward, with lights after her, Count LODOVICO, GIOVANNI,
GUID-ANTONIO *and others waiting on her; she kneels down as to*
prayers, then draws the curtain of the picture, does three reverences
to it, and kisses it thrice. She faints and will not suffer them to come
near it; dies. Sorrow expressed in GIOVANNI *and in Count*
LODOVICO; *she's conveyed out solemnly.*

BRACHIANO
    Excellent, then she's dead.

CONJUROR   She's poisoned
    By the fumed picture: 'twas her custom nightly,   25
    Before she went to bed, to go and visit
    Your picture, and to feed her eyes and lips
    On the dead shadow; Doctor Julio
    Observing this infects it with an oil
    And other poisoned stuff, which presently   30
    Did suffocate her spirits.

BRACHIANO   Methought I saw
    Count Lodowick there.

CONJUROR   He was, and by my art
    I find he did most passionately dote
    Upon your Duchess – now turn another way,
    And view Camillo's far more politic face,   35
    Strike louder music from this charmed ground,
    To yield, as fits the act, a tragic sound.

    as evidence of Webster's revision, such characters may also suggest Webster's acute
    theatrical awareness. Not only are silent figures thus clearly individualized, they may
    also have been doubled for significant visual effect. For example, Julio and
    Christophero, the murderers of Isabella, may have been doubled with Antonelli and
    Gasparo, the murderers of Brachiano, to emphasize the play's retributive pattern.
    s.d.2 *BRACHIANO's* ed. (Brachian's Q)

25 *fumed* exposed to ammonia vapour

28 *dead shadow* lifeless image

35 *face* Q4 emends 'face' to 'fate', which may be correct. However, Q may stand if
    'politic face' (sagacious visage) is taken to apply ironically to Camillo (cf.
    Flamineo's remark about Camillo at I.ii.45–8).

36 *Strike . . . music* Webster gives no stage direction to indicate what sort of music was
    provided, but it would have been appropriate if it issued from beneath the stage
    (NCW II.ii.36–7 n.).

37 s.d.2 *vaulting-horse* For this detail Webster may have either misunderstood, or
    knowingly literalized, Monte Cavallo, the actual place where Francesco Peretti,
    Camillo's historical counterpart, was murdered. The vaulting horse may also furnish

THE SECOND DUMB SHOW

Enter FLAMINEO, MARCELLO, CAMILLO *with four more as Captains, they drink healths and dance, a vaulting-horse is brought into the room,* MARCELLO *and two more whispered out of the room, while* FLAMINEO *and* CAMILLO *strip themselves into their shirts, as to vault; compliment who shall begin; as* CAMILLO *is about to vault,* FLAMINEO *pitcheth him upon his neck, and with the help of the rest, writhes his neck about, seems to see if it be broke, and lays him folded double as 'twere under the horse; makes shows to call for help.* MARCELLO *comes in, laments, sends for the Cardinal and Duke, who come forth with armed men, wonder at the act, commands the body to be carried home, apprehends* FLAMINEO, MARCELLO, *and the rest, and go as 'twere to apprehend* VITTORIA.

BRACHIANO
'Twas quaintly done, but yet each circumstance
I taste not fully.
CONJUROR   O 'twas most apparent,
You saw them enter charged with their deep healths   40
To their boon voyage, and to second that,
Flamineo calls to have a vaulting-horse
Maintain their sport. The virtuous Marcello
Is innocently plotted forth the room
Whilst your eye saw the rest, and can inform you   45
The engine of all.
[BRACHIANO]   It seems Marcello and Flamineo
Are both committed.
CONJUROR   Yes, you saw them guarded,
And now they are come with purpose to apprehend
Your mistress, fair Vittoria; we are now
Beneath her roof: 'twere fit we instantly   50
Make out by some back postern.

     an obscene visual joke at Camillo's expense – since 'vaulting' can mean 'mounting sexually' (as in *Cymbeline* I.vi.134), Camillo's ignominious position under the vaulting-horse is a visual sign of his sexual inadequacy.
38   *quaintly* skilfully, ingeniously
41   *boon* prosperous (as in 'bon voyage')
46   *engine* means, contrivance s.p. BRACHIANO ed. (MAR. Q)
47–51   The distanced perspective of the magical dumb shows is suddenly foreshortened; typically in Webster, observers are never safe from involvement in the action of the drama, as one perspective can shift into another with dizzying rapidity.

BRACHIANO   Noble friend,
  You bind me ever to you; this shall stand
  As the firm seal annexed to my hand.
  It shall enforce a payment.
CONJUROR   Sir I thank you.

Exit BRACHIANO

  Both flowers and weeds spring when the sun is warm,   55
  And great men do great good, or else great harm.

Exit

[ACT III, SCENE i]

Enter FRANCISCO, *and* MONTICELSO, *their* CHANCELLOR
and REGISTER

FRANCISCO
  You have dealt discreetly to obtain the presence
  Of all the grave lieger ambassadors
  To hear Vittoria's trial.
MONTICELSO   'Twas not ill,
  For sir you know we have nought but circumstances
  To charge her with, about her husband's death;   5
  Their approbation therefore to the proofs
  Of her black lust, shall make her infamous
  To all our neighbouring kingdoms. I wonder
  If Brachiano will be here.
FRANCISCO   O fie,
  'Twere impudence too palpable.   10

[*Exeunt*]

52–3   *this . . . hand* i.e. this token (money, a jewel, or simply, a handshake) will stand for
       the seal attached to my signature
  54   s.d. ed. (to r. of l. 53 in Q)
  56   s.d. *Exit* ed. (Exit Con. Q)

   0   s.d.1 As Francisco and Monticelso converse, their chancellor and register may be
       setting properties in place for the arraignment: a table (III.ii.8), and probably one
       or two raised chairs or 'states' for Monticelso and Francisco (NCW III.i.0.1 n.).
       s.d.2 REGISTER registrar (scribe or secretary)
   2   *lieger* resident
9–10   *If . . . fie/'Twere . . . palpable* ed. (one line in Q)

Enter FLAMINEO *and* MARCELLO *guarded, and a* LAWYER

LAWYER

What, are you in by the week? So; I will try now whether thy
wit be close prisoner: methinks none should sit upon thy sister
but old whore-masters.

FLAMINEO

Or cuckolds, for your cuckold is your most terrible tickler of
lechery: whore-masters would serve, for none are judges at   15
tilting, but those that have been old tilters.

LAWYER

My lord Duke and she have been very private.

FLAMINEO

You are a dull ass; 'tis threatened they have been very public.

LAWYER

If it can be proved they have but kissed one another—

FLAMINEO

What then?

LAWYER   My lord cardinal will ferret them.   20

FLAMINEO

A cardinal I hope will not catch conies.

LAWYER

For to sow kisses (mark what I say), to sow kisses, is to reap
lechery, and I am sure a woman that will endure kissing is
half won.

FLAMINEO

True, her upper part by that rule; if you will win her nether   25
part too, you know what follows.

[*Sennet offstage*]

11   *in by the week* ensnared, caught
12   *sit upon* sit in judgement on, with possibly an obscene suggestion of 'sit astride, mount'
14–15   *tickler* chastiser, punisher; also, provoker, inciter (cf. I.ii.90–2, where the jealous
     cuckold promotes his own betrayal)
16   *tilting* literally, jousting or thrusting as in a tournament; here, with a sexual innu-
     endo of thrusting as in copulation
17   *private* intimate; secretive, secluded
18   *public* open to general observation, conspicuous; also promiscuous (a 'public
     woman' was a prostitute: cf. *Othello* IV.ii.73: 'O thou public commoner')
20   *ferret* literally, to hunt (rabbits, etc.) with ferrets; metaphorically, to hunt down or
     question searchingly
21   *catch conies* literally, catch rabbits (as above); and punning on the senses swindle or
     dupe people; fornicate with women (a 'cony' could be applied to a woman either
     endearingly or indecently)

LAWYER

    Hark, the ambassadors are lighted.

FLAMINEO

    [*Aside*] I do put on this feigned garb of mirth

    To gull suspicion.

MARCELLO   O my unfortunate sister!

    I would my dagger's point had cleft her heart   30

    When she first saw Brachiano. You, 'tis said,

    Were made his engine, and his stalking-horse

    To undo my sister.

FLAMINEO   I made a kind of path

    To her and mine own preferment.

MARCELLO   Your ruin.

FLAMINEO

    Hum! thou art a soldier,   35

    Followest the great Duke, feedest his victories,

    As witches do their serviceable spirits,

    Even with thy prodigal blood. What hast got?

    But like the wealth of captains, a poor handful,

    Which in thy palm thou bear'st, as men hold water–   40

    Seeking to gripe it fast, the frail reward

    Steals through thy fingers.

MARCELLO   Sir–

FLAMINEO   Thou hast scarce maintenance

    To keep thee in fresh chamois.

MARCELLO   Brother–

FLAMINEO   Hear me.

    And thus when we have even poured ourselves

    Into great fights, for their ambition   45

    Or idle spleen, how shall we find reward,

---

32   *engine* instrument

    stalking-horse originally, a trained horse used by a fowler to get within easy reach of
    the game without being observed; hence, a person whose participation in an action
    is used to disguise its real design

37   *As . . . spirits* Witches were commonly supposed to nourish their spirits or familiars
    (usually beasts sent by the devil) with their own milk or blood from supernumary
    teats.

38   *prodigal* wastefully used

43   *chamois* supple leather jerkins worn beneath armour

But as we seldom find the mistletoe
Sacred to physic on the builder oak
Without a mandrake by it, so in our quest of gain.
Alas the poorest of their forced dislikes   50
At a limb proffers, but at heart it strikes:
This is lamented doctrine.

MARCELLO   Come, come.

FLAMINEO
When age shall turn thee
White as a blooming hawthorn—

MARCELLO   I'll interrupt you.
For love of virtue bear an honest heart,   55
And stride over every politic respect,
Which where they most advance they most infect.
Were I your father, as I am your brother,
I should not be ambitious to leave you
A better patrimony.

Enter SAVOY [AMBASSADOR]

FLAMINEO   I'll think on't—   60
The lord ambassadors.

---

47   *mistletoe* parasitic European plant sacred to the Druids which, when found growing
      on the oak, was thought to be able to cure illness
48   *on* ed. (: Or Q) *builder* which builds itself up, or is used for building
49   *mandrake* plant with narcotic and medicinal properties whose forked root resem-
      bles a human form and attracted superstition: it reputedly shrieked when pulled
      out of the ground and grew under the gallows (or the gallows-tree, the oak). The
      mandrake in Webster feeds, like the witch's familiars, on blood (cf. III.iii.112–13),
      and drives men mad (cf. *The Duchess of Malfi* II.v.1–2).
50–1 *Alas . . . strikes* i.e. the most insignificant of their feigned dislikes appears to injure
      only superficially but in fact it wounds deeply and irrecoverably (because it results
      in loss of favour)
60   s.d. ed. (opposite l. 60 in Q)
60–1 *A better . . . on't / The . . . ambassadors* ed. (one line in Q)
61   s.d.2 *Enter French Ambassador* ed. (Enter French Embassadours Q)
      Though the stage directions are slightly confusing, the procession is probably led by
      Savoy, who is followed by the French ambassador, the English ambassador, the
      Spanish ambassador and two more. This takes its place among processions over the
      stage, by which Webster highlights pivotal events of his drama (the arraignment,
      the papal election, the wedding of Brachiano and Vittoria). Typically, visual specta-
      cle is counterpointed by verbal commentary, and perspectives are always shifting:
      the ambassadors are now observed, now observers of the action (cf. IV.iii.4–32).

*Here there is a passage of the lieger Ambassadors over
the stage severally. Enter* FRENCH AMBASSADOR

LAWYER

O my sprightly Frenchman, do you know him? He's an admirable tilter.

FLAMINEO

I saw him at last tilting; he showed like a pewter candle-stick fashioned like a man in armour, holding a tilting staff in his 65 hand little bigger than a candle of twelve i'th'pound.

LAWYER

O but he's an excellent horseman.

FLAMINEO

A lame one in his lofty tricks; he sleeps o' horseback like a poulter.

Enter ENGLISH *and* SPANISH [AMBASSADORS]

LAWYER

Lo you my Spaniard. 70

FLAMINEO

He carries his face in's ruff, as I have seen a serving-man carry glasses in a cypress hat-band, monstrous steady for fear of breaking. He looks like the claw of a black-bird, first salted and then broiled in a candle.

Exeunt

63   *tilter* Cf. l. 16 above.
68–9   *he . . . poulter* 'lame' could mean 'impotent': i.e. all his attempts at (sexual) acrobatics result only in impotence; like poulterers who often fell asleep on the way to market. France was famous for both horsemanship and syphilis, which could lead to impotence.
72   *cypress hat-band* cobweb lawn or crepe used as a band for the hat
73–4   *He . . . candle* an ingenious analogy, in which the wide ruffs sported by the Spanish are compared to the claw of the blackbird which is spread wide when prepared for grilling
74   s.d. Flamineo, Marcello and the lawyer exit only to re-enter immediately in the larger group, thus emphasizing visually their loss of dramatic control as the arraignment begins.

[ACT III, SCENE ii]

THE ARRAIGNMENT OF VITTORIA

Enter FRANCISCO, MONTICELSO, *the six lieger* AMBASSADORS,
BRACHIANO, VITTORIA, [ZANCHE, FLAMINEO, MARCELLO,
SERVANT,] LAWYER, *and a* GUARD

MONTICELSO

[*To* BRACHIANO] Forbear my lord, here is no place assigned
   you,
This business by his holiness is left
To our examination.

BRACHIANO   May it thrive with you.

                              Lays a rich gown under him

---

0   s.d.1 *MONTICELSO* ed. (Montcelso Q)
    s.d.2–3 *ZANCHE . . . MARCELLO* ed. (Isabella Q)
    The title and mass entry signal the central importance of the arraignment for read-
    ers. The third act is divided into scenes for the convenience of readers, but may be
    considered a single unbroken dramatic unit on the stage. In fact, the stage is prob-
    ably never cleared in Act III, and the ambassadors, Flamineo, Marcello and the
    lawyer simply take their places, while the others enter. Judging from a title-page
    woodcut depicting a courtroom scene from *Swetnam the Woman Hater*, a Red Bull
    play staged about 1619, the original staging may have had Monticelso seated on a
    throne, facing the standing Vittoria (and possibly Zanche), while the ambassadors,
    court officials and Francisco, seated on low stools, were symmetrically placed on
    either side; Brachiano probably sat (conspicuously) on the floor, close to the audi-
    ence (NCW, pp. 101–3).
       The entry for Isabella – who has just been killed in the previous act – is usually
    dismissed as an irrational slip, but may be explained by the doubling of Isabella
    with Zanche (omitted in the stage direction but present in the scene). An actor who
    had just played Isabella may still have been identified in Webster's mind with that
    part. When Isabella reappears as a ghost in IV.i (obviously not in the blackface
    required for Zanche), she may have been shrouded (Francisco replaces his 'dead
    sister's face' with her more general 'figure' in his imagination, IV.i.98–101) or even
    played by another actor. Such a doubling would serve not only theatrical economy
    but also aesthetic design, linking Vittoria with Isabella through Zanche and further
    blurring the play's black/white, good/evil polarities.
1   *assigned* ed. (assing'd Q)
3   s.d. Brachiano's action may recall I.ii.186ff., where the two lovers rest on 'fair cush-
    ions' as they embrace. If so, the lovers' adultery is recalled even as it is about to be
    punished.

FRANCISCO

    A chair there for his lordship.

BRACHIANO

    Forbear your kindness; an unbidden guest   5

    Should travail as Dutch women go to church:

    Bear their stools with them.

MONTICELSO   At your pleasure sir.

    Stand to the table gentlewomen. Now signior,

    Fall to your plea.

[LAWYER]

    Domine judex converte oculos in hanc pestem mulierum   10

    corruptissimam.

VITTORIA

    What's he?

FRANCISCO A lawyer that pleads against you.

VITTORIA

    Pray my lord, let him speak his usual tongue.

    I'll make no answer else.

FRANCISCO   Why you understand Latin.

VITTORIA

    I do sir, but amongst this auditory   15

    Which come to hear my cause, the half or more

    May be ignorant in't.

---

8   *Stand . . . gentlewomen* Though many editors emend to 'gentlewoman', Monticelso may be referring to Vittoria and Zanche in these dignified terms with heavy irony, since the trial will reveal his contempt for both of them. The women are condemned together (ll. 263–4). The analogies between them that are later suggested would be strengthened by their appearing here side by side. On the other hand, if Vittoria appeared solo (requiring emendation of the text), that would strengthen parallels and contrasts with I.i and II.i, where Lodovico and Brachiano face social disapproval alone. The choice is left to the director.

10   s.p. *LAWYER* ed. (not in Q). The comically ineffectual lawyer may originally have been doubled with Camillo, 'thus failing twice to bring Vittoria to book' (Thomson, p. 28).

10–11 *Domine . . . corruptissimam* 'Lord Judge, turn your eyes upon this plague, the most corrupted of women.'

14 *Why . . . Latin* Probably a taunt, for in early modern England women rarely learned Latin. While Vittoria disdains the use of Latin, however, she pointedly uses it at l. 200.

15–16 *this . . . cause* probably a reference to the theatre audience (rather than to the well-educated ambassadors), some of whom would also be sitting on the stage at the Red Bull; an early indication of the metadramatic control Webster gives Vittoria

MONTICELSO   Go on sir.
VITTORIA   By your favour,
  I will not have my accusation clouded
  In a strange tongue: all this assembly
  Shall hear what you can charge me with.
FRANCISCO   Signior,   20
  You need not stand on't much; pray change your language.
MONTICELSO
  O for God sake: gentlewoman, your credit
  Shall be more famous by it.
LAWYER   Well then have at you.
VITTORIA
  I am at the mark sir, I'll give aim to you,
  And tell you how near you shoot.   25
LAWYER
  Most literated judges, please your lordships,
  So to connive your judgements to the view
  Of this debauched and diversivolent woman
  Who such a black concatenation
  Of mischief hath effected, that to extirp   30
  The memory of't must be the consummation
  Of her and her projections—
VITTORIA   What's all this?
LAWYER
  Hold your peace.
  Exorbitant sins must have exulceration.
VITTORIA
  Surely my lords this lawyer here hath swallowed   35

21 *stand on't* insist on it
22 *credit* reputation
24 *give aim* in archery, to guide someone's aim by informing him of the result of a pre-
    vious shot
27 *connive your judgements* a malapropism (for 'conduct your judgments'?) caused by
    the lawyer's pompous search for elaborate terms ('connive' means to shut one's eyes
    to, to be complicit in, injustice)
28 *diversivolent* wishing strife (a nonce-word, presumably inspired by the lawyer's avid
    search for Latinisms in place of Latin)
32 *projections* projects
34 *Exorbitant . . . exulceration* i.e. outrageous sins require punishment (ulcers must be
    lanced)

Some pothecary's bills, or proclamations.
And now the hard and undigestible words
Come up like stones we use give hawks for physic.
Why this is Welsh to Latin.

LAWYER   My lords, the woman
Knows not her tropes nor figures, nor is perfect   40
In the academic derivation
Of grammatical elocution.

FRANCISCO   Sir your pains
Shall be well spared, and your deep eloquence
Be worthily applauded amongst those
Which understand you.

LAWYER   My good lord.

FRANCISCO (*Speaks this as in scorn*)   Sir,   45
Put up your papers in your fustian bag—
Cry mercy sir, 'tis buckram – and accept
My notion of your learn'd verbosity.

LAWYER
I most graduatically thank your lordship.
I shall have use for them elsewhere.   [*Exit*]   50

---

36 *pothecary's bills* medical prescriptions, often inflated and long-winded. Cf. Webster's
    'Character' of a 'Quacksalver': 'a Mountebanke of a larger bill then a Taylor; if
    he can but come by names enow of Diseases, to stuffe it with, tis all the skill hee
    studies for'.
    proclamations formal orders issued in the name of the sovereign, often written in
    inflated prose
38 *Come up* Are vomited
    stones . . . physic 'If your Hawke by over-flying, or too soone flying, be heated and
    inflamed in her body, as they are much subject thereunto, you shall then to coole
    their bodies, give them stones' (Gervase Markham, *Cheape and Good Husbandry*
    (1614) S3).
39 *Welsh to Latin* Renaissance dramatists often used Welsh as the prototype of an
    unintelligible language (cf. *A Chaste Maid in Cheapside* IV.i.100–65, *1 Henry IV*
    III.i.187–240).
40 *tropes . . . figures* in rhetoric, the figurative use of words or phrases
42 *elocution* oratory: the art of appropriate and effective expression
45 s.d. ed. (to r. of ll. 46–7 in Q)
46 *fustian* a pun: coarse cloth made of cotton and flax; inflated, bombastic language
    composed of high-sounding words and phrases
47 *buckram* coarse, stiff linen traditionally used for lawyers' bags (as Francisco would
    know)
49 *graduatically* a nonce-word, meaning as a graduate should

MONTICELSO

    I shall be plainer with you, and paint out
    Your follies in more natural red and white
    Than that upon your cheek.

VITTORIA   O you mistake.
    You raise a blood as noble in this cheek
    As ever was your mother's.   55

MONTICELSO

    I must spare you till proof cry whore to that;
    Observe this creature here my honoured lords,
    A woman of a most prodigious spirit
    In her effected.

VITTORIA   Honourable my lord,
    It doth not suit a reverend cardinal   60
    To play the lawyer thus.

MONTICELSO

    O your trade instructs your language!
    You see my lords what goodly fruit she seems,
    Yet like those apples travellers report
    To grow where Sodom and Gomorrah stood: 65
    I will but touch her and you straight shall see
    She'll fall to soot and ashes.

VITTORIA

    Your envenomed pothecary should do't.

51–3   *plainer . . . cheek* The Cardinal is invoking the misogynist stereotype of the 'painted'
       woman (cf. *Hamlet* III.i.143–4: 'God hath given you one face and you make your-
       selves another'), and claiming he will use the 'plain' style to 'paint' (show) Vittoria
       by contrast.

  58   *spirit* courage; perhaps punning on the bawdy senses 'semen' or 'erection' (as in
       Romeo and Juliet II.i.23–4: ' 'Twould anger him / To raise a spirit in his mistress'
       circle')

  59   *effected* brought about, produced (a weak and redundant ending to Monticelso's
       grand rhetorical flourish – here he sounds like the kind of lawyer Vittoria accuses
       him of playing); ejaculated (NCW III.ii.59 n.)

64–7   *apples . . . ashes* The original source is Deuteronomy 32:32: 'their vine is of the vine
       of Sodom, and of the fields of Gomorrah; their grapes are grapes of gall, their clus-
       ters are bitter'. This detail about apples turning to ashes is apocryphal, but
       frequently invoked by authors such as Sir John Mandeville (*Travels*, p. xxx), who
       interprets it as a sign of God's vengeance in burning up the cities.

  68   *Your . . . do't* i.e. your poisonous apothecary, not you, should reduce me to ashes.
       Vittoria cleverly turns Monticelso's metaphor against him – his or his apothecary's
       touch, rather than her nature, is 'envenomed'.

MONTICELSO

    I am resolved.

    Were there a second paradise to loose   70

    This devil would betray it.

VITTORIA   O poor charity!

    Thou art seldom found in scarlet.

MONTICELSO

    Who knows not how, when several night by night

    Her gates were choked with coaches and her rooms

    Outbraved the stars with several kind of lights,   75

    When she did counterfeit a prince's court

    In music, banquets and most riotous surfeits,

    This whore, forsooth, was holy?

VITTORIA   Ha? Whore, what's that?

MONTICELSO

    Shall I expound whore to you? Sure I shall;

    I'll give their perfect character. They are first   80

    Sweetmeats which rot the eater: in man's nostril

    Poisoned perfumes. They are coz'ning alchemy,

    Shipwrecks in calmest weather! What are whores?

    Cold Russian winters, that appear so barren

    As if that nature had forgot the spring.   85

    They are the true material fire of hell,

    Worse than those tributes i'th'Low Countries paid,

    Exactions upon meat, drink, garments, sleep;

    Ay even on man's perdition, his sin.

    They are those brittle evidences of law   90

    Which forfeit all a wretched man's estate

    For leaving out one syllable. What are whores?

    They are those flattering bells have all one tune,

---

72   *scarlet* colour of a cardinal's vestments and a lawyer's robes

78   *holy?* ed. (holy Q)

80   *character* formal description of a character-type based on the classical models of Theophrastus. Webster himself contributed several to the second edition of Overbury's *Characters*.

82   *Poisoned perfumes* a fleeting verbal reminder of Brachiano's murder of Isabella, which is still undiscovered; Brachiano's unpunished crimes are recalled as Vittoria is tried simply for 'black lust' (III.i.7).

     alchemy the process of transforming baser metals into gold, often requiring the investment of vast sums of money by hopefuls (cf. I.ii.138)

87–9 *Worse ... sin* At this time in the Low Countries taxes, especially those on wine, often equalled or exceeded the value of the commodity itself.

At weddings, and at funerals: your rich whores
Are only treasuries by extortion filled, 95
And emptied by curs'd riot. They are worse,
Worse than dead bodies, which are begged at gallows
And wrought upon by surgeons, to teach man
Wherein he is imperfect. What's a whore?
She's like the guilty counterfeited coin 100
Which whosoe'er first stamps it brings in trouble
All that receive it.

VITTORIA   This character scapes me.

MONTICELSO
You, gentlewoman,
Take from all beasts, and from all minerals
Their deadly poison.

VITTORIA   Well what then?

MONTICELSO   I'll tell thee. 105
I'll find in thee a pothecary's shop
To sample them all.

FRENCH AMBASSADOR   She hath lived ill.

ENGLISH AMBASSADOR
True, but the cardinal's too bitter.

MONTICELSO
You know what whore is; next the devil, Adult'ry,
Enters the devil, Murder.

FRANCISCO   Your unhappy husband 110
Is dead.

VITTORIA O he's a happy husband
Now he owes nature nothing.

FRANCISCO
And by a vaulting engine.

MONTICELSO   An active plot;
He jumped into his grave.

97–9   *dead . . . imperfect* The Barber-Surgeons were legally allowed four executed felons a
year for the purpose of instructing students in anatomy; others may have been
'begged'.

100   *guilty* probably with a play on 'gilt'

100–1   *counterfeited . . . it* For counterfeiting as a metaphor for illicit intercourse, cf.
Measure for Measure II.iv.45–6.

101   *brings* ed. (bring Q)

109   *whore . . . Adult'ry* ed. (Whore is next the devell; Adultry. Q)

FRANCISCO   What a prodigy was't,
   That from some two yards' height a slender man   115
   Should break his neck?
MONTICELSO   I'th'rushes.
FRANCISCO   And what's more,
   Upon the instant lose all use of speech,
   All vital motion, like a man had lain
   Wound up three days. Now mark each circumstance.
MONTICELSO
   And look upon this creature was his wife.   120
   She comes not like a widow: she comes armed
   With scorn and impudence. Is this a mourning habit?
VITTORIA
   Had I foreknown his death as you suggest,
   I would have bespoke my mourning.
MONTICELSO   O you are cunning.
VITTORIA
   You shame your wit and judgement   125
   To call it so. What, is my just defence
   By him that is my judge called impudence?
   Let me appeal then from this Christian court
   To the uncivil Tartar.
MONTICELSO   See my lords,
   She scandals our proceedings.
VITTORIA [*Kneeling*]   Humbly thus,   130
   Thus low, to the most worthy and respected
   Lieger ambassadors, my modesty
   And womanhood I tender; but withal
   So entangled in a cursed accusation
   That my defence, of force, like Perseus   135

116 *rushes* commonly strewn on the floor in private houses and on the stage
117 *lose* ed. (loose Q)
119 *Wound up* wrapped in a winding-sheet or shroud
122 Vittoria is wearing a sumptuous gown.
128 *Christian* ecclesiastical; civilized (not barbarous)
129 *uncivil* uncivilized. The Tartars were infamous for barbarism and cruelty.
130 *scandals* disgraces s.d. Vittoria may curtsy here; however, kneeling seems an appropriate demonstration of her humility and courage (cf. *The Duchess of Malfi* IV.ii.230) and echoes I.ii.261.
135 *of force* of necessity
     Perseus son of Zeus and Danae. Perseus cut off the head of the Gorgon Medusa and saved Andromeda from the sea monster. In Jonson's *Masque of Queens* (1609),

Must personate masculine virtue to the point.
Find me but guilty, sever head from body:
We'll part good friends: I scorn to hold my life
At yours or any man's entreaty, sir.

ENGLISH AMBASSADOR
She hath a brave spirit.   140

MONTICELSO
Well, well, such counterfeit jewels
Make true ones oft suspected.

VITTORIA   You are deceived.
For know that all your strict combined heads,
Which strike against this mine of diamonds,
Shall prove but glassen hammers, they shall break;   145
These are but feigned shadows of my evils.
Terrify babes, my lord, with painted devils,
I am past such needless palsy, for your names
Of Whore and Murd'ress, they proceed from you,
As if a man should spit against the wind,   150
The filth returns in's face.

MONTICELSO
Pray you mistress satisfy me one question:
Who lodged beneath your roof that fatal night
Your husband brake his neck?

BRACHIANO   That question
Enforceth me break silence: I was there.   155

MONTICELSO
Your business?

BRACHIANO   Why I came to comfort her,
And take some course for settling her estate,
Because I heard her husband was in debt
To you my lord.

MONTICELSO   He was.

BRACHIANO   And 'twas strangely feared
That you would cozen her.

Perseus, 'expressing heroique and masculine Vertue', routs the antimasque of
witches and celebrates the virtues of twelve famous queens.

136 *personate* imitate; symbolize, emblematically represent *virtue* moral excellence;
physical courage, valour *to the point* exactly, in every detail

143 *strict combined heads* literally, the joint force of your hammer-heads; figuratively,
your closely allied military forces

148 *palsy* trembling (with fear)

MONTICELSO	Who made you overseer?	160

BRACHIANO
Why my charity, my charity, which should flow
From every generous and noble spirit,
To orphans and to widows.

MONTICELSO   Your lust.

BRACHIANO
Cowardly dogs bark loudest. Sirrah priest,
I'll talk with you hereafter, – Do you hear?   165
The sword you frame of such an excellent temper,
I'll sheathe in your own bowels:
There are a number of thy coat resemble
Your common post-boys.

MONTICELSO   Ha?

BRACHIANO   Your mercenary post-boys.
Your letters carry truth, but 'tis your guise   170
To fill your mouths with gross and impudent lies.

                                        [*He makes for the exit*]

SERVANT
My lord your gown.

BRACHIANO   Thou liest, 'twas my stool.
Bestow't upon thy master that will challenge
The rest o'th'household stuff, for Brachiano
Was ne'er so beggarly, to take a stool   175
Out of another's lodging: let him make
Valance for his bed on't, or a demi-foot-cloth,
For his most reverent moil; Monticelso,

---

161 *charity* Cf. l. 71: Brachiano supplies the 'charity' which (as Vittoria remarks)
     Monticelso should show. While it targets Monticelso, the line also exposes Brachiano
     as a liar and possibly a coward, since he is providing himself with an alibi.

166 *sword* metaphoric weapon against Brachiano, which he declares he will use as a
     sword of justice *temper* referring to Monticelso, anger; referring to the sword, the
     resilient strength imparted to steel by tempering

168 *coat* clerical profession

169 *post-boys* letter-carriers

173 *challenge* lay claim to

177 *Valance* drapes around a bed canopy
     demi-foot-cloth half-length covering for a horse, used by lesser dignitaries; an insult
     (NCW III.ii.177 n.)

178 *moil* mule (traditional mount for cardinals)

Nemo me impune lacessit.   *Exit*

MONTICELSO
   Your champion's gone.

VITTORIA   The wolf may prey the better.   180

FRANCISCO
   My lord there's great suspicion of the murder,
   But no sound proof who did it: for my part
   I do not think she hath a soul so black
   To act a deed so bloody; if she have,
   As in cold countries husbandmen plant vines   185
   And with warm blood manure them, even so
   One summer she will bear unsavoury fruit,
   And ere next spring wither both branch and root.
   The act of blood let pass, only descend
   To matter of incontinence.

VITTORIA   I discern poison   190
   Under your gilded pills.

MONTICELSO
   [*Showing a letter*] Now the Duke's gone I will produce a letter,
   Wherein 'twas plotted he and you should meet
   At an apothecary's summer-house,
   Down by the river Tiber: view't my lords: 195
   Where after wanton bathing and the heat
   Of a lascivious banquet – I pray read it,
   I shame to speak the rest.

VITTORIA   Grant I was tempted,
   Temptation to lust proves not the act,
   Casta est quam nemo rogavit,   200
   You read his hot love to me, but you want
   My frosty answer.

---

179 *Nemo me impune lacessit* 'No one wounds me with impunity.' *lacessit* ed. (lacescit Q)
     s.d. *Exit* ed. (Exit Brachiano Q)

190–1 *poison . . . pills* Apothecaries sometimes covered pills with gold in order to increase
     their prices.

193 *he* ed. (her Q)

195 At several points during the scene (ll. 57, 107–8, 119–20, 130–3, 140), the audi-
     ence's attention is drawn away from the sparring combatants to the ambassadors,
     allowing a more detached assessment of the scene.

200 *Casta est nemo rogavit* 'Chaste is she whom no man has asked' (from Ovid,
     Amores I.viii.43). The context of the line is ironic since it occurs in a speech
     designed to persuade a woman to take many lovers.

MONTICELSO   Frost i'th'dog-days! Strange!

VITTORIA

    Condemn you me for that the Duke did love me,
    So may you blame some fair and crystal river
    For that some melancholic distracted man   205
    Hath drowned himself in't.

MONTICELSO   Truly drowned indeed.

VITTORIA

    Sum up my faults I pray, and you shall find
    That beauty and gay clothes, a merry heart,
    And a good stomach to feast, are all,
    All the poor crimes that you can charge me with: 210
    In faith my lord you might go pistol flies,
    The sport would be more noble.

MONTICELSO   Very good.

VITTORIA

    But take you your course, it seems you have beggared me first
    And now would fain undo me; I have houses,
    Jewels, and a poor remnant of crusadoes,   215
    Would those would make you charitable.

MONTICELSO   If the devil

    Did ever take good shape behold his picture.

VITTORIA

    You have one virtue left,
    You will not flatter me.

FRANCISCO   Who brought this letter?

VITTORIA

    I am not compelled to tell you.   220

MONTICELSO

    My lord Duke sent to you a thousand ducats,
    The twelfth of August.

VITTORIA   'Twas to keep your cousin
    From prison; I paid use for't.

MONTICELSO   I rather think
    'Twas interest for his lust.

---

202   *dog-days* very hot and oppressive weather when Sirius the Dog-star is high, and
      when malignant influences including lust were supposed to prevail
215   *crusadoes* Portuguese coins of gold or silver bearing the figure of a cross
223   *use* interest

VITTORIA

Who says so but yourself? If you be my accuser   225
Pray cease to be my judge, come from the bench,
Give in your evidence 'gainst me, and let these
Be moderators; my lord cardinal,
Were your intelligencing ears as long
As to my thoughts, had you an honest tongue   230
I would not care though you proclaimed them all.

MONTICELSO

Go to, go to.
After your goodly and vain-glorious banquet
I'll give you a choke-pear.

VITTORIA   O' your own grafting?

MONTICELSO

You were born in Venice, honourably descended   235
From the Vitelli; 'twas my cousin's fate—
Ill may I name the hour – to marry you;
He bought you of your father.

VITTORIA   Ha?

MONTICELSO

He spent there in six months
Twelve thousand ducats, and to my acquaintance   240
Received in dowry with you not one julio:
'Twas a hard penny-worth, the ware being so light.
I yet but draw the curtain now to your picture:
You came from thence a most notorious strumpet,
And so you have continued.

227   *these* i.e. the ambassadors, or more broadly, the theatre audience
229   *intelligencing* spying
       long ed. (louing Q)
234   *choke-pear* rough, unpalatable pear, difficult to swallow; a severe reproof
       grafting literally, with trees and plants, the action of inserting a shoot or scion into a
       groove or slit made in another stock, so as to allow the sap of the latter to circulate
       through the former; with an obvious bawdy sense (as in *The Duchess of Malfi*
       II.i.148–9)
235–6 *born . . . Vitelli* The real Vittoria was descended from the Accoramboni and born at
       Gubbio, but Webster may have wanted to associate her with Venice, famed for its
       prostitutes.
241   *julio* silver coin struck by Pope Julius II (1503–13), formerly current in Italy. There
       may be an unintended ironic reference to 'Doctor Julio' (cf. II.ii.28) as Vittoria's real
       'dowry' or gift to Camillo, especially since the word is italicized like other proper
       names in the copy.
242   *light* not heavy; wanton, unchaste

VITTORIA	My lord.	
MONTICELSO	Nay hear me,	245

    You shall have time to prate – my lord Brachiano–
    Alas I make but repetition,
    Of what is ordinary and Rialto talk,
    And ballated, and would be played o'th'stage,
    But that vice many times finds such loud friends   250
    That preachers are charmed silent.
    You gentlemen Flamineo and Marcello,
    The court hath nothing now to charge you with,
    Only you must remain upon your sureties
    For your appearance.

FRANCISCO   I stand for Marcello.   255

FLAMINEO

    And my lord Duke for me.

MONTICELSO

    For you Vittoria, your public fault,
    Joined to th'condition of the present time,
    Takes from you all the fruits of noble pity.
    Such a corrupted trial have you made   260
    Both of your life and beauty, and been styled
    No less in ominous fate than blazing stars
    To princes; here's your sentence: you are confined
    Unto a house of convertites and your bawd–

FLAMINEO

    [*Aside*] Who I?

MONTICELSO   The Moor.

FLAMINEO [*Aside*]   O I am a sound man again.   265

---

246   *prate . . . Brachiano* – ed. (no punctuation in Q)
      prate tell or repeat to little purpose
248   *Rialto talk* talk of the Exchange, or meeting-place
249   *ballated* turned into a ballad (and thus made notorious)
      would . . . stage As many contemporary scandals were in Webster's time.
254   *sureties* persons who will make themselves liable for another's appearance in court
257   *public* Cf. III.i.18n.
262   *blazing stars* comets, considered signs of ill omen, especially for great men
263   *To . . . here's* ed. (To Princes heares; Q)
264   *Unto* ed. (VIT. Unto Q)
      house of convertites The real-life Vittoria was imprisoned in Castel Sant' Angelo in
      Rome, though a contemporary account, translated by John Florio, claims she was
      'put into a monasterie of Nunnes'. In Jacobean London the 'house of correction' for
      reformed prostitutes was Bridewell.

VITTORIA
  A house of convertites, what's that?
MONTICELSO   A house
  Of penitent whores.
VITTORIA   Do the noblemen in Rome
  Erect it for their wives, that I am sent
  To lodge there?
FRANCISCO
  You must have patience.
VITTORIA   I must first have vengeance.   270
  I fain would know if you have your salvation
  By patent, that you proceed thus.
MONTICELSO   Away with her.
  Take her hence.   [GUARD *leads* VITTORIA *away*]
VITTORIA   A rape, a rape!
MONTICELSO   How?
VITTORIA
  Yes, you have ravished Justice,
  Forced her to do your pleasure.
MONTICELSO   Fie, she's mad.   275
VITTORIA
  Die with these pills in your most cursed maws,
  Should bring you health, or while you sit o'th'bench,
  Let your own spittle choke you.
MONTICELSO   She's turned fury.
VITTORIA
  That the last day of judgement may so find you,
  And leave you the same devil you were before,   280
  Instruct me some good horse-leech to speak treason,
  For since you cannot take my life for deeds,
  Take it for words. O woman's poor revenge
  Which dwells but in the tongue; I will not weep,

266–7   *A . . . Rome* ed. (A . . . that? / MON . . . whoores./Do . . . Rome, Q)
269–70 *To . . . there? / You . . . vengeance* ed. (To . . . patience / I . . . vengeance Q)
  272   *patent* special licence
  276   *maws* throats, gullets
276–7   *Die . . . health* probably a reference to the 'gilded pills' (l. 191) or apparently pious
          words uttered by her enemies
  281   *horse-leech* literally, blood-sucker; a cunning rhetorician (as in Erasmus, *Praise of
          Folly* (1509): 'the rhetoricians of our day who consider themselves as good as gods
          if like horse-leeches they can seem to have two tongues' (trans. Clarence Miller,
          1979: p. 14))

No I do scorn to call up one poor tear   285
To fawn on your injustice; bear me hence,
Unto this house of – what's your mitigating title?

MONTICELSO

Of convertites.

VITTORIA

It shall not be a house of convertites.
My mind shall make it honester to me   290
Than the Pope's palace, and more peaceable
Than thy soul, though thou art a cardinal.
Know this, and let it somewhat raise your spite,
Through darkness diamonds spread their richest light.

Exit [with ZANCHE, *guarded]*

Enter BRACHIANO

BRACHIANO

Now you and I are friends sir, we'll shake hands,   295
In a friend's grave, together: a fit place,
Being the emblem of soft peace t'atone our hatred.

FRANCISCO

Sir, what's the matter?

BRACHIANO

I will not chase more blood from that loved cheek,
You have lost too much already; fare you well.   [*Exit*]   300

FRANCISCO

How strange these words sound? What's the interpretation?

FLAMINEO

[*Aside*] Good, this is a preface to the discovery of the Duchess'
death. He carries it well. Because now I cannot counterfeit a
whining passion for the death of my lady, I will feign a mad
humour for the disgrace of my sister, and that will keep off idle   305
questions. Treason's tongue hath a villainous palsy in't; I will talk

288–9   ed. (one line in Q)
294   s.d. *Exit* ed. (Exit Vittoria Q)
295–339 Webster again employs the simultaneous staging which allows him to develop
        visual parallels (cf. II.i.282–322); the ambassadors silently confer with Monticelso
        (about the trial) while Francisco and Giovanni react to news of Isabella's death:
        thus Vittoria's 'disgrace' is juxtaposed with Isabella's 'death' (as in Flamineo's
        speech, ll. 303–6), and cause and effect are reversed in the dramatic sequence
306   *palsy* nervous disease characterized by involuntary tremors.

to any man, hear no man, and for a time appear a politic
madman. [*Exit*]

Enter GIOVANNI, *Count* LODOVICO

FRANCISCO
How now my noble cousin, what in black?
GIOVANNI
Yes uncle, I was taught to imitate you   310
In virtue, and you must imitate me
In colours for your garments; my sweet mother
Is–
FRANCISCO How? Where?
GIOVANNI
Is there – no, yonder; indeed sir I'll not tell you,
For I shall make you weep.
FRANCISCO   Is dead.   315
GIOVANNI
Do not blame me now,
I did not tell you so.
LODOVICO   She's dead my lord.
FRANCISCO
Dead?
MONTICELSO
Blessed lady; thou art now above thy woes.
[*To* AMBASSADORS] Wilt please your lordships to withdraw a
    little?   320
GIOVANNI
What do the dead do, uncle? Do they eat,
Hear music, go a-hunting, and be merry,
As we that live?
FRANCISCO
No coz; they sleep.
GIOVANNI   Lord, Lord, that I were dead–
I have not slept these six nights. When do they wake?   325
FRANCISCO
When God shall please.

---

319 *Blessed ... woes* ed. (Dead? ... Lady/Thou ... woes Q)
322–3 ed. (one line in Q)

GIOVANNI   Good God let her sleep ever.
  For I have known her wake an hundred nights,
  When all the pillow, where she laid her head,
  Was brine-wet with her tears. I am to complain to you sir.
  I'll tell you how they have used her now she's dead: 330
  They wrapped her in a cruel fold of lead,
  And would not let me kiss her.
FRANCISCO   Thou didst love her.
GIOVANNI
  I have often heard her say she gave me suck,
  And it should seem by that she dearly loved me,
  Since princes seldom do it.   335
FRANCISCO
  O all of my poor sister that remains!
  Take him away for God's sake—
                      [*Exeunt* GIOVANNI *and* LODOVICO]
MONTICELSO   How now my Lord?
FRANCISCO
  Believe me I am nothing but her grave,
  And I shall keep her blessed memory
  Longer than thousand epitaphs.   340
                                          [*Exeunt*]

---

327 *For* ed. (GIO. For I Q) s.p. misplaced
331 *fold of lead* covering made of lead (an aristocratic addition to the more permeable
     winding sheet made of linen in which all corpses were wrapped); a leaden coffin
     moulded to the shape of the body (designed to preserve the corpse)
333 *she ... suck* No mean boast among the English or Italian upper classes, whose
     infants were usually sent out to wet-nurses. Much of the domestic conduct litera-
     ture recommended that mothers nurse their own children: 'How can a mother
     better expresse her love to her young babe, then by letting it sucke of her owne
     breasts?' (William Gouge, *Of Domesticall Duties* (1612) p. 509).

Enter FLAMINEO *as distracted* [, MARCELLO *and* LODOVICO]

FLAMINEO

We endure the strokes like anvils or hard steel,
Till pain itself make us no pain to feel.
Who shall do me right now? Is this the end of service?
I'd rather go weed garlic; travail through France, and be mine
own ostler; wear sheep-skin linings; or shoes that stink of   5
blacking; be entered into the list of the forty thousand pedlars
in Poland.

Enter SAVOY [AMBASSADOR]

Would I had rotted in some surgeon's house at Venice, built
upon the pox as well as on piles, ere I had served Brachiano.

SAVOY AMBASSADOR

You must have comfort.   10

FLAMINEO

Your comfortable words are like honey. They relish well in your
mouth that's whole; but in mine that's wounded they go down
as if the sting of the bee were in them. O they have wrought
their purpose cunningly, as if they would not seem to do it of
malice. In this a politician imitates the devil, as the devil imitates   15

---

   0   s.d. *as distracted* The s.d. ('as distracted') may indicate gestures or dress befitting
the 'distracted' person. The s.d. at V.iv.88 reads 'Cornelia doth this in several forms
of distraction', suggesting, perhaps, such conventionalized gestures as wringing the
hands and beating the breast.

   5   *ostler* groom, stable-boy *linings* underclothing

6–7   *forty . . . Poland* The Poles were proverbially poor.

   9   *built . . . piles* i.e. built on a fortune made from curing syphilis, as well as haemor-
rhoids (with a pun on 'piles' as pillars or timbers, especially necessary as
foundations in Venice)

12–14   *they . . . them* lines borrowed from an unidentified translation of Seneca, *Epistles*
109, 7: 'Some there are to whom honey seemeth bitter in regard of their sicknesse'
(trans. Lodge). Cf. Pierre Matthieu, *The History of Lewis the Eleventh* (1611):
'Honey how sweet soever it be, is sharpe and offensive to a mouth ulcered with passion and slander' (p. 25).

a cannon. Wheresoever he comes to do mischief, he comes with
his backside towards you.

Enter the FRENCH [AMBASSADOR]

FRENCH AMBASSADOR
The proofs are evident.

FLAMINEO
Proof! 'Twas corruption. O Gold, what a god art thou! And O
man, what a devil art thou to be tempted by that cursed   20
mineral! Yon diversivolent lawyer – mark him, knaves turn
informers, as maggots turn to flies; you may catch gudgeons
with either. A cardinal – I would he would hear me – there's
nothing so holy but money will corrupt and putrify it, like
victual under the line.   25

Enter ENGLISH AMBASSADOR

You are happy in England, my lord; here they sell justice with
those weights they press men to death with. O horrible salary!

ENGLISH AMBASSADOR
Fie, fie, Flamineo.

FLAMINEO
Bells ne'er ring well till they are at their full pitch, and I hope
yon cardinal shall never have the grace to pray well, till he come   30
to the scaffold.

[*Exeunt* AMBASSADORS]

16–17 *Wheresoever . . . you* Showing one's back is not threatening but, as with a cannon,
    one has only to turn to face someone to be a threat.
  21 *Yon* ed. (You Q)
    diversivolent Flamineo uses the lawyer's word against him (cf. III.ii.28).
    turn turn into
  22 *gudgeons* small fish much used for bait; credulous gulls
  25 *victual . . . line* food at the equator
    line ed. (live Q)
  25 s.d. ed. (*Enter English Embassador* l. margin opposite l. 27 in Q)
    here . . . with ironic, since it was English law which devised the *peine forte et dure*, or
    torture of the press, for those who remained mute when required to plead at trial.
    Prisoners who were thus starved and crushed under heavy iron weights died in
    slow agony, though their property could not be confiscated from their heirs
    because they could not be convicted.
  27 *salary* reward
  29 *full pitch* highest point (of a bell-tower)

If they were racked now to know the confederacy! But your
noblemen are privileged from the rack; and well may. For a little
thing would pull some of them a' pieces afore they came to their
arraignment. Religion; oh how it is commeddled with policy.   35
The first bloodshed in the world happened about religion.
Would I were a Jew.

MARCELLO

Oh, there are too many.

FLAMINEO

You are deceived. There are not Jews enough, priests enough,
nor gentlemen enough.   40

MARCELLO

How?

FLAMINEO

I'll prove it. For if there were Jews enough, so many Christians
would not turn usurers; if priests enough, one should not have six
benefices; and if gentlemen enough, so many early mushrooms,
whose best growth sprang from a dunghill, should not aspire to   45
gentility. Farewell. Let others live by begging. Be thou one of
them; practise the art of Wolner in England to swallow all's given
thee; and yet let one purgation make thee as hungry again as
fellows that work in a sawpit. I'll go hear the screech-owl.   *Exit*

LODOVICO

[*Aside*] This was Brachiano's pander, and 'tis strange   50
That in such open and apparent guilt
Of his adulterous sister, he dare utter
So scandalous a passion. I must wind him.

---

33   *well may* with good reason
34   *pull . . . pieces* dismember on the rack; reduce to a state of confusion
35   *commeddled* mixed together
     policy intrigue
36   *first . . . religion* a reference to Cain's murder of his brother Abel, possibly fore-
     shadowing Flamineo's murder of Marcello (cf. V.vi.13–14)
39   *Jews* synonymous with usurers, as in *The Merchant of Venice*
44   *early mushrooms* young upstarts
47–8 *practise . . . thee* Wolner was a famous Elizabethan glutton who consumed iron, glass,
     oyster shells, raw meat and raw fish. He died of eating raw eel. Flamineo is very likely
     reiterating his cynical view of Marcello's exploitation by Francisco (cf. III.i.38–43).
49   *a sawpit* ed. (sawpit Q)
     screech-owl bird of evil omen
53   *wind* find out about

Enter FLAMINEO

FLAMINEO
  [*Aside*] How dares this banished count return to Rome,
  His pardon not yet purchased? I have heard   55
  The deceased Duchess gave him pension,
  And that he came along from Padua
  I'th'train of the young prince. There's somewhat in't.
  Physicians, that cure poisons, still do work
  With counterpoisons.
MARCELLO [*Aside*]   Mark this strange encounter.   60
FLAMINEO
  The god of melancholy turn thy gall to poison,
  And let the stigmatic wrinkles in thy face
  Like to the boisterous waves in a rough tide
  One still overtake another.
LODOVICO   I do thank thee
  And I do wish ingeniously for thy sake   65
  The dog-days all year long.
FLAMINEO   How croaks the raven?
  Is our good Duchess dead?
LODOVICO   Dead.
FLAMINEO   O fate!
  Misfortune comes like the crowner's business,
  Huddle upon huddle.
LODOVICO
  Shalt thou and I join housekeeping?
FLAMINEO   Yes, content.   70
  Let's be unsociably sociable.

  55 *purchased* obtained
  56 *pension* salary, wages
60–129 This 'strange encounter' brings the play's two tool-villains into parallel relation:
      both are the miserable dependants of great men, though Lodovico does not share
      Flamineo's complex ambivalence about his position.
  61 *gall* gall bladder, supposed source of bitterness and choler
  62 *stigmatic* branded, deformed, ugly
  65 *ingeniously* cleverly (usual sense): also used, mistakenly, to mean ingenuously, can-
      didly
  66 *dog-days* Cf. III.ii.202 n.
      raven another bird of ill omen
  68 *crowner's* coroner's
  69 *Huddle upon huddle* 'tumbling in heaps one over the other' (Lucas, p. 235)
69–70 ed. (Huddle . . . housekeeping?/FLA. Yes, . . . content. Q)

LODOVICO

Sit some three days together, and discourse.

FLAMINEO

Only with making faces;
Lie in our clothes.

LODOVICO

With faggots for our pillows.

FLAMINEO   And be lousy.   75

LODOVICO

In taffeta linings; that's gentle melancholy;
Sleep all day.

FLAMINEO   Yes; and like your melancholic hare
Feed after midnight.

Enter ANTONELLI [*and* GASPARO, *laughing*]

We are observed: see how yon couple grieve.

LODOVICO

What a strange creature is a laughing fool,   80
As if man were created to no use
But only to show his teeth.

FLAMINEO   I'll tell thee what,
It would do well instead of looking-glasses
To set one's face each morning by a saucer
Of a witch's congealed blood.

74–5   ed. (Lie . . . pillowes./FLA. And . . . lowsie. Q)
   75   *faggots* bundles of sticks
         lousy full of lice; filthy, vile
   76   *taffeta linings* glossy silk underclothing (supposed to protect against lice)
         gentle ed. (gentile Q)
77–8   *melancholic . . . midnight* Hares were supposed to be among the most melancholy
         beasts, sleeping all day and feeding at night (because 'their hart and bloode is cold',
         explains Topsell in *The Historie of Four-footed Beasts* (1607)).
   78   s.d. *Enter Antonelli* ed. (to r. of l. 90 in Q)
   79   *We . . . grieve* Q offers no s.d., though there is space for one. The likeliest explana-
         tion is that Antonelli's entry has been misplaced to 11 lines later (to correspond
         with his speech), and Gasparo's entry omitted. It is less likely, though possible, that
         two ambassadors have remained on stage as witnesses to the comic 'flyting', or
         exchange of insults.
         grieve probably intended ironically, given Lodovico's subsequent remark
   84   *saucer* receptacle for blood in blood-letting

LODOVICO   Precious girn, rogue.   85
  We'll never part.

FLAMINEO   Never: till the beggary of courtiers,
  The discontent of churchmen, want of soldiers,
  And all the creatures that hang manacled,
  Worse than strappadoed, on the lowest felly
  Of Fortune's wheel, be taught in our two lives   90
  To scorn that world which life of means deprives.

ANTONELLI
  My lord, I bring good news. The Pope on's death-bed,
  At th'earnest suit of the great Duke of Florence,
  Hath signed your pardon, and restored unto you—

LODOVICO
  I thank you for your news. Look up again   95
  Flamineo, see my pardon.

FLAMINEO   Why do you laugh?
  There was no such condition in our covenant.

LODOVICO   Why?

FLAMINEO
  You shall not seem a happier man than I;
  You know our vow sir, if you will be merry,
  Do it i'th'like posture, as if some great man   100
  Sat while his enemy were executed:
  Though it be very lechery unto thee,
  Do't with a crabbed politician's face.

---

85 *witch's ... blood* Witches were supposed to be melancholy (Scot, *Discoverie of Witchcraft* (1584) p. 7), hence cold and dry, which caused their blood to congeal. (Cf. *The Taming of the Shrew* Induction ii.132: '... too much sadness hath congeal'd your blood'.)

    girn, rogue ed. (gue Q) 'Girn' meant 'the act of showing the teeth; a snarl', and Marston's *Antonio and Mellida* contains a parallel passage; after 'setting of faces' in a looking glass, Balurdo cries: 'O that girn kills, it kills' (III.ii.125–6). Lodovico may be reacting to Flamineo distorting his visage. Altered during press correction from 'grine rogue' to 'gue', the latter (from French *gueux*, beggar), meaning 'rogue, sharper', is rarely accepted as authoritative; 'gue' (which looks like the end of 'rogue') may be the result of a botched attempt at correcting the spelling of both words. Perhaps the compositor mistook the press-corrector's transposition sign for a deletion (see NCW III.iii.82 n.).

89 *strappadoed* hoisted from the ground by the hands when tied across the back, a torture
    felly felloe or section of the rim of a wheel

90 *Fortune's wheel* The proverbial turning of this wheel might raise one to prosperity or lower one to misfortune. For this reason it was frequently conflated, as here, with a torture-wheel (cf. *King Lear* IV.vii.45–6: 'I am bound/Upon a wheel of fire').

LODOVICO

Your sister is a damnable whore.

FLAMINEO   Ha?

LODOVICO

Look you; I spake that laughing.   105

FLAMINEO

Dost ever think to speak again?

LODOVICO   Do you hear?

Wilt sell me forty ounces of her blood,

To water a mandrake?

FLAMINEO   Poor lord, you did vow

To live a lousy creature.

LODOVICO   Yes.

FLAMINEO   Like one

That had for ever forfeited the daylight,   110

By being in debt.

LODOVICO   Ha, ha!

FLAMINEO

I do not greatly wonder you do break:

Your lordship learnt long since. But I'll tell you—

LODOVICO

What?

FLAMINEO And't shall stick by you.

LODOVICO   I long for it.

FLAMINEO

This laughter scurvily becomes your face;   115

If you will not be melancholy, be angry.   *Strikes him*

See, now I laugh too.

MARCELLO

[*Seizing* FLAMINEO] You are to blame, I'll force you hence.

LODOVICO [*To* ANTONELLI *and* GASPARO]   Unhand me.

                              Exit MAR[CELLO] & FLAM[INEO]

107–8 *forty . . . mandrake?* Cf. III.i.49 n. Lodovico implies that Vittoria will be executed.
  110 *for ever . . . daylight* i.e. been imprisoned for life
  112 *break* break your covenant (cf. l. 97); become bankrupt (as in previous line)
  113 *learnt* ed. (learn't Q)
  114 *stick* remain in your memory; with a suggestion of 'stab, pierce' (though Flamineo clearly uses his fist, not a sword)
  118 *Unhand me* Antonelli and Gasparo restrain Lodovico physically as they restrain him verbally in I.i.

That e'er I should be forced to right myself
Upon a pander.

ANTONELLI   My lord.   120

LODOVICO

H'had been as good met with his fist a thunderbolt.

GASPARO

How this shows!

LODOVICO   Ud's death, how did my sword miss him?
These rogues that are most weary of their lives
Still scape the greatest dangers;
A pox upon him: all his reputation—   125
Nay all the goodness of his family—
Is not worth half this earthquake.
I learnt it of no fencer to shake thus;
Come, I'll forget him, and go drink some wine.

                                        Exeunt

[ACT IV, SCENE i]

Enter FRANCISCO *and* MONTICELSO

MONTICELSO

Come, come my lord, untie your folded thoughts,
And let them dangle loose as a bride's hair.
Your sister's poisoned.

FRANCISCO   Far be it from my thoughts
To seek revenge.

MONTICELSO   What, are you turned all marble?

FRANCISCO

Shall I defy him, and impose a war   5
Most burdensome on my poor subjects' necks,
Which at my will I have not power to end?
You know; for all the murders, rapes, and thefts,
Committed in the horrid lust of war,

---

123   *Ud's death* (By) God's death, an oath

2   *loose . . . hair* Jacobean virgin brides wore their hair loose. Loose or dishevelled hair
    was also a conventional sign for distraction or grief.

81

He that unjustly caused it first proceed 10
Shall find it in his grave and in his seed.

MONTICELSO

That's not the course I'd wish you: pray, observe me.
We see that undermining more prevails
Than doth the cannon. Bear your wrongs concealed,
And, patient as the tortoise, let this camel 15
Stalk o'er your back unbruised: sleep with the lion,
And let this brood of secure foolish mice
Play with your nostrils, till the time be ripe
For th' bloody audit and the fatal gripe:
Aim like a cunning fowler, close one eye, 20
That you the better may your game espy.

FRANCISCO

Free me my innocence from treacherous acts:
I know there's thunder yonder: and I'll stand
Like a safe valley which low bends the knee
To some aspiring mountain: since I know 25
Treason, like spiders weaving nets for flies,
By her foul work is found, and in it dies.
To pass away these thoughts, my honoured lord,
It is reported you possess a book
Wherein you have quoted, by intelligence, 30
The names of all notorious offenders
Lurking about the city.

MONTICELSO   Sir I do;
And some there are which call it my black book.

15–16   *patient . . . unbruised* In George Wither's *Collection of Emblems* (1635), the tortoise
represents self-sufficient virtue: 'If any at his harmlesse person strike;/Himselfe hee
streight contracteth, Torteis-like, /To make the Shell of Suffrance, his defence;/And
counts it Life, to die with Innocence' (p. 86). The application of the image in this
context is thus highly ironic.

19   *audit* searching inspection

20   *fowler* hunter of fowl

22   *from* ed. (fro Q)

23–5   *I . . . mountain* Though Francisco's words imply that he leaves vengeance to heaven,
his actions (perhaps gesturing towards and bowing before Monticelso) may appeal
to Monticelso himself as that 'aspiring mountain'.

30   *quoted* noted, set down *by intelligence* by secret information

33   *black book* an official register bound in black; a record of those liable to censure. In
his *Disputation* (1592), Robert Greene promised to publish a pamphlet called *The
Blacke Booke* to expose the knaves of London.

Well may the title hold: for though it teach not
The art of conjuring, yet in it lurk   35
The names of many devils.

FRANCISCO   Pray let's see it.

MONTICELSO

I'll fetch it to your lordship.   *Exit*

FRANCISCO   Monticelso,
I will not trust thee, but in all my plots
I'll rest as jealous as a town besieged.
Thou canst not reach what I intend to act;   40
Your flax soon kindles, soon is out again,
But gold slow heats, and long will hot remain.

Enter MONT[ICELSO,] *presents* FRAN[CISCO] *with a book*

MONTICELSO

'Tis here my lord.

FRANCISCO

First your intelligencers, pray let's see.

MONTICELSO

Their number rises strangely,   45
And some of them
You'd take for honest men.
Next are panders.
These are your pirates: and these following leaves,
For base rogues that undo young gentlemen   50
By taking up commodities; for politic bankrupts;
For fellows that are bawds to their own wives,

---

35 *conjuring* the 'black art' of calling up devils to do one's bidding (cf. *Doctor Faustus*
    I.i.154, where Faustus is advised to consult books by famed magicians like Bacon in
    order to conjure)

37 s.d. *Exit* ed. (Exit Monticelso Q)

39 *jealous* vigilant

42 *heats* ed. (heat's Q)
    s.d. ed. (to r. of ll. 43–4 in Q)

45–8 The sequence of half-lines is unusual, and may indicate pauses in Monticelso's speech
      as he turns the pages and points to sections of his black book (Brown IV.i.45–8 n.)

51 *taking up commodities* To circumvent laws against high rates of interest, swindlers
    lent cheap commodities, at a highly inflated value, instead of money. Then the
    gullible borrower, required to repay the alleged value of the commodities, often
    ended up in debtors' prison.
    politic bankrupts those who feign bankruptcy in order to avoid creditors

83

Only to put off horses and slight jewels,
Clocks, defaced plate, and such commodities,
At birth of their first children.
FRANCISCO   Are there such?   55
MONTICELSO
These are for impudent bawds
That go in men's apparel; for usurers
That share with scriveners for their good reportage:
For lawyers that will antedate their writs:
And some divines you might find folded there,   60
But that I slip them o'er for conscience' sake.
Here is a general catalogue of knaves.
A man might study all the prisons o'er
Yet never attain this knowledge.
FRANCISCO   Murderers.
Fold down the leaf I pray;   65
Good my lord let me borrow this strange doctrine.
MONTICELSO
[*Handing him the book*] Pray use't my lord.
FRANCISCO   I do assure your
    lordship,
You are a worthy member of the state,
And have done infinite good in your discovery
Of these offenders.
MONTICELSO   Somewhat sir.
FRANCISCO   O God!   70
Better than tribute of wolves paid in England,
'Twill hang their skins o'th'hedge.

53–5 *Only . . . commodities* i.e. men who prostituted their own wives in exchange for
       goods sold at an inflated price to their wives' lovers
56–7 *impudent . . . apparel* a reference to the contemporary controversy surrounding
       women crossdressing as men, some of whom were prostitutes, all of whom were
       attacked in antifeminist tracts
57–8 *usurers . . . reportage* i.e. moneylenders who give a 'cut' to scriveners (who supplied
       those who wanted to raise money on security) in exchange for their recommenda-
       tion, their good report
  59 *antedate . . . writs* i.e. produce a phony legal document (alleging an offence) ante-
       dated so as to take precedence over, and thus displace, a genuine one (cf. II.i.291–5)
  71 *tribute . . . England* The Welsh were supposedly ordered by King Edgar (944–75) to
       pay a tribute of three hundred wolves a year as a means of controlling the wolf
       population in Wales.

MONTICELSO   I must make bold
  To leave your lordship.
FRANCISCO   Dearly sir, I thank you;
  If any ask for me at court, report
  You have left me in the company of knaves.   75

                                    Exit MONT[ICELSO]

  I gather now by this, some cunning fellow
  That's my lord's officer, one that lately skipped
  From a clerk's desk up to a justice' chair,
  Hath made this knavish summons; and intends,
  As th'Irish rebels wont were to sell heads,   80
  So to make prize of these. And thus it happens,
  Your poor rogues pay for't, which have not the means
  To present bribe in fist: the rest o'th'band
  Are razed out of the knaves' record; or else
  My lord he winks at them with easy will,   85
  His man grows rich, the knaves are the knaves still.
  But to the use I'll make of it; it shall serve
  To point me out a list of murderers,
  Agents for any villainy. Did I want
  Ten leash of courtesans, it would furnish me;   90
  Nay laundress three armies. That in so little paper
  Should lie th'undoing of so many men!
  'Tis not so big as twenty declarations.
  See the corrupted use some make of books:
  Divinity, wrested by some factious blood,   95
  Draws swords, swells battles, and o'erthrows all good.
  To fashion my revenge more seriously,
  Let me remember my dead sister's face:
  Call for her picture: no; I'll close mine eyes,
  And in a melancholic thought I'll frame   100

---

  80 *Irish ... heads* A bounty was paid by Elizabeth I's officers for heads in the Irish
      rebellions.
  90 *leash* set of three (animals or birds used in hunting)
  91 *laundress* furnish with laundresses (reputedly of easy virtue) *in so* ed. (so in Q)
  93 *declarations* official proclamations
  95 *wrested ... blood* i.e. stirred by some violent, seditious passion
  100 s.d. *Enter* ISABELLA's *Ghost* Francisco's view of the ghost as a figment of his own
      imagination is in tension with a long stage tradition of unquestioned presentation
      of ghosts. This one is highly ambiguous, unlike the ghost of Brachiano which
      appears in V.iv.

Enter ISABEL[L]A*'s Ghost*

Her figure 'fore me. Now I ha't – d'foot! How strong
Imagination works! How she can frame
Things which are not! Methinks she stands afore me;
And by the quick idea of my mind,
Were my skill pregnant, I could draw her picture.   105
Thought, as a subtle juggler, makes us deem
Things supernatural which have cause
Common as sickness. 'Tis my melancholy;
How cam'st thou by thy death? How idle am I
To question my own idleness? Did ever   110
Man dream awake till now? Remove this object,
Out of my brain with't: what have I to do
With tombs, or death-beds, funerals, or tears,
That have to meditate upon revenge?

          [Exit Ghost]

So now 'tis ended, like an old wives' story.   115
Statesmen think often they see stranger sights
Than madmen. Come, to this weighty business.
My tragedy must have some idle mirth in't,
Else it will never pass. I am in love,
In love with Corombona, and my suit   120
Thus halts to her in verse. –   *Writes*
I have done it rarely: O the fate of princes!

---

101 *ha't – d'foot.* ed. (– ha'te Q) The uncorrected Q reads 'Now I – d'foot' ('by God's
  foot', an oath). The editors of NCW hypothesize (IV.i.99 n.) that the mark of inclu-
  sion for 'ha'te' led the corrector to think that 'd'foot' was being struck out. If both
  words stand, the actor can register more effectively the shock of opening his eyes to
  find a real ghost before him.

104 *quick* active, vital

105 *pregnant* fertile, imaginative

106 *juggler* conjuror, magician

108 *melancholy* During the Renaissance, melancholy was believed to be a physiological
  disease caused by an excess of black bile which often produced visual hallucina-
  tions: 'From the fuming melancholy of our spleen mounteth that hot matter into
  the higher region of the brain, whereof many fearful visions are framed' (Thomas
  Nashe, *Terrors of the Night* (1594)).

110 *idleness* folly; delirium

121 *halts* is defective in rhyme and measure (like this line)
  s.d. ed. (opposite l. 123 in Q)
  s.d. *Writes* ed. (he writes Q)

I am so used to frequent flattery,
That being alone I now flatter myself;
But it will serve; 'tis sealed.

Enter SERVANT

              Bear this   125
To th'house of convertites; and watch your leisure
To give it to the hands of Corombona,
Or to the matron, when some followers
Of Brachiano may be by. Away.

                                Exit SERVANT
He that deals all by strength, his wit is shallow: 130
When a man's head goes through, each limb will follow.
The engine for my business, bold Count Lodowick;
'Tis gold must such an instrument procure,
With empty fist no man doth falcons lure.
Brachiano, I am now fit for thy encounter.   135
Like the wild Irish I'll ne'er think thee dead
Till I can play at football with thy head.
Flectere si nequeo superos, Acheronta movebo.   *Exit*

[ACT IV, SCENE ii]

Enter the MATRON, *and* FLAMINEO

MATRON
    Should it be known the Duke hath such recourse
    To your imprisoned sister, I were like
    T'incur much damage by it.

131 *When . . . follow* proverbial image for a cunning fox or snake, here applied to a man
134 *lure* i.e. train a falcon to come to the lure (a bunch of feathers held by the falconer resembling its prey); hence entice, tempt
136–7 *Like . . . head* The Irish were notoriously cruel and bloodthirsty.
138 *Flectere . . . movebo* 'If I cannot prevail upon the gods above, I will move the gods of the infernal regions' (Virgil, *Aeneid* VII, 312). This was a stock remark for villains in the drama.
    s.d. *Exit* ed. (Exit Mon. Q)

FLAMINEO   Not a scruple.
The Pope lies on his death-bed, and their heads
Are troubled now with other business   5
Than guarding of a lady.

Enter SERVANT [*with the letter*]

SERVANT
[*Aside*] Yonder's Flamineo in conference
With the Matrona. [*To the* MATRON] Let me speak with you.
I would entreat you to deliver for me
This letter to the fair Vittoria–   10
MATRON
I shall sir.

Enter BRACHIANO

SERVANT   With all care and secrecy;
Hereafter you shall know me, and receive
Thanks for this courtesy.   [*Exit*]
FLAMINEO   How now? What's that?
MATRON
A letter.
FLAMINEO To my sister: I'll see't delivered.
                     [*Takes the letter. Exit* MATRON]
BRACHIANO
What's that you read Flamineo?
FLAMINEO   Look.   15
                     [*Gives him the letter*]
BRACHIANO
Ha? [*Reads*] 'To the most unfortunate his best respected
  Vittoria –'
Who was the messenger?

---

3   *scruple* very small quantity; with a play on the usual modern sense, a thought that
    troubles the conscience
4   *Pope . . . death-bed* Gregory XIII, historically responsible for Vittoria's imprison-
    ment in a monastery, died on 10 April 1585.
10 *letter . . . Vittoria* Francisco's letter to Vittoria becomes an important prop in this
    scene; passed rapidly from one character to another, it triggers explosive feeling and
    reinforces gesturally the heated verbal exchanges.

FLAMINEO   I know not.
BRACHIANO
  No! Who sent it?
FLAMINEO   Ud's foot, you speak as if a man
  Should know what fowl is coffined in a baked meat
  Afore you cut it up.   20
BRACHIANO
  I'll open't, were't her heart. What's here subscribed–
  Florence? This juggling is gross and palpable.
  I have found out the conveyance; read it, read it.
                      [*Thrusts the letter at* FLAMINEO]
FLAMINEO
  (*Reads the letter*) 'Your tears I'll turn to triumphs, be but mine.
  Your prop is fall'n; I pity that a vine   25
  Which princes heretofore have longed to gather,
  Wanting supporters, now should fade and wither.'
  Wine i'faith, my lord, with lees would serve his turn.
  'Your sad imprisonment I'll soon uncharm,
  And with a princely uncontrolled arm   30
  Lead you to Florence, where my love and care
  Shall hang your wishes in my silver hair.'
  A halter on his strange equivocation.
  'Nor for my years return me the sad willow:

---

18   *Ud's foot* (By) God's foot (see III.iii.128)
19   *coffined . . . meat* i.e. enclosed in pastry or in a pie
22   ed. (Florence? / This Q)
      juggling . . . palpable i.e. this deception is plain and manifest
23   *conveyance* means of communication; cunning contrivance; document by which
      property (i.e. Vittoria) is transferred from one person to another (NCW IV.ii.24 n.)
24   s.d. *Reads the letter* ed. (outer r. margin ll. 24–5 in Q)
24–7   *Your . . . wither* Cf. III.ii.185–8, where Francisco describes Vittoria as a vine in a
      much less complimentary context; cf. also II.i.391–3, where in Francisco's analogy
      Brachiano is the vine and Vittoria the withered, rotting elm.
28   *Wine . . . turn* Flamineo mockingly takes Francisco's analogy literally: wine with its
      dregs (lees) can be made by gathering vines.
30   *uncontrolled* ungoverned, not subjected to control
33   *halter . . . equivocation* Flamineo calls for a rope with a noose (a halter) to empha-
      size Francisco's 'equivocation', his possibly duplicitous use of the word 'hang' (as a
      threat as well as a promise).
34   *willow* sign of a rejected lover

Who prefer blossoms before fruit that's mellow?'   35
Rotten on my knowledge with lying too long i'th' bed-straw.
'And all the lines of age this line convinces:
The gods never wax old, no more do princes.'
A pox on't, tear it, let's have no more atheists for God's sake.

BRACHIANO
Ud's death, I'll cut her into atomies   40
And let th'irregular north-wind sweep her up
And blow her int' his nostrils. Where's this whore?

FLAMINEO
That –? What do you call her?

BRACHIANO   O, I could be mad,
Prevent the curst disease she'll bring me to,
And tear my hair off. Where's this changeable stuff?   45

FLAMINEO
O'er head and ears in water, I assure you,
She is not for your wearing.

BRACHIANO   In you pander!

FLAMINEO
[*Facing him*] What me, my lord, am I your dog?

BRACHIANO
A bloodhound: do you brave? Do you stand me?

36   *Rotten . . . bed-straw* Fruit was ripened in straw; people could grow melancholy and
        lousy by lying too long in bed (where straw served as a mattress); cf. III.iii.74–7.
37   *all . . . convinces* i.e. all the wrinkles of age this line refutes; all the maxims of old
        this maxim confutes
39   *atheists* Here, Francisco is an 'atheist' because he appears to deny the Christian God
        by invoking the classical gods. Flamineo again wittily reacts with shock not to
        Francisco's attempted seduction of Vittoria but to his stale analogies.
40   *atomies* minute particles, motes
41   *irregular* disorderly
43   *That –?* ed. (That? Q)
44–5 *Prevent . . . off* i.e. forestall the hair loss caused by venereal disease I'll contract from
        her by tearing out my own hair
45   *changeable stuff* inconstant whore; material such as shot or watered silk that shows
        different colours under different aspects (a sense unintended by Brachiano, played
        on by Flamineo)
46–7 *O'er . . . wearing* i.e. literally, in deep water, thus unfit to be worn (whereas watered
        silk would be); figuratively, absorbed in weeping, and thus unfit for Brachiano's
        offered destruction
49   *bloodhound* hunter for blood (for lifeblood and for sexual passion, as in the case of
        a pander)
        brave defy
        stand withstand

FLAMINEO

Stand you? Let those that have diseases run;   50
I need no plasters.

BRACHIANO

Would you be kicked?

FLAMINEO   Would you have your neck broke?
I tell you duke, I am not in Russia;
My shins must be kept whole.

BRACHIANO   Do you know me?

FLAMINEO

O my lord! Methodically.   55
As in this world there are degrees of evils:
So in this world there are degrees of devils.
You're a great Duke; I your poor secretary.
I do look now for a Spanish fig, or an Italian sallet daily.

BRACHIANO

Pander, ply your convoy, and leave your prating.   60

FLAMINEO

All your kindness to me is like that miserable courtesy of
Polyphemus to Ulysses; you reserve me to be devoured last. You
would dig turves out of my grave to feed your larks: that would
be music to you. Come, I'll lead you to her.   [*Walks backwards*]

---

50 *run* as in the usual sense, move away quickly; also, ooze (as from a 'running' sore, requiring plasters)

51–2 *I . . . plasters / Would . . . broke?* ed. (I . . . kickt? / FLA. Would . . . broke? Q)

52 *Would . . . broke?* Flamineo threateningly reminds Brachiano of his expert murder of Camillo (II.ii.37).

53–4 *I . . . whole* The Russians reputedly punished those who refused to pay their debts ('politic bankrupts') by beating them on the shins.

55 *Methodically* in accordance with a prescribed method

59 *Spanish fig* insulting gesture of thrusting thumb between two closed fingers or into the mouth; also poison; *Italian sallet* Italian salad; poisonous concoction – Italians being notorious in Renaissance tragedy for clever ways to kill

60 *ply . . . convoy* i.e. get on with your business (of pandering)

61–3 *miserable . . . last* In Homer's *Odyssey* (IX, 369–70), Polyphemus, a Cyclops (a savage one-eyed giant), promised Ulysses a hospitable gift, which turned out to be the vow to eat him last. In the end, Ulysses blinded the Cyclops.

63 *turves* pl. of turf.

62–3 *You . . . larks* i.e. you would dig grassy slabs from my grave to feed your ethereal birds; figuratively, you would mutilate my body to feed your soul

BRACHIANO

Do you face me? 65

FLAMINEO

O sir, I would not go before a politic enemy with my back
towards him, though there were behind me a whirlpool.

Enter VITTORIA *to* BRACHIANO *and* FLAMINEO

BRACHIANO

[*Showing the letter*] Can you read, mistress? Look upon that letter;
There are no characters nor hieroglyphics.
You need no comment, I am grown your receiver; 70
God's precious, you shall be a brave great lady,
A stately and advanced whore.

VITTORIA   Say, sir.

BRACHIANO

Come, come, let's see your cabinet, discover
Your treasury of love-letters. Death and furies,
I'll see them all.

VITTORIA   Sir, upon my soul, 75
I have not any. Whence was this directed?

BRACHIANO

Confusion on your politic ignorance.
You are reclaimed; are you? I'll give you the bells
And let you fly to the devil.   [*Gives her the letter*]

---

65 *face* stand facing; brave, defy
67 s.d. Flamineo offers to 'lead' Brachiano to Vittoria, but the s.d. suggests that Vittoria
      enters (perhaps via the discovery space). An unsummoned entry, imitating the
      force of the 'whirlpool' (l. 67), would immediately give her dramatic control.
69 *characters* cabbalistic or magical signs
70 *comment* commentary, explanation (of the 'hieroglyphics')
      receiver procurer, pimp
71 *God's precious* i.e. by God's precious blood (an oath)
73 *cabinet* case for letters or jewels, casket
78 *reclaimed* redeemed from a wrong course of action; (in falconry) called back,
      tamed after being let fly
78–9 *I'll . . . devil* In falconry, bells attached to the hawk's legs aided recovery of the prey.
      In his disgust, Brachiano rejects everything associated with Vittoria.
79 *Ware hawk* either, simply, 'Watch out for what *this* hawk might do (when she gets
      angry)' or 'Beware the officer who pounces upon rogues' (warning Brachiano against
      Vittoria's retaliation), or an imitation of the hunting call used by the falconer when
      patiently training a hawk to enjoy the rewards of its own kill (Dent, pp. 124–5;
      implying that Brachiano should reward her with his attentions?)

FLAMINEO   Ware hawk, my lord.

VITTORIA

Florence! This is some treacherous plot, my lord,   80
To me he ne'er was lovely I protest,
So much as in my sleep.

BRACHIANO   Right: they are plots.
Your beauty! O, ten thousand curses on't.
How long have I beheld the devil in crystal?
Thou hast led me, like an heathen sacrifice,   85
With music and with fatal yokes of flowers
To my eternal ruin. Woman to man
Is either a god or a wolf.

VITTORIA [*Weeps*]   My lord.

BRACHIANO   Away.
We'll be as differing as two adamants:
The one shall shun the other. What? Dost weep?   90
Procure but ten of thy dissembling trade,
Ye'd furnish all the Irish funerals
With howling, past wild Irish.

FLAMINEO   Fie, my lord.

BRACHIANO

That hand, that cursed hand, which I have wearied
With doting kisses! O my sweetest Duchess   95
How lovely art thou now! [*To* VITTORIA] Thy loose thoughts
Scatter like quicksilver. I was bewitched;
For all the world speaks ill of thee.

VITTORIA   No matter.
I'll live so now I'll make that world recant
And change her speeches. You did name your Duchess.   100

---

81   *lovely* amorous, affectionate; lovable, attractive
84   *devil in crystal* a common expression signifying self-deception, easy credulity
87–8 *Woman . . . wolf* used proverbially for the relation of man to man, and applied by
      Montaigne to marriage (*Essays*, trans. Florio III, v)
89   *adamants* loadstones, magnets
92–3 *furnish . . . Irish* According to contemporary accounts, the Irish hired women to
      mourn the dead; 'for some small recompence given them, [they] will furnish the
      cry, with greater shriking and howling, then those that are grieved indeede'. 'To
      weep Irish' thus meant 'to weepe at pleasure, without cause, or griefe' (Rich, *A New
      Description of Ireland* (1610), p. 13).
94–5 The gesture recalls Brachiano's divorce from Isabella by kissing her hand (II.i.192).

BRACHIANO
Whose death God pardon.

VITTORIA   Whose death God revenge
On thee, most godless Duke.

FLAMINEO   Now for two whirlwinds.

VITTORIA
What have I gained by thee but infamy?
Thou hast stained the spotless honour of my house,
And frighted thence noble society: 105
Like those which, sick o'th'palsy, and retain
Ill-scenting foxes 'bout them, are still shunned
By those of choicer nostrils. What do you call this house?
Is this your palace? Did not the judge style it
A house of penitent whores? Who sent me to it?   110
Who hath the honour to advance Vittoria
To this incontinent college? Is't not you?
Is't not your high preferment? Go, go brag
How many ladies you have undone, like me.
Fare you well sir; let me hear no more of you.   115
I had a limb corrupted to an ulcer,
But I have cut it off: and now I'll go
Weeping to heaven on crutches. For your gifts,
I will return them all; and I do wish
That I could make you full executor   120
To all my sins – O that I could toss myself
Into a grave as quickly: for all thou art worth
I'll not shed one tear more – I'll burst first.
                    Throws herself [face down] upon a bed [and weeps]

BRACHIANO
I have drunk Lethe. Vittoria?

102   *two* ed. (tow Q)
108   *those ... nostrils* Foxes, known for their foul odour, were commonly used in the
       treatment of the palsy (a disease characterized by involuntary tremors or paralysis).
113   *preferment* promotion
116   *I ... ulcer* The historic Brachiano had a malignant ulcer in his leg.
116–18 *I ... crutches* An echo of St Mark 9.45: 'And if thy foot offend thee, cut it off: it is
       better for thee to enter halt into life, than having two feet to be cast into hell'.
123   s.d. *Throws* ed. (She throws Q)
       s.d. *Throws ... bed* The bed may be thrust out on the stage at the beginning of
       the scene, or, perhaps, upon Vittoria's entry (l. 67). Vittoria's dramatic physical
       gesture, more than her words, seems to precipitate Brachiano's abrupt change of heart.
124   *Lethe* river of oblivion, forgetfulness

94

My dearest happiness? Vittoria? 125
What do you ail my love? Why do you weep?

VITTORIA
[*Turns to him*] Yes, I now weep poniards, do you see.

BRACHIANO
Are not those matchless eyes mine?

VITTORIA   I had rather
They were not matches.

BRACHIANO   Is not this lip mine?

VITTORIA
[*Turning away*] Yes: thus to bite it off, rather than give it thee. 130

FLAMINEO
Turn to my lord, good sister.

VITTORIA   Hence you pander.

FLAMINEO
Pander! Am I the author of your sin?

VITTORIA
Yes: he's a base thief that a thief lets in.

FLAMINEO
We're blown up, my lord—

BRACHIANO   Wilt thou hear me?
Once to be jealous of thee is t'express 135
That I will love thee everlastingly,
And never more be jealous.

VITTORIA   O thou fool,
Whose greatness hath by much o'ergrown thy wit!
What dar'st thou do that I not dare to suffer,
Excepting to be still thy whore? For that, 140
In the sea's bottom sooner thou shalt make
A bonfire.

FLAMINEO O, no oaths for God's sake.

BRACHIANO
Will you hear me?

124–5   *I . . . Vittoria?* ed. (I . . . Lethe / Vittoria? . . . Vittoria? Q)
  127   *poniards* daggers (suggesting her anger as well as grief)
128–9   *I . . . matches* a play on 'matchless' as 'not matches'. i.e. I had rather my eyes were
           not symmetrical. Vittoria's desire to thwart an unwanted lover by mutilating herself
           recalls Celia's in *Volpone* III.vii.251–7.
  134   *blown up* shattered, as by the explosion of a mine

VITTORIA Never.

FLAMINEO

What a damned imposthume is a woman's will?
Can nothing break it? Fie, fie, my lord.   145
Women are caught as you take tortoises,
She must be turned on her back. Sister, by this hand
I am on your side. Come, come, you have wronged her.
What a strange credulous man were you, my lord,
To think the Duke of Florence would love her?   150
Will any mercer take another's ware
When once 'tis toused and sullied? And yet sister,
How scurvily this frowardness becomes you!
Young leverets stand not long; and women's anger
Should, like their flight, procure a little sport;   155
A full cry for a quarter of an hour;
And then be put to th'dead quat.

BRACHIANO   Shall these eyes,
Which have so long time dwelt upon your face,
Be now put out?

FLAMINEO   No cruel landlady i'th'world,
Which lends forth groats to broom-men, and takes use for them 160
Would do't.
Hand her, my lord, and kiss her: be not like
A ferret to let go your hold with blowing.

144   *imposthume* abscess, festering sore
144–67 Flamineo is playing his part as pander by encouraging each of the lovers to move
        towards reconciliation; it is unclear, however, whether his lines are asides directed
        at Brachiano and Vittoria in turn or delivered openly in the hearing of both. The
        choice is ultimately the actor's; however, given Flamineo's generally open misogyny
        (cf. I.ii.106–10, 180–2), the latter seems more likely.
146–7   *Women . . . back* To catch tortoises one need only turn them on their backs.
151   *mercer* merchant dealing in silks, velvets and other costly materials
152   *toused* rumpled; (of a woman) abused, roughly handled
153   *frowardness* naughtiness, perversity
154   *leverets* young hares (once thought to be all female); mistresses *stand* hold out (in
        the hunt)
156   *full cry* full pursuit (of the hounds); open weeping
157   *quat* squat (position taken by a cornered hare)
160   i.e. who lends pennies to street-sweepers and earns interest on them
        them ed. (the Q)
162   *Hand* fondle
162–3   *be . . . blowing* Blowing at a ferret forces it to let go of the thing its teeth are fixed in.

BRACHIANO

Let us renew right hands.

VITTORIA   Hence.

BRACHIANO

Never shall rage, or the forgetful wine,   165

Make me commit like fault.

FLAMINEO

Now you are i'th'way on't, follow't hard.

BRACHIANO

Be thou at peace with me; let all the world

Threaten the cannon.

FLAMINEO   Mark his penitence.

Best natures do commit the grossest faults   170

When they're giv'n o'er to jealousy; as best wine

Dying makes strongest vinegar. I'll tell you;

The sea's more rough and raging than calm rivers,

But nor so sweet nor wholesome. A quiet woman

Is a still water under a great bridge.   175

A man may shoot her safely.

VITTORIA

O ye dissembling men!

FLAMINEO   We sucked that, sister,

From women's breasts in our first infancy.

VITTORIA

To add misery to misery.

BRACHIANO   Sweetest.

VITTORIA

Am I not low enough?   180

Ay, ay, your good heart gathers like a snowball

Now your affection's cold.

FLAMINEO   Ud's foot, it shall melt

To a heart again, or all the wine in Rome

Shall run o'th'lees for't.

---

165   *forgetful* inducing forgetfulness

175   *great bridge* like London Bridge, which was impassable when tides ran high

176   *shoot* descend (a river) swiftly (in a boat or other vessel); penetrate sexually

176–9   ed. (A Man . . . men! / Wee . . . first / first . . . Sweetest. Q)

182   *Ud's foot* ed. (Ud'foot Q)

VITTORIA

    Your dog or hawk should be rewarded better   185

    Than I have been. I'll speak not one word more.

FLAMINEO

    Stop her mouth

    With a sweet kiss, my lord.

                    [BRACHIANO *embraces* VITTORIA]

    So now the tide's turned the vessel's come about.

    He's a sweet armful. O we curled-haired men   190

    Are still most kind to women. This is well.

BRACHIANO

    [*To* VITTORIA] That you should chide thus!

FLAMINEO   O, sir, your little

    chimneys

    Do ever cast most smoke. I sweat for you.

    Couple together with as deep a silence

    As did the Grecians in their wooden horse.   195

    My lord, supply your promises with deeds.

    'You know that painted meat no hunger feeds.'

BRACHIANO

    Stay – ingrateful Rome.

FLAMINEO

    Rome! It deserves to be called Barbary, for our villainous usage.

BRACHIANO

    Soft; the same project which the Duke of Florence   200

    (Whether in love or gullery I know not)

    Laid down for her escape, will I pursue.

FLAMINEO

    And no time fitter than this night, my lord;

---

185   *rewarded* (in hunting) given part of the prey they have helped to kill (and thus
       encouraged to continue hunting)

191   *still* always

195   *Grecians . . . horse* The Greeks won the Trojan war by presenting a large wooden
       horse as a gift to the Trojans. It was taken into Troy and the Greeks hidden inside it
       emerged to effect a victory.

198   *Stay . . . Rome* ed. (Stay ingratefull Rome. Q) Rome was proverbially ungrateful to
       Romans.

199   *Barbary* land of barbarians (in northern Africa)

201   *gullery* deception

The Pope being dead; and all the cardinals entered
The conclave for th'electing a new Pope;   205
The city in a great confusion;
We may attire her in a page's suit,
Lay her post-horse, take shipping, and amain
For Padua.

BRACHIANO

I'll instantly steal forth the Prince Giovanni,   210
And make for Padua. You two with your old mother
And young Marcello that attends on Florence,
If you can work him to it, follow me.
I will advance you all: for you Vittoria,
Think of a Duchess' title.

FLAMINEO   Lo you sister.   215
Stay, my lord, I'll tell you a tale. The crocodile, which lives in the
river Nilus, hath a worm breeds i'th'teeth of 't, which puts it to
extreme anguish: a little bird, no bigger than a wren, is barber-
surgeon to this crocodile; flies into the jaws of 't; picks out the
worm; and brings present remedy. The fish, glad of ease but   220
ingrateful to her that did it, that the bird may not talk largely of
her abroad for non-payment, closeth her chaps intending to
swallow her and so put her to perpetual silence. But nature
loathing such ingratitude, hath armed this bird with a quill or
prick on the head, top o'th'which wounds the crocodile   225
i'th'mouth, forceth her open her bloody prison, and away flies
the pretty tooth-picker from her cruel patient.

BRACHIANO

Your application is, I have not rewarded
The service you have done me.

FLAMINEO   No my lord.

208–9 *Lay ... Padua* i.e. provide her with relays of post-horses, embark and sail with all
       speed to Padua
216–27 *Stay ... patient* Webster borrows this tale from Topsell, *History of Serpents* (1608),
       pp. 135–6, and possibly from Africanus, *History and Description of Africa* (1600).
       He invents the crocodile's motive for wanting to swallow the bird ('that the bird
       may not talk-largely of her abroad for non-payment'), adding a human concern for
       reward (clearly at stake in the scene) to a story of animal savagery. Brachiano and
       Flamineo suggest different interpretations of the tale; critics have found still others.
       Its precise meaning is less important than the symbiosis among the characters it
       illuminates: all three are locked into complex relationships in which desire and
       self-interest, love and cruelty, are inextricable.
218–19 *barber-surgeon* Barbers acted as dentists in Webster's time.

You sister are the crocodile: you are blemished in your fame, 230
my lord cures it. And though the comparison hold not in every
particle; yet observe, remember, what good the bird with the
prick i'th'head hath done you; and scorn ingratitude.
[*Aside*] It may appear to some ridiculous
Thus to talk knave and madman; and sometimes 235
Come in with a dried sentence, stuffed with sage.
But this allows my varying of shapes,
'Knaves do grow great by being great men's apes.'

Exeunt

[ACT IV, SCENE iii]

Enter LODOVICO, GASPARO, *and six* AMBASSADORS. *At
another door* [FRANCISCO] *the Duke of Florence*

FRANCISCO

[*To* LODOVICO] So, my lord, I commend your diligence –
Guard well the conclave, and, as the order is,
Let none have conference with the cardinals.

---

236 *sentence* aphorism, maxim
    sage culinary herb; wisdom (cf. I.ii.124)

  0 s.d. ed. (Enter Francisco, Lodovico, Gasper, and sixe Embassadours Q)
    This scene is unique in the play for its indebtedness to a single source, Hierome
    Bignon's *A Briefe, but an Effectuall Treatise of the Election of Popes*. This eyewitness
    account of a papal election in Rome in 1605 (just seven years before the first per-
    formance of *The White Devil*) furnishes many of the details in the scene, and may
    even suggest stage action Webster had in mind but failed to record fully in the
    printed text.
1–3 Webster opens the scene at a dramatic point in the papal election. Francisco inter-
    cepts Lodovico as he guards the ambassadors' passage from the conclave after they
    have solicited the cardinals on behalf of their own rulers. The conclave must
    now be completely sealed off from the outside world until a new Pope is elected
    (cf. ll. 27–32).
  2 *conclave* place in which the cardinals meet in private for the election of a Pope. In
    Rome, the conclave is in the Sistine chapel.

LODOVICO
   I shall, my lord. Room for the ambassadors—

   [*The* AMBASSADORS *pass over the stage*]

GASPARO
   They're wondrous brave today: why do they wear   5
   These several habits?
LODOVICO   O sir, they're knights
   Of several orders.
   That lord i'th'black cloak with the silver cross
   Is Knight of Rhodes; the next Knight of S. Michael;
   That of the Golden Fleece; the Frenchman there   10
   Knight of the Holy Ghost; my lord of Savoy
   Knight of th'Annunciation; the Englishman
   Is Knight of th'honoured Garter, dedicated

4 s.d. The theatrical spectacle of the passage of the ambassadors, magnificently dressed as knights of venerable orders, allows Webster to feast the eyes of the Red Bull audience while emphasizing by implied contrast the sinister perversion of honour and ceremony by Monticelso and Francisco. (I am indebted to NCW III.i.61 n. for identification of ambassadors with knights.)

4–17 Like Monticelso in III.ii.320–40, Francisco may be conversing with the ambassadors while they are observed by Lodovico and Gasparo from a peripheral position on the stage.

5 *brave* finely dressed

6 *several* various

9 *Rhodes* The order of the Knights of St John of Jerusalem, founded during the First Crusade, moved from Jerusalem to Rhodes, and finally to Malta, granted by Charles V in 1530. According to W. Segar's *Honour, Military and Civil* (1602), they wore 'a white Crosse upon a blacke garment' (p. 97).
    S. Michael Knights of this order (founded in 1469 by Louis XI) wore a richly embroidered mantle and hood of cloth of silver over white doublet, hose and shoes.

10 *Golden Fleece* Spanish ambassador. Knights of this order (founded in 1429 by Philip Duke of Burgundy) wore a hood and mantle of crimson velvet with a border of flames and fleeces; from their distinctive collar hung a fleece of wrought gold ('which signifieth *Iustice uncorrupted*' (Segar, p. 80)).

11 *Holy Ghost* French ambassador. Knights of this order (founded in 1578 by Henry III) wore mantles of black velvet embroidered with gold and silver and decorated with capes of embroidered green cloth of silver, lined with orange satin, over white doublet and hose.

12 *Annunciation* Savoy ambassador. Knights of this order (founded in 1362 by Amadeus VI of Savoy and the highest order of knights in Italy) wore white satin with a cloak of purple velvet along with the gold collar of their order.

13 *Garter* English ambassador. Knights of this order (founded in 1350 by Edward III) wore a mantle of purple velvet over a gown of crimson velvet; over the right

Unto their saint, S. George. I could describe to you
Their several institutions, with the laws   15
Annexed to their orders, but that time
Permits not such discovery.
FRANCISCO   Where's Count Lodowick?
LODOVICO
  Here my lord.
FRANCISCO   'Tis o'th'point of dinner time;
  Marshal the cardinals' service.
LODOVICO   Sir, I shall.

Enter SERVANTS *with several dishes covered*

  Stand, let me search your dish; who's this for?   20
SERVANT
  For my Lord Cardinal Monticelso.
LODOVICO
  Whose this?
SERVANT   For my Lord Cardinal of Bourbon.
FRENCH AMBASSADOR
  Why doth he search the dishes? To observe
  What meat is dressed?
ENGLISH AMBASSADOR No sir, but to prevent
  Lest any letters should be conveyed in   25
  To bribe or to solicit the advancement
  Of any cardinal; when first they enter
  'Tis lawful for the ambassadors of princes
  To enter with them, and to make their suit
  For any man their prince affecteth best;   30
  But after, till a general election
  No man may speak with them.
LODOVICO
  You that attend on the lord cardinals
  Open the window, and receive their viands.

shoulder hung a hood of crimson velvet lined with white. Around their necks these
knights wore a pure gold chain worked in garters and knots, and enamelled with
white and red roses, from which hung the image of St George, worked in precious
stones. Around their left legs they wore a garter worked in gold, pearl and stones,
with the motto HONI SOIT QUI MAL Y PENSE ('Shame to him that evill thinketh').
  19 s.d. ed. (to r. of ll. 19–22 in Q)
  24 *meat* food
       dressed prepared

A CARDINAL

[*At the window*] You must return the service; the lord cardinals   35
Are busied 'bout electing of the Pope;
They have given o'er scrutiny, and are fallen
To admiration.

LODOVICO   Away, away.

                     [*Exeunt* SERVANTS *with dishes*]

FRANCISCO

I'll lay a thousand ducats you hear news
Of a Pope presently – hark; sure he's elected–   40

    [*The*] *Cardinal* [*of* ARRAGON *appears*] *on the terrace*

Behold! My Lord of Arragon appears
On the church battlements.

ARRAGON

[*Holding up a cross*] *Denuntio vobis gaudium magnum.*
Reverendissimus Cardinalis Lorenzo de Monticelso electus est in
sedem apostolicam, et elegit sibi nomen Paulum quartum.   45

OMNES

Vivat Sanctus Pater Paulus Quartus.

---

35   s.d. *window* probably a grating or wicket in a stage door, or perhaps a stage-level window (NCW IV.iii. 35 n.)

37   *scrutiny* taking of individual votes. The cardinals voted until a two-thirds majority elected a new Pope.

38   *admiration* adoration: means of papal election by divine inspiration. The cardinals turned and kneeled before the one they desired to be made Pope; when they saw that two-thirds had done so, the Pope was elected. Bignon comments that this method is not as lawful as voting, 'because by meanes of contentions, and partialities, there may be some fraude or violence committed therein, in that the weaker side may be drawne to Adoration by the example of those more mightie, and those fearful, induced by them more resolute' (Brown, p. 196). Papal elections (like that of the real Montalto) were often decided in this way.

40   s.d. ed. (to r. of ll. 39–40 in Q) *terrace* i.e. the upper stage

42   s.d. Since Webster follows Bignon closely verbally here, he may intend the accompanying action: 'he shewes forth a Crosse'.

43–6   *Denuntio . . . Quartus* i.e. 'I announce to you tidings of great joy. The Most Reverend Cardinal Lorenzo di Monticelso has been elected to the Apostolic See, and has chosen for himself the name of Paul IV.' ALL: 'Long live the Holy Father Paul IV.' In fact, the historical Cardinal Montalto became Pope Sixtus V.

[Enter SERVANT]

SERVANT
  Vittoria my lord–
FRANCISCO   Well: what of her?
SERVANT
  Is fled the city–
FRANCISCO   Ha?
SERVANT   With Duke Brachiano.
FRANCISCO
  Fled? Where's the Prince Giovanni?
SERVANT   Gone with his father.
FRANCISCO
  Let the Matrona of the convertites   50
  Be apprehended: fled – O damnable!

                                        [*Exit* SERVANT]

  How fortunate are my wishes. Why? 'Twas this
  I only laboured. I did send the letter
  T'instruct him what to do. Thy fame, fond Duke,
  I first have poisoned; directed thee the way   55
  To marry a whore; what can be worse? This follows.
  The hand must act to drown the passionate tongue,
  I scorn to wear a sword and prate of wrong.

          Enter MONTICELSO *in state* [*in pontifical robes*]

MONTICELSO
  Concedimus vobis apostolicam benedictionem et remissionem
  peccatorum.   60

                        [FRANCISCO *whispers to him*]
  My lord reports Vittoria Corombona
  Is stol'n from forth the house of convertites
  By Brachiano, and they're fled the city.

47–9 ed. (*Vittoria . . . Lord. /* FRAN. Wel . . . Ha? / SER. With . . . *Giovanni /* SER. Gone . . .
      father. Q)
50–2 The speech illustrates the gap between public and private. Francisco's first two lines
      are spoken for the benefit of the ambassadors; the rest are addressed to Lodovico
      and the audience (NCW IV.iii.52, 53 n.).
  54 *fond* foolish; infatuated
59–60 *Concedimus . . . peccatorum* 'We grant you the Apostolic blessing and remission of
      sins.' This Latin benediction was added by Webster during press correction, perhaps
      a verbal expansion of stage business already implicit in Monticelso's entry 'in state'.
  64 *seat* technical term for the throne or office of a Pope. Monticelso may be carried on
      and offstage in the 'great and high Pontificall Chayre' described by Bignon.

Now, though this be the first day of our seat,
We cannot better please the divine power   65
Than to sequester from the holy church
These cursed persons. Make it therefore known,
We do denounce excommunication
Against them both: all that are theirs in Rome
We likewise banish. Set on.   70

Exeunt [all except FRANCISCO *and* LODOVICO]

FRANCISCO
Come dear Lodovico.
You have ta'en the sacrament to prosecute
Th'intended murder.
LODOVICO   With all constancy.
But, sir, I wonder you'll engage yourself,
In person, being a great prince.
FRANCISCO   Divert me not.   75
Most of his court are of my faction,
And some are of my counsel. Noble friend,
Our danger shall be 'like in this design;

Enter MONTICELSO

Give leave, part of the glory may be mine.   [*Bows*]
                                                 Exit

MONTICELSO
Why did the Duke of Florence with such care   80
Labour your pardon? Say.
LODOVICO
[*Kneeling*] Italian beggars will resolve you that
Who, begging of an alms, bid those they beg of
Do good for their own sakes; or't may be
He spreads his bounty with a sowing hand,   85
Like kings, who many times give out of measure
Not for desert so much as for their pleasure.
MONTICELSO
I know you're cunning. Come, what devil was that
That you were raising?

---

79 *Exit* ed. (Exit Fran. Q)
80–1 Cf. III.iii.96.
  85 *sowing* scattering (like seed); presumably, in hope of reaping
  86 *out of measure* excessively
  88 *cunning* sly, crafty; possessing magical skill (to raise or conjure devils)

LODOVICO	Devil, my lord?	
[MONTICELSO]	I ask you	

How doth the Duke employ you, that his bonnet   90
Fell with such compliment unto his knee
When he departed from you?

LODOVICO   Why, my lord,
He told me of a resty Barbary horse
Which he would fain have brought to the career,
The 'sault, and the ring-galliard. Now, my lord,   95
I have a rare French rider.

MONTICELSO   Take you heed:
Lest the jade break your neck. Do you put me off
With your wild horse-tricks? Sirrah you do lie.
O, thou'rt a foul black cloud, and thou dost threat
A violent storm.

LODOVICO   Storms are i'th'air, my lord;   100
I am too low to storm.

MONTICELSO   Wretched creature!
I know that thou art fashioned for all ill,
Like dogs that once get blood, they'll ever kill.
About some murder? Was't not?

LODOVICO   I'll not tell you;
And yet I care not greatly if I do;   105
Marry with this preparation. Holy Father,
I come not to you as an intelligencer,
But as a penitent sinner. What I utter
Is in confession merely; which you know
Must never be revealed.

MONTICELSO   You have o'erta'en me.   110

---

89   MONTICELSO . . . you ed. (I aske you / MONT. How . . . bonnet Q)
93   resty restive, intractable, stubborn
      Barbary horse small, swift and hot-tempered horse from Barbary
94   career a gallop at full speed brought up short
95   'sault leaps and vaults
      ring-galliard a mixture of bounding forward and lashing out with the heels
96   French rider The French were supposed to be excellent horsemen and promiscuous
      lovers (hence prone to syphilis).
97   jade ill-tempered horse; woman (used pejoratively)
98   horse-tricks exercises in the horse's manage; horseplay
101   I . . . storm Lodovico refers both to his social status and (perhaps) to his physical
      position as he kneels before Monticelso.
107   intelligencer spy, informer
110   o'erta'en i.e. caught, ensnared (with an unexpected event)

LODOVICO

  Sir I did love Brachiano's Duchess dearly;
  Or rather I pursued her with hot lust,
  Though she ne'er knew on't. She was poisoned;
  Upon my soul she was: for which I have sworn
  T'avenge her murder.

MONTICELSO   To the Duke of Florence?   115

LODOVICO

  To him I have.

MONTICELSO   Miserable creature!
  If thou persist in this, 'tis damnable.
  Dost thou imagine thou canst slide on blood
  And not be tainted with a shameful fall?
  Or, like the black, and melancholic yew-tree,   120
  Dost think to root thyself in dead men's graves,
  And yet to prosper? Instruction to thee
  Comes like sweet showers to over-hard'ned ground:
  They wet, but pierce not deep. And so I leave thee
  With all the Furies hanging 'bout thy neck,   125
  Till by thy penitence thou remove this evil,
  In conjuring from thy breast that cruel devil.   *Exit*

LODOVICO

  I'll give it o'er. He says 'tis damnable:
  Besides I did expect his suffrage
  By reason of Camillo's death.   130

Enter SERVANT *and* FRANCISCO [*standing apart*]

FRANCISCO

  Do you know that count?

SERVANT   Yes, my lord.

---

118 *slide* slip
119 *tainted* injured; convicted, proven guilty
120 *yew-tree* Cf. I.ii.236. For the audience, the image may connect Lodovico with his
     victim, Brachiano (the yew/you of I.ii).
125 *Furies* Cf. I.ii.252 n.
127 s.d. ed. (to r. of l. 128 in Q)
     s.d. *Exit* ed. (Exit Mon. Q)
129 *suffrage* support, assistance; prayers, liturgical intercessory petitions
130 s.d. ed. (to r. of ll. 130–1 in Q)

FRANCISCO

Bear him these thousand ducats to his lodging;
Tell him the Pope hath sent them. Happily
That will confirm more than all the rest.   [*Exit*]

SERVANT [*Giving money to* LODOVICO]   Sir.

LODOVICO

To me sir?   135

SERVANT

His Holiness hath sent you a thousand crowns,
And wills you if you travel, to make him
Your patron for intelligence.

LODOVICO   His creature
Ever to be commanded.

                                              [*Exit* SERVANT]

Why now 'tis come about. He railed upon me;   140
And yet these crowns were told out and laid ready
Before he knew my voyage. O the art,
The modest form of greatness! That do sit
Like brides at wedding dinners, with their looks turned
From the least wanton jests, their puling stomach   145
Sick of the modesty, when their thoughts are loose,
Even acting of those hot and lustful sports
Are to ensue about midnight: such his cunning!
He sounds my depth thus with a golden plummet;
I am doubly armed now. Now to th'act of blood;   150
There's but three Furies found in spacious hell;
But in a great man's breast three thousand dwell.   [*Exit*]

---

134   s.d. Francisco may exit or withdraw to observe (NCW IV.iii.135 n.).
137   *wills* ed. (will Q)
138   *intelligence* secret information or news
138–9 *Your ... commanded* ed. (one line in Q)
141   *told out* counted out
142   *art* ed. (Art Q)
143   *form* customary method; outward appearance
144–8 Lodovico's simile anticipates the wedding that opens Act V.
145   *puling* weak, sickly
146   *loose* unchaste
149   *plummet* ball of lead attached to a line to measure depth (here, money)
151–2 *There's ... dwell* These lines turn Monticelso's own words (ll. 125–8) back on himself.

[ACT V, SCENE i]

A passage over the stage of BRACHIANO, FLAMINEO,
MARCELLO, HORTENSIO, [VITTORIA] COROMBONA,
CORNELIA, ZANCHE *and others*

[Exeunt all but FLAMINEO *and* HORTENSIO]

FLAMINEO

In all the weary minutes of my life
Day ne'er broke up till now. This marriage
Confirms me happy.

HORTENSIO   'Tis a good assurance.
Saw you not yet the Moor that's come to court?

FLAMINEO

Yes, and conferred with him i'th'Duke's closet;   5
I have not seen a goodlier personage
Nor ever talked with man better experienced
In state affairs or rudiments of war.
He hath by report served the Venetian
In Candy these twice seven years, and been chief   10
In many a bold design.

HORTENSIO   What are those two
That bear him company?

FLAMINEO

Two noblemen of Hungary, that living in the emperor's service
as commanders, eight years since, contrary to the expectation
of all the court entered into religion, into the strict order of   15

---

0 s.d. This is probably a wedding procession, with Brachiano and Vittoria splendidly
dressed (the latter with her hair flowing loose and sprinkled with arras powder).
Though Lodovico's final speech in IV.iii, on the hypocrisy of apparently virtuous
brides, must cast a shadow over this procession, the presence of Marcello and
Cornelia – and possibly, among the 'others', the ambassadors (ll. 55–60), still
dressed in magnificent robes – emphasizes the lovers' new stature, despite their
excommunication in the previous scene. Typically in Webster, a formal public
moment rapidly gives way to private commentary.

2 *up till* until

10 *Candy* Crete, and, by ironic metaphoric extension, death. Flamineo's apparent
obliviousness to the pun he himself made earlier (cf. II.i.289) suggests his new loss
of linguistic and thus dramatic control.

Capuchins: but being not well settled in their undertaking they
left their order and returned to court: for which being after
troubled in conscience, they vowed their service against the
enemies of Christ; went to Malta; were there knighted; and in
their return back, at this great solemnity, they are resolved for   20
ever to forsake the world, and settle themselves here in a house
of Capuchins in Padua.

HORTENSIO

'Tis strange.

FLAMINEO

One thing makes it so. They have vowed for ever to wear next
their bare bodies those coats of mail they served in.   25

HORTENSIO

Hard penance. Is the Moor a Christian?

FLAMINEO

He is.

HORTENSIO

Why proffers he his service to our Duke?

FLAMINEO

Because he understands there's like to grow
Some wars between us and the Duke of Florence,   30
In which he hopes employment.
I never saw one in a stern bold look
Wear more command, nor in a lofty phrase
Express more knowing, or more deep contempt
Of our slight airy courtiers. He talks   35
As if he had travelled all the princes' courts
Of Christendom; in all things strives t'express,
That all that should dispute with him may know:
Glories, like glow-worms, afar off shine bright
But looked to near, have neither heat nor light.   40
The Duke.

---

16   *Capuchins* order of monks established in 1528 to restore the original austerity and
      simplicity of the Franciscans. The pun on the name of the Duke of Florence, here
      submerged, surfaces at V.iii.38. Capuchins derived their name from their long,
      pointed hoods, a useful disguise for Gasparo and Lodovico. This circular account of
      the career of the supposed Capuchins, with its alternation of militarism and religious
      devotion, is probably designed to arouse suspicion in the minds of the audience.

26–7 *Hard . . . is* ed. (ued . . . penance/Is . . . is. Q)

31   no s.d. ed. (Enter Duke Brachiano Q)

39–40 *Glories . . . light* Fond of this phrase (borrowed from Alexander's *Alexandrean
      Tragedy*), Webster reused it in *The Duchess of Malfi* (IV.ii.141–2). Here, Flamineo

Enter BRACHIANO, [FRANCISCO, *Duke of*] *Florence disguised*
like Mulinassar; LODOVICO, ANTONELLI, GASPARO
[*all disguised*]; FERNESE *bearing their swords and helmets;*
[CARLO *and* PEDRO]

BRACHIANO

You are nobly welcome. We have heard at full
Your honourable service 'gainst the Turk.
To you, brave Mulinassar, we assign
A competent pension: and are inly sorrow,   45
The vows of those two worthy gentlemen
Make them incapable of our proffered bounty.
Your wish is you may leave your warlike swords
For monuments in our chapel. I accept it
As a great honour done me, and must crave   50
Your leave to furnish out our Duchess' revels.
Only one thing, as the last vanity
You e'er shall view, deny me not to stay
To see a barriers prepared tonight.
You shall have private standings: it hath pleased   55
The great ambassadors of several princes

again misses the dramatic irony of his own words on the deceptiveness of outward
appearances. Since Alexander's lines are a comment on the futility of princely
ambition, the irony may also encompass Francisco as well as Brachiano (a 'glow-
worm' or 'proud fool' was applied contemptuously to persons after 1624), as they
both enter while Flamineo speaks.

41   s.d. CARLO ... PEDRO While it is possible (and some editors maintain) that Carlo
     and Pedro (who appear in speech prefixes at ll. 61 and 63) are names taken by
     Lodovico and Gasparo in disguise, it is more likely that they are separate characters,
     members of Brachiano's court who are of Francisco's faction (IV.iii.76). Thus the
     'moles' welcome Francisco and his travelling companions at l. 63 (with 'all things
     ready' for the murder), witness Marcello's death – possibly bearing his body to
     Cornelia's lodging (V.ii.69) – and appear in the final masque and murder to 'strike
     [Flamineo, Vittoria and Zanche] with a joint motion' (V.vi.227–8) and taste the
     justice of Giovanni (V.vi.288). The presence of conspirators inside Brachiano's own
     court may emphasize his self-destruction; in *Antony and Cleopatra*, Caesar plants
     defectors in the front lines 'That Antony may seem to spend his fury/Upon himself'
     (IV.vi.9–10).

54   *barriers* Cf I.ii.27. In January 1610 and again in January 1612 (probably just before
     the first performance of *The White Devil*), Prince Henry fought at barriers at
     Whitehall (carefully staged by Ben Jonson and Inigo Jones in 1610). Webster com-
     posed an elegy (*A Monumental Columne*) for Prince Henry after his sudden death
     in 1612, mourning the loss of this popular chivalric hero.

In their return from Rome to their own countries
To grace our marriage, and to honour me
With such a kind of sport.

FRANCISCO   I shall persuade them
To stay, my lord.

[BRACHIANO]   Set on there to the presence.   60

          Exeunt BRACHIANO, FLAMINEO *and* [HORTENSIO]

CARLO [*To* FRANCISCO]
Noble my lord, most fortunately welcome,

                The conspirators here embrace

You have our vows sealed with the sacrament
To second your attempts.

PEDRO   And all things ready.
He could not have invented his own ruin,
Had he despaired, with more propriety.   65

LODOVICO
You would not take my way.

FRANCISCO   'Tis better ordered.

LODOVICO
T'have poisoned his prayer book, or a pair of beads,
The pommel of his saddle, his looking-glass,
Or th'handle of his racket – O that, that!
That while he had been bandying at tennis,   70
He might have sworn himself to hell, and struck
His soul into the hazard! O my lord!

---

60 ed. (To ... Lord/Set ... presence Q) Most editors assign the final command to
    Brachiano, but Webster may want to suggest Francisco's control in Brachiano's
    court.
    presence presence chamber
    s.p. *BRACHIANO* ed. (not in Q)
    s.d. *HORTENSIO* ed. (Marcello Q). Unless Marcello remains silent, he probably
    passes over the stage and exits with the rest at the opening of the scene. The exit is
    probably intended for Hortensio, who has spoken, rather than Marcello.
61 s.d. ed. (to r. of ll. 63–5 in Q)
68 *pommel ... saddle* Edward Squire, a Catholic conspirator, was hanged in 1598 for
    poisoning the pommel of the Queen's saddle. The contemporary allusion strength-
    ens Webster's association of Brachiano with legitimate power and his enemies with
    popish heresy.
70–2 *bandying ... hazard* Brachiano has earlier been identified with the aristocratic
    game of tennis (II.i.53). Here Lodovico, like Hamlet, is bent on destroying his

I would have our plot be ingenious,
And have it hereafter recorded for example
Rather than borrow example.

FRANCISCO   There's no way   75
More speeding than this thought on.

LODOVICO   On then.

FRANCISCO
And yet methinks that this revenge is poor,
Because it steals upon him like a thief;
To have ta'en him by the casque in a pitched field,
Led him to Florence!

LODOVICO   It had been rare. – And there 80
Have crowned him with a wreath of stinking garlic.
T'have shown the sharpness of his government,
And rankness of his lust. Flamineo comes.

      Exeunt LODOVICO, ANTONELLI [*and*
      GASPARO, FERNESE, CARLO, PEDRO]

    [FRANCISCO *stands apart*]
   Enter FLAMINEO, MARCELLO *and* ZANCHE

MARCELLO
Why doth this devil haunt you? Say.

FLAMINEO   I know not.
For by this light I do not conjure for her.   85
'Tis not so great a cunning as men think
To raise the devil: for here's one up already;
The greatest cunning were to lay him down.

MARCELLO
She is your shame.

---

  enemy's soul as well as his body. In the image, Brachiano's soul is a tennis ball
  struck into the 'hazard' (an opening in the inner wall of the royal tennis court; also
  risk or peril).

79 *ta'en . . . field* i.e. seized him by the helmet in a field planned for battle; the honor-
  able military alternative

83 ed. (And . . . lust/Flamineo comes. Q)
  s.d. ed. (to r. of ll. 82–4 in Q)

87–8 *raise . . . down* The joke is Flamineo's bawdy attempt to defend his mistress (cf.
  Romeo and Juliet II.i.23–9): the 'devil' is not (as first appears) Zanche, but
  Flamineo's own erection, which must be laid down through his mistress's 'cunning'.

113

FLAMINEO   I prithee pardon her.
In faith you see, women are like to burs;   90
Where their affection throws them, there they'll stick.

ZANCHE
[*Motioning towards* FRANCISCO] That is my countryman, a
     goodly person;
When he's at leisure I'll discourse with him
In our own language.

FLAMINEO   I beseech you do—

                                              Exit ZANCHE

How is't brave soldier? O that I had seen   95
Some of your iron days! I pray relate
Some of your service to us.

FRANCISCO
'Tis a ridiculous thing for a man to be his own chronicle; I did
never wash my mouth with mine own praise for fear of getting
a stinking breath.   100

MARCELLO
You're too stoical. The Duke will expect other discourse from you.

FRANCISCO
I shall never flatter him, I have studied man too much to do that.
What difference is between the Duke and I? No more than
between two bricks; all made of one clay. Only 't may be one is
placed on the top of a turret; the other in the bottom of a well by   105
mere chance; if I were placed as high as the Duke, I should stick
as fast; make as fair a show; and bear out weather equally.

FLAMINEO
If this soldier had a patent to beg in churches, then he would
tell them stories.

MARCELLO
I have been a soldier too.   110

FRANCISCO
How have you thrived?

---

  94   s.d. (to r. of l. 93 in Q)
103–7   *What ... equally* These apparently egalitarian remarks, borrowed from Stefano
        Guazzo's *Civil Conversation* (trans. Pettie 1581), mask a deeper irony: there is in
        fact no difference in class between the two dukes, and both are, literally, 'fair' or
        white-skinned.
  108   *soldier ... churches* Beggars often claimed to be soldiers without employment
        (cf. ll. 130–2); without a licence, they could be arrested and whipped as vagabonds.

MARCELLO

Faith, poorly.

FRANCISCO

That's the misery of peace. Only outsides are then respected: as
ships seem very great upon the river, which show very little
upon the seas: so some men i'th'court seem Colossuses in a   115
chamber, who if they came into the field would appear pitiful
pigmies.

FLAMINEO

Give me a fair room yet hung with arras, and some great
cardinal to lug me by th'ears as his endeared minion.

FRANCISCO

And thou may'st do – the devil knows what villainy.   120

FLAMINEO

And safely.

FRANCISCO

Right; you shall see in the country in harvest time, pigeons,
though they destroy never so much corn, the farmer dare not
present the fowling-piece to them! Why? Because they belong to
the Lord of the Manor; whilst your poor sparrows that belong   125
to the Lord of heaven, they go to the pot for't.

FLAMINEO

I will now give you some politic instruction. The Duke says he
will give you pension; that's but bare promise: get it under his
hand. For I have known men that have come from serving
against the Turk; for three or four months they have had   130
pension to buy them new wooden legs and fresh plasters; but
after 'twas not to be had. And this miserable courtesy shows as if
a tormentor should give hot cordial drinks to one three-quarters
dead o'th'rack, only to fetch the miserable soul again to endure
more dog-days.   135

113–17 *misery ... pigmies* a common sentiment. Cf. *Measure for Measure* I.ii.14–16:
     'There's not a soldier of us all, that in the thanksgiving before meat, do relish the
     petition well that prays for peace'.
116–17 *pitiful pigmies* ed. (pittifull. Pigmies. Q)
  118 *arras* tapestry adorning rooms at court (behind which one might hide unsuspected,
     as in *Hamlet* III.iv.7)
122–5 *pigeons ... Manor* Pigeons, though considered pests, were raised for their ready
     value on the open market.
  132 *miserable* compassionate; miserly; wretched
  135 *dog-days* Cf. III.ii.202.

Enter HORTENSIO, *a* YOUNG LORD, ZANCHE *and two more*

How now, gallants; what, are they ready for the barriers?

[*Exit* FRANCISCO]

YOUNG LORD

Yes: the lords are putting on their armour.

[HORTENSIO *and* FLAMINEO *stand apart*]

HORTENSIO

What's he?

FLAMINEO

A new upstart: one that swears like a falc'ner, and will lie in the
Duke's ear day by day like a maker of almanacs; and yet I knew   140
him since he came to th'court smell worse of sweat than an
under-tennis-court-keeper.

HORTENSIO

Look you, yonder's your sweet mistress.

FLAMINEO

Thou art my sworn brother, I'll tell thee – I do love that Moor,
that witch, very constrainedly: she knows some of my villainy; I   145
do love her, just as a man holds a wolf by the ears. But for fear
of turning upon me, and pulling out my throat, I would let her
go to the devil.

HORTENSIO

I hear she claims marriage of thee.

FLAMINEO

'Faith, I made to her some such dark promise and in seeking to   150
fly from't I run on, like a frighted dog with a bottle at's tail that
fain would bite it off and yet dares not look behind him. [*To*
ZANCHE] Now my precious gipsy!

135   s.d. Flamineo's cynical commentary on the court is punctuated by the arrival of the
      young lord, who epitomizes the sycophancy which Flamineo both desires and despises.
137   s.d. All except Flamineo and Hortensio are very likely setting up the barriers on
      stage (NCW V.i.134.I n.).
140   *maker of almanacs* fortune-teller, astrologer
146   *holds . . . ears* common proverb. Cf. Philip Sidney, *Arcadia, Works* II, 12: 'like them
      that holde the wolfe by the eares, bitten while they hold, and slaine if they loose'.
153   *gipsy* Like Cleopatra, Zanche is 'with Phoebus' amorous pinches black' (*Antony and
      Cleopatra* I.v.28) – as dark-skinned as the gipsies, who arrived in England in the
      early sixteenth century and were thought to come from Egypt.

ZANCHE

Ay, your love to me rather cools than heats.

FLAMINEO

Marry, I am the sounder lover – we have many wenches about   155
the town heat too fast.

HORTENSIO

What do you think of these perfumed gallants then?

FLAMINEO

Their satin cannot save them. I am confident
They have a certain spice of the disease,
For they that sleep with dogs shall rise with fleas.   160

ZANCHE

Believe it! A little painting and gay clothes
Make you loathe me.

FLAMINEO

How? Love a lady for painting or gay apparel? I'll unkennel one
example more for thee. Aesop had a foolish dog that let go the
flesh to catch the shadow. I would have courtiers be better diners.   165

ZANCHE

You remember your oaths.

FLAMINEO

Lovers' oaths are like mariners' prayers, uttered in extremity; but
when the tempest is o'er and that the vessel leaves tumbling, they
fall from protesting to drinking. And yet amongst gentlemen
protesting and drinking go together, and agree as well as   170
shoemakers and Westphalia bacon. They are both drawers on:
for drink draws on protestation and protestation draws on
more drink. Is not this discourse better now than the morality
of your sunburnt gentleman?

154 *cools* abates, declines (as used by Zanche); allays, cools down (implied by Flamineo)
155 *sounder lover* ed. (sounder, lover Q)
156 *heat* become sexually aroused; contract venereal disease
158 *satin* with a pun on 'Satan'
161–2 *A little . . . me* i.e. women who wear makeup and dress well attract you, and lead
       you to reject me
164–5 *Aesop . . . diners* i.e. a bird in the hand is worth two in the bush; only a fool gives up
       what he has for what he desires
165 *diners* ed. (*Diuers.* Q)
168 *tumbling* tossing and rolling about (as a ship in a storm; as in sexual intercourse)
170–1 *agree . . . bacon* Bacon draws men on to drink, and shoemakers draw shoes on to feet.
173 *morality* ed. (mortality Q)

117

Enter CORNELIA

CORNELIA

Is this your perch, you haggard? [*Strikes* ZANCHE] Fly to th'stews. 175

FLAMINEO

You should be clapped by th'heels now: strike i'th'court!

[*Exit* CORNELIA]

ZANCHE

She's good for nothing but to make her maids
Catch cold o'nights; they dare not use a bedstaff
For fear of her light fingers.

MARCELLO   You're a strumpet.

An impudent one.   [*Kicks* ZANCHE]

FLAMINEO   Why do you kick her? Say,   180
Do you think that she's like a walnut-tree?
Must she be cudgelled ere she bear good fruit?

MARCELLO

She brags that you shall marry her.

FLAMINEO   What then?

MARCELLO

I had rather she were pitched upon a stake
In some new-seeded garden, to affright   185
Her fellow crows thence.

---

174 s.d. *Enter* CORNELIA Flamineo's complacent misogyny is abruptly and dramaticall
disturbed by Cornelia's violent entrance, which recalls her interruption at I.ii.252
and signals the disruption of the apparent harmony of the wedding procession, in
which Cornelia and Zanche appeared together.

175 *haggard* wild female hawk, often applied to a promiscuous, intractable woman
stews brothel

176 *clapped . . . heels* put in irons or in the stocks
strike . . . court Striking and drawing blood at court was severely punished: offenders might be imprisoned for life or have their right hands chopped off.

178–9 *they . . . fingers* Bed-staves were either slats supporting the bedding or sticks used in
making beds, well known as ready weapons; Zanche's bed-staff is a potential
weapon or a warm male companion. She dare not use either because (she implies)
Cornelia covets both.

181–2 *Do . . . fruit?* The source from which Webster lifted this common proverb reads: 'A
woman, an asse, and a walnut tree / Bring the more fruit, the more beaten they bee'
(Pettie-III.39). The same text counters it with this: 'He God offendes, and holy love
undoes / Which on his wife doth fasten churlish bloes'.

184–6 *pitched . . . thence* Marcello conflates images of Zanche as a witch ('upon a stake')
and a crow (the black scavenger so hated by English farmers).

185 *new-seeded garden* Cf. I.ii.257.

FLAMINEO   You're a boy, a fool,
  Be guardian to your hound, I am of age.
MARCELLO
  If I take her near you I'll cut her throat.
FLAMINEO
  With a fan of feathers?
MARCELLO   And for you, I'll whip
  This folly from you.
FLAMINEO   Are you choleric?   190
  I'll purge't with rhubarb.
HORTENSIO   O your brother—
FLAMINEO   Hang him.
  He wrongs me most that ought t'offend me least.
  [To MARCELLO] I do suspect my mother played foul play
  When she conceived thee.
MARCELLO   Now by all my hopes,
  Like the two slaughtered sons of Oedipus,   195
  The very flames of our affection
  Shall turn two ways. Those words I'll make thee answer
  With thy heart blood.
FLAMINEO   Do like the geese in the progress;
  You know where you shall find me –   [Exit]
MARCELLO   Very good.
  And thou beest a noble friend, bear him my sword,   200
  And bid him fit the length on't.

186   *You're* ed. (Your Q)
189   *fan of feathers* appropriate to the courtier Marcello has become, not the soldier he
      has been
190   *choleric* Choler was one of the four humours of early physiology, hot and dry, and
      supposed to cause irascibility. Flamineo here treats it as a digestive malady,
      attended with bilious diarrhoea and vomiting, remedied by purging. Rhubarb was
      a commonly prescribed purgative (cf. *The Duchess of Malfi* II.v.12–13, 'Rhubarb, O
      for rhubarb / To purge this choler').
195–7 *two ... ways* After the two sons of Oedipus, Eteocles and Polinices, were killed in
      combat for their father's throne, their bodies were burnt together; the flames
      miraculously parted, showing that death did not end their mutual hatred.
198   *geese* ed. (gesse Q) prostitutes. The word 'gesses' is a technical term for the stopping
      places on a royal progress, and may be intended (Lucas, p. 251). But prostitutes
      plied their trade during progresses, and Flamineo's bawdy remark is typical. The
      syntax is ambiguous, however, and so the line may read 'Do as the prostitutes do in
      a progress, who know where their victims are to be found', or 'Do – I shall be found
      as easily as prostitutes in a progress'.
201   s.d. ed. (to r. of ll. 222–3 in Q)

119

YOUNG LORD   Sir I shall.

[*Exeunt all but* ZANCHE]

Enter FRANCISCO *the Duke of Florence* [*disguised*]

ZANCHE

[*Aside*] He comes. Hence petty thought of my disgrace–
[*To* FRANCISCO] I ne'er loved my complexion till now,
Cause I may boldly say without a blush
I love you.

[FRANCISCO] Your love is untimely sown;   205
There's a spring at Michaelmas, but 'tis but a faint one–
I am sunk in years, and I have vowed never to marry.

ZANCHE

Alas! Poor maids get more lovers than husbands. Yet you may
mistake my wealth. For, as when ambassadors are sent to
congratulate princes, there's commonly sent along with them a   210
rich present; so that though the prince like not the ambassador's
person nor words, yet he likes well of the presentment. So I may
come to you in the same manner, and be better loved for my
dowry than my virtue.

[FRANCISCO]

I'll think on the motion.   215

ZANCHE

Do, I'll now detain you no longer. At your better leisure
I'll tell you things shall startle your blood.
Nor blame me that this passion I reveal;
Lovers die inward that their flames conceal.

[FRANCISCO]

[*Aside*] Of all intelligence this may prove the best,   220
Sure I shall draw strange fowl, from this foul nest.

Exeunt

205, 215, 220 s.p. *FRANCISCO* ed. (FLA Q)
 206–7 ed. (Ther's . . . sunck / In . . . marry. Q)
   206 *spring . . . one* Michaelmas is 29 September.
   214 *motion* offer, proposal

Enter MARCELLO *and* CORNELIA [*and a* PAGE]

CORNELIA
I hear a whispering all about the court,
You are to fight; who is your opposite?
What is the quarrel?
MARCELLO   'Tis an idle rumour.
CORNELIA
Will you dissemble? Sure you do not well
To fright me thus – you never look thus pale,   5
But when you are most angry. I do charge you
Upon my blessing; nay I'll call the Duke,
And he shall school you.
MARCELLO   Publish not a fear
Which would convert to laughter; 'tis not so–
Was not this crucifix my father's?
CORNELIA   Yes.   10
MARCELLO
I have heard you say, giving my brother suck,
He took the crucifix between his hands,
And broke a limb off.
CORNELIA   Yes: but 'tis mended.

Enter FLAMINEO

FLAMINEO
I have brought your weapon back.

FLAMINEO *runs* MARCELLO *through*

CORNELIA   Ha, O my horror!
MARCELLO
You have brought it home indeed.

  2 *You* ed. (Your Q)
 10 *crucifix* Cornelia wears this around her neck, probably from the beginning of the
     play, immediately identifying her (along with the Cardinal) as a guardian of tradi-
     tional Christian values.
 13 s.d. ed. (to r. of l. 12 in Q). The sudden violence of Flamineo's entrance and subse-
     quent assault imitates precisely Cornelia's attack on Zanche (V.i.175). Thus Flamineo
     makes clear that his action is a direct response to his mother's rigid morality.

CORNELIA   Help – O he's murdered.   15

FLAMINEO

Do you turn your gall up? I'll to sanctuary,
And send a surgeon to you.   [*Exit*]

Enter CARL[O,] HORT[ENSIO,] PEDRO

HORTENSIO   How? O'th'ground?

MARCELLO

O mother now remember what I told
Of breaking off the crucifix: farewell–
There are some sins which heaven doth duly punish   20
In a whole family. This it is to rise
By all dishonest means. Let all men know
That tree shall long time keep a steady foot
Whose branches spread no wider than the root.

CORNELIA

O my perpetual sorrow!

HORTENSIO   Virtuous Marcello.   25

He's dead: pray leave him lady; come, you shall.

CORNELIA

Alas he is not dead: he's in a trance.
Why here's nobody shall get anything by his death. Let me call
him again for God's sake.

CARLO

I would you were deceived.   30

16   *turn . . . up* probably a witty extension of Flamineo's earlier remark about purging
     Marcello's choler (supposed to have its seat in the gall). Since bloodletting was a
     remedy for choler (like purgation), Flamineo may be humorously expressing sur-
     prise that Marcello's irascibility is increased by being stabbed. He then offers to
     send a doctor to complete the cure.

17   s.d. ed. (to r. of ll. 19–20 in Q). The entrance of Carlo and Pedro, 'moles' in
     league with Francisco, as witnesses to Flamineo's fratricide emphasizes the self-
     determination of Brachiano and his allies; the revenge plot is unexpectedly
     superseded in the final act.

23–4 *That . . . root* Cf. I.ii.233–7, where the 'yew' of Vittoria's dream strikes Isabella and
     Camillo dead with one of its branches.

24   *wider* ed. (wilder Q)

26   Carlo, Pedro and Hortensio force Cornelia away from the body of Marcello, and
     she struggles to free herself.

CORNELIA

O you abuse me, you abuse me, you abuse me. How many have
gone away thus for lack of tendance; rear up's head, rear up's
head; his bleeding inward will kill him.

HORTENSIO

You see he is departed.

CORNELIA

Let me come to him; give me him as he is, if he be turned 35
to earth; let me but give him one hearty kiss, and you shall put
us both into one coffin. Fetch a looking-glass, see if his breath
will not stain it; or pull out some feathers from my pillow,
and lay them to his lips – will you lose him for a little painstaking? 40

HORTENSIO

Your kindest office is to pray for him.

CORNELIA

Alas! I would not pray for him yet. He may live to lay me
i'th'ground, and pray for me, if you'll let me come to him.

Enter BRACHIANO *all armed, save the beaver, with* FLAMINEO,
[LODOVICO *disguised and* FRANCISCO *disguised
as* MULINASSAR]

BRACHIANO

Was this your handiwork?

FLAMINEO

It was my misfortune. 45

CORNELIA

He lies, he lies, he did not kill him: these have killed him, that
would not let him be better looked to.

BRACHIANO

Have comfort my grieved mother.

CORNELIA

O you screech-owl.

36–9 *earth . . . lips* Webster is borrowing from *King Lear* (V.iii.262–6): 'She's dead as
earth. Lend me a looking-glass, / If that her breath will mist or stain the stone, /
Why then she lives . . . This feather stirs; she lives!'
39 *lose* ed. (loose Q)
43 s.d. ed. (to r. of ll. 45–7 in Q)
49 *screech-owl* bird of ill-omen. The line is addressed either to Brachiano, who has
attempted to comfort her, or to Flamineo.

123

HORTENSIO

    [*Restraining her*] Forbear, good madam.   50

CORNELIA

    [*Shaking him off*] Let me go, let me go.

> *She runs to* FLAMINEO *with her knife drawn and*
> *coming to him lets it fall*

    The God of heaven forgive thee. Dost not wonder
    I pray for thee? I'll tell thee what's the reason—
    I have scarce breath to number twenty minutes;
    I'd not spend that in cursing. Fare thee well—   55
    Half of thyself lies there: and may'st thou live
    To fill an hour-glass with his mouldered ashes,
    To tell how thou shouldst spend the time to come
    In blest repentance.

BRACHIANO   Mother, pray tell me

    How came he by his death? What was the quarrel?   60

CORNELIA

    Indeed my younger boy presumed too much
    Upon his manhood; gave him bitter words;
    Drew his sword first; and so I know not how,
    For I was out of my wits, he fell with's head
    Just in my bosom.

PAGE   This is not true madam.   65

CORNELIA

    I pray thee peace.
    One arrow's grazed already; it were vain
    T'lose this: for that will ne'er be found again.

BRACHIANO

    Go, bear the body to Cornelia's lodging:

---

51 s.d. ed. (to r. of ll. 51–5 in Q)

61 *younger boy* Marcello. Younger brothers were frequently angry about their disen-
    franchised position (cf. Orlando in *As You Like It*); Cornelia may be capitalizing on
    the choleric reputation of younger brothers.

67 *grazed* probably 'grassed' (lost in the grass) with the secondary meaning 'grazed' (to
    cut the surface of, as in a wound). The idea of shooting a second arrow to find the
    first was a common metaphor for ambition.

And we command that none acquaint our Duchess 70
With this sad accident: for you Flamineo,
Hark you, I will not grant your pardon.
FRANCISCO   No?
BRACHIANO
Only a lease of your life. And that shall last
But for one day. Thou shalt be forced each evening
To renew it, or be hanged.
FLAMINEO   At your pleasure. 75

LODOVICO *sprinkles* BRACHIANO's *beaver with a poison*

Your will is law now, I'll not meddle with it.
BRACHIANO
You once did brave me in your sister's lodging;
I'll now keep you in awe for't. Where's our beaver?
FRANCISCO
[*Aside*] He calls for his destruction. Noble youth,
I pity thy sad fate. Now to the barriers. 80
This shall his passage to the black lake further,
The last good deed he did, he pardoned murder.

Exeunt

74–5 *But . . . pleasure* ed. (But . . . it,/ or . . . pleasure Q)
   75 s.d. *beaver* lower portion of the face-guard of a helmet. The poisoning of
        Brachiano's mouthpiece recalls the dumb show in II.ii.23, when Dr Julio washed
        the lips of Brachiano's picture in order to poison Isabella when she kissed it.
   77 *You . . . lodging* Cf. IV.ii.48–9.
   81 *black lake* probably Acheron, black river of the underworld

[ACT V, SCENE iii]

Charges and shouts. They fight at barriers; first single pairs, then three to three

Enter BRACHIANO *and* FLAMINEO *with others*
[GIOVANNI, VITTORIA, *and* FRANCISCO
disguised as MULINASSAR]

BRACHIANO
An armourer! Ud's death, an armourer!
FLAMINEO
Armourer; where's the armourer?
BRACHIANO
Tear off my beaver.
FLAMINEO　　　　　　　Are you hurt, my lord?
BRACHIANO
O my brain's on fire,

Enter ARMOURER

　　　　　　　the helmet is poisoned.
ARMOURER　　　　　　　　　　　　　　　　　　5
My lord upon my soul–
BRACHIANO
Away with him to torture.

　　　　　　　　　　[*Exit* ARMOURER, *guarded*]
There are some great ones that have hand in this,
And near about me.
VITTORIA　　　　　　O my loved lord, poisoned?
FLAMINEO
Remove the bar: here's unfortunate revels–
Call the physicians;

---

  0 s.d. The fight at barriers, a spectacle for the Red Bull stage, was a highly formal ceremonial combat (frequently allegorized as, for example, Truth vs. Opinion) rapidly disappearing from courtly life. Here, it gives Webster the opportunity to juxtapose chivalric courtly ideals with the Machiavellian revenge plot. The scene opens with six combatants jousting in full armour (probably Brachiano and five of the ambassadors; cf. l. 12); they may be observed (perhaps, from the upper stage) by an audience which includes Francisco, Lodovico, Gasparo, Vittoria, Zanche, Giovanni and Flamineo (so NCW V.iii.0.1–2 n.).

  4 *O . . . poisoned* ed. (O . . . fire/The . . . soule Q)

  9 *bar* probably the barrier, still on the stage

Ent[er] 2 PHYSICIANS

a plague upon you; 10
We have too much of your cunning here already.
I fear the ambassadors are likewise poisoned.

BRACHIANO

O I am gone already: the infection
Flies to the brain and heart. O thou strong heart!
There's such a covenant 'tween the world and it, 15
They're loth to break.

GIOVANNI   O my most loved father!

BRACHIANO

Remove the boy away.

                    [GIOVANNI *is led offstage*]

Where's this good woman? Had I infinite worlds
They were too little for thee. Must I leave thee?
What say yon screech-owls, is the venom mortal? 20

PHYSICIANS

Most deadly.

BRACHIANO   Most corrupted politic hangman!
You kill without book; but your art to save
Fails you as oft as great men's needy friends.
I that have given life to offending slaves
And wretched murderers, have I not power 25
To lengthen mine own a twelvemonth?
[*To* VITTORIA] Do not kiss me, for I shall poison thee.
This unction is sent from the great Duke of Florence.

FRANCISCO

Sir be of comfort.

BRACHIANO

O thou soft natural death, that art joint-twin 30

---

20   *screech-owls* the physicians, who can foretell, but not prevent, death
21–3   *Most . . . friends* This is addressed to Death, here envisaged as a schemer who kills by
        rote (without book), but lacks the ability to save life as great men lack friends. This
        speech reveals that, while Brachiano knows he is Francisco's victim (in a revenge
        tragedy), he nonetheless sees himself as the great victim of Fate (in a *de casibus*
        tragedy), and thus ignores the disguised Duke of Florence to focus on larger forces.
24–5   *I . . . murderers* Cf. V.ii.82.
27   *Do . . . me* Brachiano protects Vittoria from the poisoned kiss which, in picture,
        killed Isabella (II.ii.23).
30–1   *death . . . slumber* Sleep is 'death's second self, that seals up all in rest' (Shakespeare,
        Sonnet 73).

To sweetest slumber: no rough-bearded comet
Stares on thy mild departure: the dull owl
Beats not against thy casement: the hoarse wolf
Scents not thy carrion. Pity winds thy corse,
Whilst horror waits on princes.   35

VITTORIA

[*Wailing*] I am lost for ever.

BRACHIANO

How miserable a thing it is to die,
'Mongst women howling!

[*Enter* LODOVICO *and* GASPARO *disguised as Capuchins*]

                    What are those?
FLAMINEO   Franciscans.
They have brought the extreme unction.

BRACHIANO

On pain of death, let no man name death to me,   40
It is a word infinitely terrible.
Withdraw into our cabinet.
                    Exeunt [*all*] *but* FRANCISCO *and* FLAMINEO

FLAMINEO

To see what solitariness is about dying princes. As heretofore
they have unpeopled towns, divorced friends, and made great
houses unhospitable, so now, O justice! where are their flatterers   45
now? Flatterers are but the shadows of princes' bodies, the least
thick cloud makes them invisible.

FRANCISCO

There's great moan made for him.

FLAMINEO

'Faith, for some few hours salt water will run most plentifully

---

31-3 *rough-bearded . . . casement* a series of prodigies associated with the fall of kings
35-6 ed. (one line in Q)
  38 *Franciscans* a wonderful pun: the murderers are both disguised Franciscan friars
      and servants to Francisco.
  39 *extreme unction* both the anointment of the faithful before death and the most
      powerful poison of the murderers
  42 *Withdraw . . . cabinet* Brachiano, Vittoria and the disguised assassins may retreat into
      the curtained discovery space at the rear of the stage, where they are discovered at l. 81.

in every office o'th'court. But believe it; most of them do but   50
weep over their stepmothers' graves.

FRANCISCO

How mean you?

FLAMINEO

Why? They dissemble, as some men do that live within compass
o'th'verge.

FRANCISCO

Come, you have thrived well under him.   55

FLAMINEO

'Faith, like a wolf in a woman's breast; I have been fed with
poultry; but for money, understand me, I had as good a will to
cozen him, as e'er an officer of them all. But I had not cunning
enough to do it.

FRANCISCO

What did'st thou think of him? 'Faith speak freely.   60

FLAMINEO

He was a kind of statesman that would sooner have reckoned
how many cannon bullets he had discharged against a town, to
count his expense that way, than how many of his valiant and
deserving subjects he lost before it.

FRANCISCO

O, speak well of the Duke.   65

FLAMINEO

I have done. Wilt hear some of my court wisdom?

Enter LODOVICO [*disguised*]

To reprehend princes is dangerous: and to over-commend
some of them is palpable lying.

FRANCISCO

How is it with the Duke?

LODOVICO   Most deadly ill.

He's fall'n into a strange distraction.   70

He talks of battles and monopolies,

53–4 *compass . . . verge* within twelve miles of the king's court, under the jurisdiction of
the Lord High Steward

56–7 *wolf . . . poultry* The 'ulcerous wolf' (*The Duchess of Malfi* II.i.57), common par-
lance for a cancerous ulcer, was fed with fresh meat so that it would not consume
human flesh. The ulcer in the thigh of the real-life Brachiano was treated with raw
meat. There may also be a pun on 'poultry' and 'paltry' (rubbish, trash).

Levying of taxes, and from that descends
To the most brain-sick language. His mind fastens
On twenty several objects, which confound
Deep sense with folly. Such a fearful end   75
May teach some men that bear too lofty crest,
Though they live happiest, yet they die not best.
He hath conferred the whole state of the dukedom
Upon your sister, till the Prince arrive
At mature age.

FLAMINEO   There's some good luck in that yet.   80

FRANCISCO
See here he comes.

Enter BRACHIANO, *presented in a bed,* VITTORIA *and others*
[*including* GASPARO, *disguised*]

There's death in's face already.

VITTORIA
O my good lord!

*These speeches are several kinds of distractions and in the
action should appear so*

BRACHIANO   Away, you have abused me.
You have conveyed coin forth our territories,
Bought and sold offices, oppressed the poor,
And I ne'er dreamt on't. Make up your accounts;
I'll now be mine own steward.   85

FLAMINEO   Sir, have patience.

---

81 *See . . . already* ed. (See . . . comes/There's . . . allready Q)
81 s.d. ed. (to r. of l. 81 in Q) The bed recalls that in the house of convertites in
    IV.ii.123, upon which Vittoria threw herself earlier; now Brachiano, like Vittoria in
    the earlier scene, is the accuser. The bed may have been thrust out onto the main
    stage and remained for the rest of the scene.
82 s.d. ed. (to l. of ll. 83–90 in Q). This s.d. suggests that distraction was signalled by
    conventionalized gestures (cf. V.iv.89 s.d.): perhaps beating the breast or wringing
    the hands (see Thomson, p. 31). Brachiano is clearly feeling the effects of the
    poison.
83 *conveyed . . . territories* The export of money was a serious offence; Henry VIII
    published a statute forbidding it.

BRACHIANO

    Indeed I am too blame.

    For did you ever hear the dusky raven

    Chide blackness? Or was't ever known the devil

    Railed against cloven creatures?

VITTORIA   O my lord!   90

BRACHIANO

    Let me have some quails to supper.

FLAMINEO   Sir, you shall.

BRACHIANO

    No: some fried dog-fish. Your quails feed on poison—

    That old dog-fox, that politician Florence—

    I'll forswear hunting and turn dog-killer.

    Rare! I'll be friends with him: for mark you sir, one dog   95

    Still sets another a-barking: peace, peace,

    Yonder's a fine slave come in now.

FLAMINEO   Where?

BRACHIANO   Why, there.

    In a blue bonnet, and a pair of breeches

    With a great codpiece. Ha, ha, ha,

    Look you his codpiece is stuck full of pins   100

    With pearls o'th'head of them. Do not you know him?

FLAMINEO

    No my lord.

BRACHIANO   Why 'tis the devil.

    I know him by a great rose he wears on's shoe

    To hide his cloven foot. I'll dispute with him.

    He's a rare linguist.

  88–9   *raven . . . blackness* 'The raven chides blackness' is proverbial, like the pot calling the kettle black. Ravens were considered malignant: Brachiano may refer either to the dark-haired Vittoria or the dark-skinned Zanche. Francisco, disguised as Mulinassar, is a more appropriate, though unintended, target for this remark.

    91   *quails* birds supposed to feed on venomous seeds, and considered a culinary delicacy; courtesans

    92   *dog-fish* a small shark; applied opprobriously to persons

    93   *dog-fox* male fox (symbol of sly cunning and craft)

  95–6   *one . . . a-barking* It is proverbial that if one dog barks, they all do.

100–1   *codpiece . . . them* Codpieces, out of fashion in 1612, were in Henry VIII's time very prominent and highly decorated.

103–4   *rose . . . foot* Large, expensive silk rosettes on shoes became fashionable at the end of the sixteenth century.

  105   *linguist* polyglot; eloquent speaker

VITTORIA   My lord here's nothing.   105

BRACHIANO

Nothing? Rare! Nothing! When I want money,
Our treasury is empty; there is nothing,–
I'll not be used thus.

VITTORIA   O! Lie still my lord–

BRACHIANO

See, see, Flamineo that killed his brother
Is dancing on the ropes there: and he carries   110
A money-bag in each hand, to keep him even,
For fear of breaking's neck. And there's a lawyer
In a gown whipt with velvet, stares and gapes
When the money will fall. How the rogue cuts capers!
It should have been in a halter.   115
'Tis there; what's she?   [*Points to* VITTORIA]

FLAMINEO   Vittoria, my lord.

BRACHIANO

Ha, ha, ha. Her hair is sprinkled with arras powder, that makes
her look as if she had sinned in the pastry. What's he?
                              [*Points to* GASPARO *or* LODOVICO]

FLAMINEO

A divine my lord.

BRACHIANO

He will be drunk: avoid him: th'argument is fearful when   120
churchmen stagger in't. Look you; six gray rats that have lost
their tails crawl up the pillow; send for a rat-catcher.
I'll do a miracle: I'll free the court
From all foul vermin. Where's Flamineo?

FLAMINEO

I do not like that he names me so often,   125

---

110   *ropes* tightropes
113   *whipt* trimmed
114–15   *rogue . . . halter* Flamineo is the rogue cutting capers, or dancing; the rope on which
         he dances should have gone around his neck.
117   *hair . . . powder* As a new bride, Vittoria's hair would have been sprinkled with
         powdered orris, or iris root, commonly used for whitening and perfuming hair.
118   *pastry* place where pastry is made
121–2   *six . . . pillow* possibly a reference to witches, who often turned themselves into
         animals, like the witch in *Macbeth*, who promises 'Like a rat without a tail,/I'll do,
         I'll do, and I'll do' (I.iii.9–10)
122–4   *send . . . vermin* a possible allusion to the Pied Piper of Hamelin

Especially on's death-bed: 'tis a sign
I shall not live long: see he's near his end.

BRACHIANO *seems here near his end.* LODOVICO *and*
GASPARO *in the habit of Capuchins present him in his bed with a*
crucifix and hallowed candle

LODOVICO

Pray give us leave; *Attende Domine Brachiane–*

FLAMINEO

See, see, how firmly he doth fix his eye
Upon the crucifix.

VITTORIA   O hold it constant.   130

It settles his wild spirits; and so his eyes
Melt into tears.

LODOVICO

(By the crucifix) Domine Brachiane, solebas in bello tutus esse tuo
clypeo, nunc hunc clypeum hosti tuo opponas infernali.

GASPARO

(By the hallowed taper) Olim hasta valuisti in bello; nunc hanc   135
sacram hastam vibrabis contra hostem animarum.

LODOVICO

Attende Domine Brachiane si nunc quoque probas ea quae acta
sunt inter nos, flecte caput in dextrum.

GASPARO

Esto securus Domine Brachiane: cogita quantum habeas meritorum
– denique memineris meam animam pro tua oppignoratam si quid   140
esset periculi.

127   s.d. ed. (to r. of ll. 120–30 in Q). For the crucifix as a significant property cf. V.ii.10.
        The 'hallowed candle' may recall the dumb show (II.ii.23) when Dr Julio and his
        assistant burned perfumes in the 'fire' before Brachiano's picture.
128   *Attende . . . Brachiane* 'Listen, Lord Brachiano.' The fraudulent capuchins begin the
        Commendatio Animae, the commending of the soul to God, which follows the
        extreme unction in Roman ritual: in this ritual, candle and crucifix are symbols of
        hope and comfort to the dying (McLeod, *Dramatic Imagery*, p. 66).
133   s.d. ed. (to l. of ll. 133–5 in Q)
133–43   i.e. LODOVICO 'Lord Brachiano, you were accustomed to be guarded in battle by
        your shield; now this shield [the crucifix] you shall oppose against your infernal
        enemy.' – GASPARO 'Once with your spear you prevailed in battle; now this holy

LODOVICO

    Si nunc quoque probas ea quae acta sunt inter nos, flecte caput in
    loevum.
    He is departing: pray stand all apart,
    And let us only whisper in his ears   145
    Some private meditations which our order
    Permits you not to hear.

        Here the rest being departed LODOVICO *and* GASPARO
                discover themselves

GASPARO   Brachiano.

LODOVICO

    Devil Brachiano. Thou art damned.

GASPARO   Perpetually.

LODOVICO

    A slave condemned and given up to the gallows
    Is thy great lord and master.

GASPARO   True: for thou   150

    Art given up to the devil.

LODOVICO   O you slave!
    You that were held the famous politician;
    Whose art was poison.

GASPARO   And whose conscience murder.

133–43 spear [the hallowed taper] you shall wield against the enemy of souls.' – LODOVICO
       'Listen, Lord Brachiano, if you now also approve what has been done between us,
       turn your head to the right.' – GASPARO 'Rest assured Lord Brachiano: think how
       many good deeds you have done – lastly remember that my soul is pledged for
       yours if there should be any peril.' – LODOVICO 'If you now also approve what has
       been done between us, turn your head to the left.'
          The whole passage is based on Erasmus, *Funus*, an account of the death of
       Georgius Balearicus, a corrupt and wealthy man, whose death is described by
       Erasmus as 'the last acte of the comedy'. After purchasing papal remission of sins
       (and justifying all his goods 'goten by extorcyon and robbery'), Georgius himself,
       'lyke a man of warre', delivers the first two speeches which Webster gives to the
       assassins. Erasmus emphasizes the corruption and hypocrisy of the dying man;
       Webster uses the same ceremony to highlight the villainy and hypocrisy of the
       dying man's assassins.
135   s.d. ed. (to l. of ll. 135–7 in Q)
144–65 The revengers parody the *Commendatio*, by dismissing witnesses (who normally
       participated in prayers for the dying one's soul), and by commending Brachiano
       not to God but to the devil (NCW V.iii.144–7, 148–64 n.).
147   s.d. ed. (to r. of ll. 146–8 in Q)
153   *conscience* inmost thought

LODOVICO

That would have broke your wife's neck down the stairs

Ere she was poisoned.   155

GASPARO

That had your villainous sallets—

LODOVICO

And fine embroidered bottles, and perfumes

Equally mortal with a winter plague—

GASPARO

Now there's mercury—

LODOVICO   And copperas—

GASPARO   And quicksilver—

LODOVICO

With other devilish pothecary stuff   160

A-melting in your politic brains; dost hear?

GASPARO

This is Count Lodovico.

LODOVICO   This Gasparo.

And thou shalt die like a poor rogue.

GASPARO   And stink

Like a dead fly-blown dog.

LODOVICO   And be forgotten

Before thy funeral sermon.   165

BRACHIANO

Vittoria! Vittoria!

154–5   ed. (prose in Q)

        broke . . . poisoned probably an allusion to the notorious Earl of Leicester's alleged
        attempt to poison his wife, Amy Robsart, before having her thrown down the stairs
        at Cumnor Place in 1560, when she finally died. Leicester wanted to be free to
        marry Queen Elizabeth; according to the 1584 pamphlet *Leicester's Commonwealth*,
        the Earl employed a poisoner named Dr Julio as well as two 'atheists' for 'figuring
        and conjuring'. Renaissance Italy was thus not so different from Renaissance
        England.

156   *sallets* salads

157   *And . . . perfumes* ed. (And . . . bottles/And perfumes Q)

158   *winter plague* A plague which flourished during the cold months was considered
        most pernicious.

159   *mercury . . . quicksilver* Mercury *is* quicksilver (unless the poisonous plant,
        Mercurialis perennis, or wild mercury, is meant); Gasparo is trying to 'terrify him at
        the last gasp' (l. 211) through sheer emphasis. Copperas (sulphate of copper, iron
        or zinc) is fatal only when taken in quantity.

164–5   ed. (one line in Q)

LODOVICO   O the cursed devil,
    Come to himself again. We are undone.

                Enter VITTORIA *and the* ATTEND[ANTS]

GASPARO
    [*Aside to* LODOVICO] Strangle him in private.
    [*Aloud*] What? Will you call him again
    To live in treble torments? For charity,   170
    For Christian charity, avoid the chamber.
                          [*Exeunt* VITTORIA *and* ATTENDANTS]
LODOVICO
    You would prate, sir. This is a true-love knot
    Sent from the Duke of Florence.

                    BRACHIANO *is strangled*

GASPARO   What, is it done?
LODOVICO
    The snuff is out. No woman-keeper i'th'world,
    Though she had practised seven year at the pest-house,   175
    Could have done't quaintlier.

    [*Enter* VITTORIA, FRANCISCO, FLAMINEO, *and* ATTENDANTS]

                    My lord he's dead.
OMNES
    Rest to his soul.

167–76 Thomson (pp. 33–4) argues that the bustle of mass entries and exits risks bringing
        the scene close to farce on the stage; the visual movement of Vittoria with her
        attendants on and off the stage certainly emphasizes by contrast Brachiano's isola-
        tion and stillness in death.
   170 *charity* a word that echoes throughout the arraignment (cf. III.ii.71, 161)
   172 *true-love knot* the noose used to strangle Brachiano (perhaps Lodovico's waistcord
        or rosary: so NCW V.iii.171 n.). The word-play links Brachiano's death with his
        love affair, and recalls Francisco's feigned courtship of Vittoria.
   174 *snuff* proverbial: to die is to go out like a candle in a snuff (possibly punctuated by
        Lodovico snuffing out the hallowed taper)
        woman-keeper female nurse, often suspected of killing off patients
   175 *pest-house* a hospice for those sick of the plague. One was erected in London in 1594.
   176 *quaintlier* more skilfully
   177 s.d. *Exit* ed. (Exit Vittoria Q)

VITTORIA   O me! This place is hell.

                    Exit [with ATTENDANTS *and* GASPARO]

[FRANCISCO]

    How heavily she takes it.

FLAMINEO   O yes, yes;

    Had women navigable rivers in their eyes

    They would dispend them all; surely I wonder   180

    Why we should wish more rivers to the city

    When they sell water so good cheap. I'll tell thee,

    These are but moonish shades of griefs or fears,

    There's nothing sooner dry than women's tears.

    Why here's an end of all my harvest, he has given me nothing–   185

    Court promises! Let wise men count them cursed

    For while you live he that scores best pays worst.

[FRANCISCO]

    Sure, this was Florence' doing.

FLAMINEO   Very likely.

    Those are found weighty strokes which come from th'hand,

    But those are killing strokes which come from th'head.   190

    O the rare tricks of a Machiavellian!

    He doth not come like a gross plodding slave

    And buffet you to death: no, my quaint knave,

    He tickles you to death, makes you die laughing

    As if you had swallowed down a pound of saffron.   195

    You see the feat, 'tis practised in a trice–

    To teach court-honesty it jumps on ice.

178–205, 218 s.p. *FRANCISCO* ed. (FLO Q)

181–2 *Why . . . cheap* Sir Hugh Middleton's artificial New River, which was designed to supply London with water, was begun in 1608 and under way at the time of the play's first performance.

183 *moonish* changeable (like the moon)

187 *he . . . worst* i.e. he who runs up a score or debt on credit (like him who depends on promises) pays dearly for it

191 *Machiavellian* ed. (Machivillian Q, with a pun on 'villain')

193 *buffet* strike, beat
     quaint ingenious

195 *saffron* in moderation, supposed to quicken the senses and make men merry; fatal when taken in excess

197 *To . . . ice* i.e. to teach court intrigue that it is precarious and dangerous. In the *The Duchess of Malfi*, courts are 'slippery ice-pavements' on which 'men may break their necks' (V.ii.328–9).
     court-honesty honesty as practised at court – deception, intrigue

[FRANCISCO]
Now have the people liberty to talk
And descant on his vices.
FLAMINEO   Misery of princes,
That must of force be censured by their slaves!   200
Not only blamed for doing things are ill,
But for not doing all that all men will.
One were better be a thresher.
Ud's death, I would fain speak with this Duke yet.
[FRANCISCO]
Now he's dead?   205
FLAMINEO
I cannot conjure, but if prayers or oaths
Will get to th'speech of him, though forty devils
Wait on him in his livery of flames,
I'll speak to him and shake him by the hand,
Though I be blasted.   *Exit*
FRANCISCO   Excellent Lodovico!   210
What? Did you terrify him at the last gasp?
LODOVICO
Yes; and so idly, that the Duke had like
T'have terrified us.
FRANCISCO   How?

Enter [ZANCHE] *the Moor*

LODOVICO   You shall hear that hereafter.
See! Yon's the infernal that would make up sport.
Now to the revelation of that secret   215
She promised when she fell in love with you.

---

199 *descant* comment, enlarge
210 *blasted* stricken by supernatural agency
     s.d. *Exit* ed. (Exit Flamineo Q)
     s.d. ed. (to r. of l. 211 in Q)
     Lodovico, in his hooded Capuchins' robe, has been a silent witness to the preceding
     dialogue; his presence on the stage is a constant visual reminder of Francisco's
     hypocrisy.
214 *infernal* Zanche is considered devilish because she is black (the s.p. 'Moor' draws
     attention to her colour); Francisco, here in blackface as Mulinassar, may exemplify
     the proverb 'The white devil is worse than the black' (Tilley D310).
     make up sport make our fun complete

[FRANCISCO]

    You're passionately met in this sad world.

[ZANCHE]

    I would have you look up, sir; these court tears

    Claim not your tribute to them. Let those weep

    That guiltily partake in the sad cause.   220

    I knew last night by a sad dream I had

    Some mischief would ensue, yet to say truth

    My dream most concerned you.

LODOVICO   Shall's fall a-dreaming?

FRANCISCO

    Yes, and for fashion sake I'll dream with her.

[ZANCHE]

    Methought, sir, you came stealing to my bed.   225

FRANCISCO

    Wilt thou believe me sweeting? By this light

    I was a-dreamt on thee too, for methought

    I saw thee naked.

[ZANCHE]   Fie, sir! As I told you,

    Methought you lay down by me.

FRANCISCO   So dreamt I,

    And lest thou shouldst take cold, I covered thee   230

    With this Irish mantle.

[ZANCHE]   Verily I did dream

    You were somewhat bold with me; but to come to't.

LODOVICO

    How? How? I hope you will not go to't here.

FRANCISCO

    Nay, you must hear my dream out.

[ZANCHE]   Well, sir, forth.

FRANCISCO

    When I threw the mantle o'er thee, thou didst laugh   235

    Exceedingly methought.

[ZANCHE]   Laugh?

218–64 s.p. ZANCHE ed. (MOO or MOORE. Q)

221–68 This scene both illustrates visually Flamineo's words about the Machiavellian (here,
      Francisco) who 'tickles you to death' (1.198) and clearly recalls I.ii.228ff., where two
      lovers embrace and Vittoria recounts her dream, which is to lead to murder.

    231 Irish mantle blanket worn by rustic Irish in all weathers as the only covering over
        their naked bodies

FRANCISCO   And cried'st out,
   The hair did tickle thee.
[ZANCHE]   There was a dream indeed.
LODOVICO
   Mark her, I prithee: she simpers like the suds
   A collier hath been washed in.
[ZANCHE]
   Come, sir; good fortune tends you; I did tell you   240
   I would reveal a secret – Isabella
   The Duke of Florence' sister was empoisoned
   By a fumed picture and Camillo's neck
   Was broke by damned Flamineo, the mischance
   Laid on a vaulting-horse.
FRANCISCO   Most strange!
[ZANCHE]   Most true.   245
LODOVICO
   The bed of snakes is broke.
[ZANCHE]
   I sadly do confess I had a hand
   In the black deed.
FRANCISCO   Thou kept'st their counsel.
[ZANCHE]   Right.
   For which, urged with contrition, I intend
   This night to rob Vittoria.
LODOVICO   Excellent penitence!   250
   Usurers dream on't while they sleep out sermons.
[ZANCHE]
   To further our escape, I have entreated
   Leave to retire me, till the funeral,
   Unto a friend i'th'country. That excuse
   Will further our escape. In coin and jewels   255
   I shall, at least, make good unto your use
   An hundred thousand crowns.
FRANCISCO   O noble wench!

238   *simpers* with a play on 'simmers'
239   *collier* coal-carrier or coal-miner (blackened by coal dust, which would then appear in the soap suds)
243   *fumed* perfumed
245–6 ed. (Laid . . . strange!/MOO. Most . . . broke. Q)
246   *bed . . . broke* literally, the intertwined nest of snakes is untangled; figuratively, the mystery is revealed

LODOVICO
    Those crowns we'll share.
[ZANCHE]   It is a dowry,
    Methinks, should make that sunburnt proverb false,
    'And wash the Ethiop white'.
FRANCISCO   It shall, away–   260
[ZANCHE]
    Be ready for our flight.
FRANCISCO   An hour 'fore day.

                              Exit [ZANCHE] *the Moor*
    O strange discovery! Why till now we knew not
    The circumstance of either of their deaths.

                Enter [ZANCHE *the*] *Moor*

[ZANCHE]
    You'll wait about midnight in the chapel.
FRANCISCO   There.
                        [*Exit* ZANCHE]

LODOVICO
    Why, now our action's justified.
FRANCISCO   Tush for justice.   265
    What harms it justice? We now, like the partridge,
    Purge the disease with laurel, for the fame
    Shall crown the enterprise and quit the shame.

                                Exeunt

259–60 *sunburnt . . . white* The proverb is based on Jeremiah 13:23: 'Can the Ethiopian
       change his skin, or the leopard his spots?'
   261 s.d. ed. (to r. of l. 262 in Q). Zanche's exit and immediate re-entry realistically
       suggest her anxious over-insistence, as well as the precarious position of the villains
       in Brachiano's court (cf. l. 167).
   264 *You'll . . . There* ed. (You'le . . . midnight/In . . . There. Q)
266–8 *like . . . shame* According to Pliny, partridges purged themselves by eating laurel (or
       bay leaves), also a symbol of fame; Francisco declares that they will rid their crimes
       of any taint by the glory they will achieve.
   268 *quit* clear, pay off

[ACT V, SCENE iv]

Enter FLAM[INEO] *and* GASP[ARO] *at one door, another*
way GIOVANNI *attended*

GASPARO

The young Duke. Did you e'er see a sweeter prince?

FLAMINEO

I have known a poor woman's bastard better favoured. This is
behind him. Now to his face – all comparisons were hateful.
Wise was the courtly peacock, that being a great minion and
being compared for beauty, by some dottrels that stood by, to   5
the kingly eagle, said the eagle was a far fairer bird than herself,
not in respect of her feathers, but in respect of her long tallants.
His will grow out in time – [*to* GIOVANNI] My gracious lord.

GIOVANNI

I pray leave me, sir.

FLAMINEO

Your Grace must be merry: 'tis I have cause to mourn, for wot   10
you what said the little boy that rode behind his father on
horseback?

GIOVANNI

Why, what said he?

FLAMINEO

'When you are dead, father' (said he) 'I hope then I shall ride
in the saddle.' O, 'tis a brave thing for a man to sit by himself: 15
he may stretch himself in the stirrups, look about, and see the
whole compass of the hemisphere. You're now, my lord,
i'th'saddle.

GIOVANNI

Study your prayers, sir, and be penitent.
'Twere fit you'd think on what hath former bin,   20
I have heard grief named the eldest child of sin.

Exit [*with others*]

---

5   *dottrels* a variety of plover, supposed to be easy game because of their stupidity;
    term often applied to simpletons

7   *tallants* talons (with a possible pun on 'talents', natural disposition or abilities, as in
    Love's Labour's Lost IV.ii.63–4)

21 *grief . . . sin* Cf. cardinal in *The Duchess of Malfi* (V.v.53–4): 'I suffer now for what
    hath former bin/*Sorrow is held the eldest child of sin*'. s.d. *Exit* [*with others*] ed. (Exit
    Giou. Q)

FLAMINEO

Study my prayers? He threatens me divinely. I am falling to
pieces already – I care not, though, like Anacharsis, I were
pounded to death in a mortar. And yet that death were fitter for
usurers' gold and themselves to be beaten together to make a   25
most cordial cullis for the devil.
He hath his uncle's villainous look already,
In *decimo-sexto*.

Enter COURTIER

Now, sir, what are you?

COURTIER

It is the pleasure, sir, of the young Duke
That you forbear the presence, and all rooms   30
That owe him reverence.

FLAMINEO

So, the wolf and the raven are very pretty fools when they are
young. Is it your office, sir, to keep me out?

COURTIER

So the Duke wills.

FLAMINEO

Verily, master courtier, extremity is not to be used in all offices. 35
Say that a gentlewoman were taken out of her bed about
midnight and committed to Castle Angelo, to the tower yonder,
with nothing about her but her smock. Would it not show a

23 *Anacharsis* Scythian philosopher noted for his wisdom, actually killed by his
    brother with an arrow. Webster's source confuses him with Anaxarchus, pounded
    to death in a mortar with iron pestles because he challenged the authority of
    Nicocreon, tyrant of Cyprus. Anaxarchus was famous for jesting at death.
25–6 *usurers' . . . devil* A cullis, or fortifying broth, could be made by simmering together
    bruised chicken bones and pieces of gold (supposed to have medicinal value).
28 *decimo-sexto* a very small book, in which a page is one-sixteenth of a full sheet; a
    diminutive person
    s.d. ed. (to r. of l. 27 in Q)
30 *presence* presence-chamber
37 *Castle Angelo* i.e. the Castel Sant'Angelo at Rome, in which the real-life Vittoria was
    imprisoned
    tower yonder The Red Bull audience would doubtless have understood by this the
    Tower of London, where King James had recently imprisoned Arbella Stuart, his
    cousin, for marrying for love without royal permission.

cruel part in the gentleman porter to lay claim to her upper
garment, pull it o'er her head and ears, and put her in naked?   40
COURTIER
Very good: you are merry.   [*Exit*]
FLAMINEO
Doth he make a court ejectment of me? A flaming firebrand
casts more smoke without a chimney than within't. I'll smoor
some of them.

Enter [FRANCISCO, *Duke of*] *Florence*
[*disguised as* MULINASSAR]

How now? Thou art sad.   45
FRANCISCO
I met even now with the most piteous sight.
FLAMINEO
Thou met'st another here, a pitiful
Degraded courtier.
FRANCISCO   Your reverend mother
Is grown a very old woman in two hours.
I found them winding of Marcello's corse,   50
And there is such a solemn melody
'Tween doleful songs, tears, and sad elegies,
Such as old grandames watching by the dead
Were wont t'outwear the nights with, that believe me
I had no eyes to guide me forth the room,   55
They were so o'ercharged with water.
FLAMINEO   I will see them.
FRANCISCO
'Twere much uncharity in you, for your sight
Will add unto their tears.
FLAMINEO   I will see them.

---

42 *flaming firebrand* a piece of wood kindled at the fire; one who kindles strife or
    mischief; one who deserves to burn in hell. Flamineo is playing on his own name.
43 *smoor* smother, suffocate
50 *winding of . . . corse* wrapping Marcello's corpse in a shroud or winding-sheet (the
    face was usually left uncovered)
53–4 *old . . . with* The practice of watching all night over the deceased, with candles
    burning, was increasingly disappearing in seventeenth-century England, but
    persisted in rural Ireland until the twentieth century.

FRANCISCO
   They are behind the traverse. I'll discover
   Their superstitious howling.   [*Draws the traverse*]   60

   CORNELIA, [ZANCHE] *the Moor and three other Ladies*
         discovered, winding MARCELLO's *corse. A song*

CORNELIA
   This rosemary is withered, pray get fresh:
   I would have these herbs grow up in his grave
   When I am dead and rotten. Reach the bays;
   I'll tie a garland here about his head:
   'Twill keep my boy from lightning. This sheet   65
   I have kept this twenty year, and every day
   Hallowed it with my prayers – I did not think
   He should have wore it.
[ZANCHE] [*Seeing* FLAMINEO] Look you; who are yonder?
CORNELIA
   O, reach me the flowers.
[ZANCHE]
   Her ladyship's foolish.
WOMAN   Alas! Her grief   70
   Hath turned her child again.
CORNELIA (*To* FLAMINEO)   You're very welcome.
   There's rosemary for you and rue for you,
   Heart's-ease for you. I pray make much of it.
   I have left more for myself.

   59   *traverse* a curtain at the rear of the stage. The tableau thus discovered has almost
        emblematic visual significance (recalling, perhaps, as at *King Lear* V.iii.257 s.d., the
        pieta); it is held in place during the 'song'.
   61   *rosemary* evergreen herb, symbol of immortality and remembrance, customary at
        weddings and funerals
 63–5   *bays . . . lightning* Laurel wreaths were both tokens of fame and glory, and reputed
        to protect one from lightning.
   65   *sheet* i.e. winding sheet
68–76   s.p. ZANCHE ed. (MOO. Q)
 72–4   Cornelia may distribute real flowers, or be sufficiently unhinged to use imaginary
        ones (NCW IV.iv.60 ff. n.).
   71   s.d. ed. (to r. of l. 72 in Q)
 72–3   *rue . . . Heart's-ease* Rue, a perennial evergreen shrub, symbolized sorrow, repen-
        tance or compassion; the heart's-ease, or pansy, represented tranquillity.
 72–4   *There's . . . myself* an obvious echo of Ophelia in *Hamlet* IV.v.175 ff.: 'There's rose-
        mary, that's for remembrance; pray you, love, remember. And there is pansies, that's
        for thoughts . . . There's rue for you, and here's some for me.'

145

FRANCISCO   Lady, who's this?

CORNELIA

[*To* FLAMINEO] You are, I take it, the grave-maker.

FLAMINEO   So.   75

[ZANCHE]

'Tis Flamineo.

CORNELIA

Will you make me such a fool? [*Takes his hand*] Here's a white
   hand:
Can blood so soon be washed out? Let me see:
When screech-owls croak upon the chimney tops
And the strange cricket i'th'oven sings and hops,   80
When yellow spots do on your hands appear,
Be certain then you of a corse shall hear.
Out upon't, how 'tis speckled! H'as handled a toad sure.
Cowslip-water is good for the memory: pray buy me three
   ounces of't.

FLAMINEO

I would I were from hence.

CORNELIA   Do you hear, sir?   85

I'll give you a saying which my grandmother
Was wont, when she heard the bell toll, to sing o'er
Unto her lute–

---

75   *grave-maker* grave-digger. In this case, Flamineo, as Marcello's murderer, is literally
      his 'grave-maker'.

77–8 *Here's . . . out?* Cf. Lady Macbeth in *Macbeth* V.i.43: 'What, will these hands ne'er be
      clean?'

79–82 *When . . . hear* In popular superstition, these were all signs that a death was imminent.

83   *how . . . speckled* Thomas Adams, author of *The White Devil or the Hypocrite
      Uncas'd* (1612), a sermon, praises his patron for being 'free from the aspersion of
      these speckled stains' – the sins which he is about to expose.

84   *Cowslip-water* medicinal extract from the cowslip flower, reputed to be good for the
      head and sinews

84–5 ed. (Couslep . . . oun/ces . . . sir? Q)

87–8 ed. (Was . . . lute/Doe . . . doe. Q)

88   *lute* Ophelia is playing on the lute when she enters in a distracted state in Q1 of
      Hamlet IV.v.20; perhaps Cornelia has one too.
      s.d. ed. (to r. of ll. 91–3 in Q). The gestures of madness called for by the stage direc-
      tion are in tension with the elegiac, melodic strain of the dirge itself; the discordant
      effect is appropriate to the play's increasing fragmentation and despair.

FLAMINEO   Do, and you will, do.

CORNELIA *doth this in several forms of distraction*

CORNELIA
  'Call for the robin-red-breast and the wren,
  Since o'er shady groves they hover,   90
  And with leaves and flow'rs do cover
  The friendless bodies of unburied men.
  Call unto his funeral dole
  The ant, the field-mouse, and the mole
  To rear him hillocks that shall keep him warm   95
  And (when gay tombs are robbed) sustain no harm,
  But keep the wolf far thence that's foe to men,
  For with his nails he'll dig them up again.'
  They would not bury him 'cause he died in a quarrel
  But I have an answer for them.   100
  'Let holy church receive him duly
  Since he paid the church tithes truly.'
  His wealth is summed, and this is all his store:
  This poor men get and great men get no more.
  Now the wares are gone, we may shut up shop.   105
  Bless you all good people.
               Exeunt CORNELIA [, ZANCHE] *and Ladies*

FLAMINEO
  I have a strange thing in me, to th'which
  I cannot give a name, without it be
  Compassion. I pray leave me.
                      Exit FRANCISCO

---

91   *robin-red-breast . . . wren* allusion to the widespread belief that robins (and wrens, believed to be female robins) covered up and tended dead bodies
93   *dole* rites of funeral
97–8 *keep . . . again* According to popular superstition, the wolf was a minister of God's revenge, sent to dig up the corpses of those who had been murdered; cf. *The Duchess of Malfi* IV.ii.303–5: 'The wolf shall find her grave, and scrape it up;/Not to devour the corpse, but to discover/The horrid murther'.
103 *summed* reckoned *this . . . store* Cornelia may indicate the area of the stage on which Marcello lies or the winding sheet itself.
105 *shut . . . shop* Having perhaps retreated into the discovery space to sing her dirge (after talking to Flamineo), Cornelia now closes the curtains.
109 Flamineo's request that Francisco leave the stage is visual confirmation of his new interiority.

This night I'll know the utmost of my fate:	110
I'll be resolved what my rich sister means
T'assign me for my service. I have lived
Riotously ill, like some that live in court;
And sometimes, when my face was full of smiles
Have felt the maze of conscience in my breast.	115
Oft gay and honoured robes those tortures try:
'We think caged birds sing, when indeed they cry'.

Enter BRACHIA[NO's] *Ghost. In his leather cassock and breeches,*
boots, a cowl [and in his hand] a pot of lily-flowers with a
skull in't

Ha! I can stand thee. [*The Ghost approaches*] Nearer, nearer yet.
What a mockery hath death made of thee? Thou look'st sad.
In what place art thou? In yon starry gallery	120
Or in the cursed dungeon? No? Not speak?
Pray, sir, resolve me, what religion's best
For a man to die in? Or is it in your knowledge
To answer me how long I have to live?
That's the most necessary question.	125
Not answer? Are you still like some great men

---

115 *maze* labyrinth; state of confusion
116 i.e. often those who wear gay and honoured robes (i.e. courtiers) experience those tortures
117 s.d. ed. (to r. of ll. 118–24 in Q). This spectacular vision fulfils Flamineo's earlier vow to shake Brachiano 'by the hand' (V.iii.209), and confirms his private vision of the truth underlying appearances. It is highly emblematic: the lily symbolizes that which is fair in show but foul in smell, beneath which is buried the horrible symbol of mortality, the skull (revealed at 1. 128).
   s.d.1 *leather cassock* A cassock was a long coat or cloak worn by soldiers; a leather cassock was worn by ghosts in tragedies.
   s.d.2 *cowl* monastic hood or robe. In Renaissance Italy, men were commonly buried in the habit of a Franciscan friar, in the hope that it would procure a remission of their sins.
118 *stand thee* Flamineo's defiance of Brachiano here recalls IV.ii.48–9.
119 *mockery* counterfeit, shadow; object of ridicule
120–1 *starry . . . dungeon* probably theatrical terms: the gallery or upper stage; the dungeon or the area below the stage, accessible by trapdoor, from which, in other plays, devils ascended
121, 126 The ghost's silence and ominous gestures are a powerful contrast (and perhaps rebuke) to Flamineo's rapid and desperate speech (cf. ghost in *Hamlet* I.i.50, whose silence suggests that 'it is offended').

That only walk like shadows up and down
And to no purpose? Say—

The Ghost throws earth upon him and shows him the skull

What's that? O fatal! He throws earth upon me.
A dead man's skull beneath the roots of flowers.   130
I pray speak, sir. Our Italian churchmen
Make us believe dead men hold conference
With their familiars, and many times
Will come to bed to them and eat with them.
                                                            Exit Ghost
He's gone; and see, the skull and earth are vanished.   135
This is beyond melancholy. I do dare my fate
To do its worst. Now to my sister's lodging
And sum up all these horrors: the disgrace
The Prince threw on me; next the piteous sight
Of my dead brother; and my mother's dotage;   140
And last this terrible vision. All these
Shall with Vittoria's bounty turn to good,
Or I will drown this weapon in her blood.   *Exit*

[ACT V, SCENE v]

Enter FRANCISCO, LODOVICO, *and* HORTENSIO
[*overhearing them*]

LODOVICO
My lord upon my soul you shall no further:
You have most ridiculously engaged yourself
Too far already. For my part, I have paid
All my debts, so if I should chance to fall

127 *shadows* insubstantial persons
128 s.d. ed. (to r. of ll. 130–4 in Q)
136 *This . . . melancholy* i.e. this ghost is more than a figment of imagination (unlike
Isabella's ghost in IV.i.100, which Francisco believes is produced by his melancholy). According to contemporary theories, beyond melancholy lay spiritual
despair (NCW V.iv.136 n.).
143 *this weapon* Flamineo rushes off the stage waving, probably, a poniard.

My creditors fall not with me; and I vow   5
To quite all in this bold assembly
To the meanest follower. My lord, leave the city
Or I'll forswear the murder.
FRANCISCO   Farewell Lodovico.
If thou dost perish in this glorious act,
I'll rear unto thy memory that fame   10
Shall in the ashes keep alive thy name.
                        [*Exeunt* FRANCISCO *and* LODOVICO]
HORTENSIO
There's some black deed on foot. I'll presently
Down to the citadel and raise some force.
These strong court factions that do brook no checks
In the career oft break the riders' necks.   [*Exit*]   15

[ACT V, SCENE vi]

Enter VITTORIA *with a book in her hand,* ZANCHE; FLAMINEO
following them

FLAMINEO
What, are you at your prayers? Give o'er.
VITTORIA   How ruffin?
FLAMINEO
I come to you 'bout worldly business:
Sit down, sit down. Nay stay, blouze, you may hear it,
The doors are fast enough.

   6   *quite* repay, requite
  11   s.d. Lodovico and Francisco probably enter through the same door (while
       Hortensio enters through the other); here, they exit through opposite doors, having
       said their farewells. The staging thus anticipates the fracturing of the villains' plot.
  12   *presently* immediately
  15   *career* short gallop at full speed; charge in tournament or battle *oft* ed. (of't Q)

   0   s.d. ed. (to 1. of ll. 1–6 in Q). Flamineo's first line indicates that the 'book' is devotional
       (perhaps a bible). One of Webster's sources claims that the murderers 'stabbed her
       where they found her at prayer'. On the stage, the reading of a book was a conven-
       tional sign of melancholy or guilt (cf. *The Duchess of Malfi* V.v.0 s.d.). Flamineo
       probably brandishes his poniard threateningly here, or otherwise menaces the women.
   1   *ruffin* devil
   3   *stay . . . it* Flamineo's words suggest that Zanche attempts to flee, a gesture of open
       rejection from his former 'sweet mistress' (V.i.143), and yet another rebuff in a series.
       blouze fat, red-faced wench (here ironic)

VITTORIA	Ha, are you drunk?	

FLAMINEO

Yes, yes, with wormwood water – you shall taste   5
Some of it presently.

VITTORIA   What intends the fury?

FLAMINEO

You are my lord's executrix and I claim
Reward for my long service.

VITTORIA   For your service?

FLAMINEO

Come therefore, here is pen and ink, set down
What you will give me.   10

                                  She writes

VITTORIA

There.

FLAMINEO Ha! Have you done already?
'Tis a most short conveyance.

VITTORIA   I will read it.

[*Reads*] 'I give that portion to thee and no other
Which Cain groaned under having slain his brother.'

FLAMINEO

A most courtly patent to beg by.

VITTORIA   You are a villain.   15

FLAMINEO

Is't come to this? They say affrights cure agues.
Thou hast a devil in thee: I will try
If I can scare him from thee. Nay, sit still:
My lord hath left me yet two case of jewels

---

5   *wormwood* plant with a bitter taste; emblem of what is bitter and grievous to the soul

6   *fury* Cf. I.ii.252, II.ii.244 and III.ii.278; normally used of an angry woman, here used ironically by Vittoria, perhaps turning Flamineo's description of Cornelia and general misogyny back on himself.

8   *service?* ed. (service Q)

10   s.d. ed. (outer margin, 1. of 1. 11 in Q)

11   *already?* ed. (already, Q)

13–14   *I . . . brother* Cf. Genesis 4:11–12: to Cain who slew his brother Abel, the Lord said: 'And now art thou cursed from the earth, which hath opened her mouth to receive thy brother's blood from thy hand; when thou tillest the ground, it shall not henceforth yield unto thee her strength; a fugitive and a vagabond shalt thou be in the earth'.

15   *courtly . . . by* Cf. V.i.108.

16   *They* ed. (the Q)

19   *case* pair (two pairs of pistols or four pistols: cf. ll. 92–5)

Shall make me scorn your bounty; you shall see them.   20

                                                        [*Exit*]

VITTORIA

Sure he's distracted.

ZANCHE   O he's desperate—

For your own safety give him gentle language.

He enters with two case of pistols

FLAMINEO

Look, these are better far at a dead lift

Than all your jewel house.

VITTORIA   And yet methinks

These stones have no fair lustre, they are ill set.   25

FLAMINEO

I'll turn the right side towards you: you shall see

How they will sparkle.

VITTORIA   Turn this horror from me!

What do you want? What would you have me do?

Is not all mine yours? Have I any children?

FLAMINEO

Pray thee good woman, do not trouble me   30

With this vain worldly business; say your prayers.

I made a vow to my deceased lord

Neither yourself nor I should outlive him

The numb'ring of four hours.

VITTORIA   Did he enjoin it?

FLAMINEO

He did, and 'twas a deadly jealousy   35

Lest any should enjoy thee after him

That urged him vow me to it. For my death,

I did propound it voluntarily, knowing

---

22   ed. (to r. of ll. 21–3 in Q)

23   *at . . . lift* in a sudden emergency (derived from pulling a heavy, or 'dead' weight),
     with an obvious play on 'dead'

27   *they* ed. (the Q)

31   *worldly* ed. (wordly Q)

35–7 A possible reference to King Herod, who ordered that his adored wife Mariam be
      killed upon his death; Lady Elizabeth Cary, the first woman playwright in England,
      dramatized the story from Mariam's point of view in *The Tragedy of Mariam, Fair
      Queen of Jewry*. Cary's play, published in 1613, circulated in manuscript, and may
      be Webster's source here.

If he could not be safe in his own court
Being a great Duke, what hope then for us?   40

VITTORIA

This is your melancholy and despair.

FLAMINEO   Away!

Fool thou art to think that politicians
Do use to kill the effects of injuries
And let the cause live. Shall we groan in irons
Or be a shameful and a weighty burden   45
To a public scaffold? This is my resolve:
I would not live at any man's entreaty
Nor die at any's bidding.

VITTORIA   Will you hear me?

FLAMINEO

My life hath done service to other men;
My death shall serve mine own turn. Make you ready.   50

VITTORIA

Do you mean to die indeed?

FLAMINEO   With as much pleasure
As e'er my father gat me.

VITTORIA [Aside to ZANCHE] Are the doors locked?

ZANCHE

Yes madam.

VITTORIA

Are you grown an atheist? Will you turn your body,
Which is the goodly palace of the soul,   55
To the soul's slaughter house? O the cursed devil,
Which doth present us with all other sins
Thrice candied o'er: despair with gall and stibium,
Yet we carouse it off – [Aside to ZANCHE] cry out for help–
Makes us forsake that which was made for man,   60

42   *Fool* ed. (Foole, Q)
47–8 *I . . . bidding* An echo of Vittoria's lines during her arraignment (III.ii.138–9): 'I
      scorn to hold my life/At yours or any man's entreaty, sir'.
54–5 *body . . . soul* Perhaps revealing her sensual nature, Vittoria inverts the usual image of
      the body as the soul's *prison* (cf. *The Duchess of Malfi* IV.ii.127–31: 'didst thou ever
      see a lark in a cage? such is the soul in the body: this world is like her little turf of
      grass, and the heaven o'er our heads, like her looking-glass, only gives us a miserable
      knowledge of the small compass of our prison'.)
58   *candied o'er* sugared over
58–9 *despair . . . off* i.e. despair (unlike other sins) is flavoured with gall (bile; venom)
      and stibium (the poison antimony), yet we drink it down (commit suicide)

The world, to sink to that was made for devils,
Eternal darkness.

ZANCHE   Help, help!

FLAMINEO   I'll stop your throat
With winter plums—

VITTORIA   I prithee yet remember
Millions are now in graves, which at last day
Like mandrakes shall rise shrieking.

FLAMINEO   Leave your prating,   65
For these are but grammatical laments,
Feminine arguments, and they move me
As some in pulpits move their auditory
More with their exclamation than sense
Of reason or sound doctrine.

ZANCHE [*Aside*]   Gentle madam   70
Seem to consent, only persuade him teach
The way to death; let him die first.

VITTORIA

[*Aside*] 'Tis good, I apprehend it.
[*Aloud*] To kill oneself is meat that we must take
Like pills, not chew't, but quickly swallow it—   75
The smart o'th'wound or weakness of the hand
May else bring treble torments.

FLAMINEO   I have held it.
A wretched and most miserable life,
Which is not able to die.

VITTORIA   O but frailty!
Yet I am now resolved: farewell, affliction!   80
Behold Brachiano, I, that while you lived
Did make a flaming altar of my heart
To sacrifice unto you, now am ready
To sacrifice heart and all. Farewell, Zanche.

62–3   *stop . . . plums* i.e. gag you with hard fruit (stop your mouth with bullets); so NCW
       V.vi.63–4 n.

   65   *mandrakes* Cf. III.i.49n.

66–7   *grammatical . . . arguments* i.e. laments composed according to formal rules, weak
       arguments

   69   *exclamation* formal declamation; emphatic speech

82–3   *flaming . . . you* A continental emblem book (Rollenhagen's *Nucleus Emblematum*,
       Cologne, 1611–13) shows a flaming heart on an altar as an image of sacrifice to
       God.

ZANCHE
    How, madam! Do you think that I'll outlive you?   85
    Especially when my best self Flamineo
    Goes the same voyage?
FLAMINEO   O most loved Moor!
ZANCHE
    Only by all my love let me entreat you:
    Since it is most necessary none of us
    Do violence on ourselves, let you or I   90
    Be her sad taster, teach her how to die.
FLAMINEO
    Thou dost instruct me nobly. Take these pistols,
    Because my hand is stained with blood already;
    Two of these you shall level at my breast,
    Th'other 'gainst your own, and so we'll die,   95
    Most equally contented. But first swear
    Not to outlive me.
VITTORIA *and* [ZANCHE] Most religiously.
FLAMINEO
    Then here's an end of me. Farewell daylight
    And O contemptible physic! That dost take
    So long a study only to preserve   100
    So short a life, I take my leave of thee.
    These are two cupping-glasses that shall draw
    All my infected blood out–
    Are you ready?
VITTORIA *and* ZANCHE Ready.   *Showing the pistols*
FLAMINEO
    Whither shall I go now? O Lucian thy ridiculous purgatory!   105

---

91   *taster* a servant whose duty it is to taste food and drink before they are served to his
        master, in order to ascertain their quality or detect poison
92–5 Flamineo offers each woman a case or pair of pistols; each of them points one at
        Flamineo, one at the other woman.
97   s.p. ed. (VIT. & MOO. Q)
102 *cupping-glasses* cup-shaped surgical vessels applied to the body, then heated to
        create a vacuum and thus draw off blood
104 s.d. ed. (to r. of ll. 102–3 in Q)
        VITTORIA and ZANCHE ed. (BOTH Q)
105 *Lucian . . . purgatory* Lucian's *Menippos* includes different examples of the ignomin-
        ious fates of great men, such as King Philip of Macedon cobbling shoes.
        purgatory! ed. (Purgatory Q)

To find Alexander the Great cobbling shoes, Pompey tagging
points, and Julius Caesar making hair buttons, Hannibal selling
blacking, and Augustus crying garlic, Charlemagne selling lists
by the dozen, and King Pippin crying apples in a cart drawn
with one horse.   110
Whether I resolve to fire, earth, water, air,
Or all the elements by scruples, I know not
Nor greatly care – Shoot, shoot,
Of all deaths the violent death is best,
For from ourselves it steals ourselves so fast   115
The pain once apprehended is quite past.

They shoot and run to him and tread upon him

VITTORIA

What, are you dropped?

FLAMINEO

I am mixed with earth already: as you are noble
Perform your vows and bravely follow me.

VITTORIA

Whither – to hell?

ZANCHE   To most assured damnation.   120

VITTORIA

O, thou most cursed devil.

ZANCHE   Thou art caught–

VITTORIA

In thine own engine. I tread the fire out
That would have been my ruin.

---

106 *Alexander ... shoes* Cf. Hamlet's different musing on the fate of Alexander
     (V.i.203–4): 'Why may not imagination trace the noble dust of Alexander, till 'a
     find it stopping a bunghole?'
106–7 *tagging points* fixing metal tags on the laces or points which held together
       Elizabethan clothing
107–10 *Julius ... horse* Flamineo increases the absurdity of his examples by giving them
        wittily appropriate activities: bald Caesar makes hair buttons, black Hannibal sells
        black polish, King Pippin (also a variety of apple) calls out the price of his apples,
        etc. (Dent, p. 165).
108 *lists* strips of cloth
112 *by scruples* by small degrees or portions
116 s.d. ed. (to r. of ll. 115–18 in Q)
120 ed. (Whither to hell, Q)
122 *engine* device

FLAMINEO

Will you be perjured? What a religious oath was Styx that the
gods never durst swear by and violate? O that we had such an   125
oath to minister, and to be so well kept in our courts of justice.

VITTORIA

Think whither thou art going.

ZANCHE   And remember
What villanies thou hast acted.

VITTORIA   This thy death
Shall make me like a blazing ominous star—
Look up and tremble.

FLAMINEO   O I am caught with a springe!   130

VITTORIA

You see the fox comes many times short home,
'Tis here proved true.

FLAMINEO   Killed with a couple of braches.

VITTORIA

No fitter offering for the infernal Furies
Than one in whom they reigned while he was living.

FLAMINEO

O, the way's dark and horrid! I cannot see—   135
Shall I have no company?

VITTORIA   O yes, thy sins
Do run before thee to fetch fire from hell
To light thee thither.

FLAMINEO   O I smell soot,
Most stinking soot, the chimney is a-fire—

---

124   *Styx* in Greek myth, a river in the underworld. The gods swore their oaths upon its
        honoured waters (*Iliad* XV, 36 ff.).
127   *Think . . . remember* ed. (Iustice . . . remeber Q)
129   *blazing . . . star* an ominous prodigy foreshadowing the fall of princes (cf. the
        'rough-bearded comet' of V.iii.31). Using light imagery (cf. the 'diamonds' of
        III.ii.294), Vittoria prophesies her own triumphant revenge.
130   *springe* snare for trapping small game and birds
131   *fox . . . home* i.e. even the cunning fox can come home without his tail (i.e. dead)
132   *with . . . braches* i.e. by a couple of bitches
133   *Furies* Cf. IV.iii.125, 151, where first Lodovico, then Monticelso, is supposed to be
        inhabited by the Furies.
138–9 *O . . . a-fire* ed. (one line in Q)
139   *stinking* ed. (sinking Q)
        chimney is ed. (chimneis Q)

My liver's parboiled like Scotch holy-bread;   140
There's a plumber laying pipes in my guts, it scalds;
Wilt thou outlive me?
ZANCHE   Yes, and drive a stake
Through thy body; for we'll give it out
Thou didst this violence upon thyself.
FLAMINEO
O cunning devils! Now I have tried your love   145
And doubled all your reaches.

Riseth

I am not wounded:
The pistols held no bullets: 'twas a plot
To prove your kindness to me and I live
To punish your ingratitude. I knew
One time or other you would find a way   150
To give me a strong potion. O men
That lie upon your death-beds and are haunted
With howling wives, ne'er trust them – they'll remarry
Ere the worm pierce your winding sheet, ere the spider
Make a thin curtain for your epitaphs.   155
How cunning you were to discharge! Do you practise at the
Artillery Yard? Trust a woman? Never, never. Brachiano be my
precedent: we lay our souls to pawn to the devil for a little
pleasure and a woman makes the bill of sale. That ever man

---

140   *liver* seat of the passions
       Scotch holy-bread according to Cotgrave's *Dictionarie of the French and English
       Tongues* (1611), a sodden sheep's liver
142–3 *drive . . . body* traditional treatment of suicides, who were then buried at crossroads
146   *doubled . . . reaches* i.e. matched your plots or contrivances
146   s.d. ed. (to r. of ll. 146–7 in Q)
       s.d. *Riseth* ed. (Flamineo riseth Q)
147   A metatheatrical joke; as Flamineo rises, Webster makes his audience (which has
       shared the women's illusions) conscious of the reality of the theatre, in which death
       is always feigned.
151–3 *men . . . wives* possibly a deliberate allusion to Brachiano's cry at V.iii. 37–8: 'How
       miserable a thing it is to die / 'Mongst women howling!'
157   *Artillery Yard* In 1610 the weekly exercise of arms and military discipline for citi-
       zens and merchants was revived in the Artillery Gardens at Bishopsgate.
158   *precedent* ed. (president Q)

should marry! For one Hypermnestra that saved her lord and   160
husband, forty-nine of her sisters cut their husbands' throats all
in one night. There was a shoal of virtuous horse-leeches.
Here are two other instruments.

Enter LOD[OVICO], GASP[ARO, *disguised*], PEDRO, CARLO

VITTORIA   Help, help!
FLAMINEO
What noise is that? Hah? False keys i'th'court!
LODOVICO
We have brought you a masque.
FLAMINEO   A matachin it seems   165
By your drawn swords. Churchmen turned revellers.
CONSPIRATORS
Isabella, Isabella!
                        [*They throw off their disguises*]
LODOVICO
Do you know us now?
FLAMINEO   Lodovico and Gasparo.
LODOVICO
Yes, and that Moor the Duke gave pension to
Was the great Duke of Florence.

160–2 *For ... night* Hypermnestra's father, Danaus, was warned by an oracle that he
would be killed by one of his brother's sons. He then persuaded his fifty daughters
to marry his brother's fifty sons, and instructed them to murder their husbands
on the wedding night. Only Hypermnestra disobeyed her father and spared her
husband.
162 *horse-leeches* bloodsuckers; double-tongued rhetoricians (cf. III.ii.281)
163 *two ... instruments* i.e. two more weapons (perhaps poniard and sword, with
which he may have intended to attack Vittoria and Zanche) probably wrested from
his grasp by the four assassins. Alternatively, this could be a contemptuous reference to Vittoria and Zanche as 'instruments' of death like Hypermnestra's sisters.
Help, help! Vittoria may be appealing to the masked conspirators to save her from
Flamineo (NCW V.vi.163–4 n.).
165 *masque* ritualistic dance of masked revellers, who invited those already present to
participate; often used by Jacobean dramatists as a means to bring on disguised
conspirators for a final massacre, to which the formality of the masque offers a
striking contrast (cf. *The Revenger's Tragedy* V.iii) *matachin* sword-dance in masks
and fantastic costumes
166–7 ed. (By ... swords./Church-men ... Isabella, Q)

VITTORIA   O we are lost.   170
FLAMINEO

You shall not take justice from forth my hands—
O let me kill her! I'll cut my safety
Through your coats of steel. Fate's a spaniel,
We cannot beat it from us: what remains now?
Let all that do ill take this precedent: 175
'Man may his fate foresee, but not prevent'.
And of all axioms this shall win the prize:
' 'Tis better to be fortunate than wise'.

GASPARO

Bind him to the pillar.

VITTORIA   O your gentle pity!
I have seen a blackbird that would sooner fly   180
To a man's bosom, than to stay the gripe
Of the fierce sparrow-hawk.

GASPARO   Your hope deceives you.

VITTORIA

If Florence be i'th'court, would he would kill me.

GASPARO

Fool! Princes give rewards with their own hands,
But death or punishment by the hands of others.   185

LODOVICO

Sirrah you once did strike me – I'll strike you
Into the centre.

FLAMINEO

Thou'lt do it like a hangman, a base hangman,
Not like a noble fellow, for thou seest
I cannot strike again.

LODOVICO   Dost laugh?   190

FLAMINEO

Wouldst have me die, as I was born, in whining?

173–4 *Fate's . . . us* Webster probably borrows this phrase from Nashe's *Lenten Stuffe*
       (1599), which explains: 'the more you thinke to crosse it, the more you blesse and
       further it'. Spaniels were reputed to fawn on those who beat them.
  175 *precedent* ed. (president Q)
  179 *Bind . . . pillar* either a freestanding stage post or one of the two pillars supporting
       the heavens
  181 *stay* wait for
  187 *centre* i.e. heart or soul
  188 *hangman* executioner

GASPARO
    Recommend yourself to heaven.
FLAMINEO
    No, I will carry mine own commendations thither.
LODOVICO
    O, could I kill you forty times a day
    And use't four year together 'twere too little: 195
    Nought grieves but that you are too few to feed
    The famine of our vengeance. What dost think on?
FLAMINEO
    Nothing, of nothing: leave thy idle questions;
    I am i'th'way to study a long silence.
    To prate were idle – I remember nothing.   200
    There's nothing of so infinite vexation
    As man's own thoughts.
LODOVICO   O thou glorious strumpet,
    Could I divide thy breath from this pure air
    When't leaves thy body, I would suck it up
    And breathe't upon some dunghill.
VITTORIA   You, my death's-man;   205
    Methinks thou dost not look horrid enough,
    Thou hast too good a face to be a hangman;
    If thou be, do thy office in right form:
    Fall down upon thy knees and ask forgiveness.
LODOVICO
    O thou hast been a most prodigious comet   210
    But I'll cut off your train: kill the Moor first.
VITTORIA
    You shall not kill her first. Behold my breast.
    I will be waited on in death; my servant
    Shall never go before me.
GASPARO
    Are you so brave?

---

196   *grieves* ed. (greeu's Q)
198   *Nothing . . . nothing* This secular response is later echoed by the Duchess in *The Duchess of Malfi* before her death (IV.ii.16). *idle* foolish, useless
208–9 It was conventional for executioners to beg a perfunctory pardon before going to work: cf. *Measure for Measure* IV.ii.49–51: 'I do find your hangman is a more penitent trade than your bawd; he doth oft'ner ask forgiveness'.
211   *train* tail of a comet, with a pun on 'attendants' (Zanche)
215–17 ed. (Shall . . . brave. / Yes . . . death / As . . . weapon / halfe . . . tremble Q)

VITTORIA   Yes, I shall welcome death   215
As princes do some great ambassadors:
I'll meet thy weapon halfway.

LODOVICO   Thou dost tremble–
Methinks fear should dissolve thee into air.

VITTORIA
O thou art deceived, I am too true a woman:
Conceit can never kill me. I'll tell thee what–   220
I will not in my death shed one base tear,
Or if look pale, for want of blood, not fear.

CARLO
Thou art my task, black fury.

ZANCHE   I have blood
As red as either of theirs; wilt drink some?
'Tis good for the falling sickness: I am proud   225
Death cannot alter my complexion,
For I shall ne'er look pale.

LODOVICO   Strike, strike
With a joint motion.

[*They strike*]

VITTORIA   'Twas a manly blow.
The next thou giv'st, murder some sucking infant
And then thou wilt be famous.

FLAMINEO   O what blade is't?   230
A Toledo or an English fox?

---

220 *Conceit* idea or imaginative apprehension (of death); vanity or pride (proverbially feminine); physical conception of a child

221 An echo of Vittoria during the arraignment (III.ii.284–6): 'I will not weep, / No I do scorn to call up one poor tear / To fawn on your injustice'.

223–4 *I . . . theirs* Red blood was a sign of courage.

225 *falling sickness* epilepsy

227–8 *Strike . . . motion* This is group tragedy, as the three are stabbed simultaneously: Flamineo by Lodovico, Vittoria by Gasparo, and Zanche by Carlo.

228–30 In the 1991 National Theatre production, Josette Simon as Vittoria met Lodovico's dagger thrusts 'as though they represented a tempestuously flattering act of copulation', and completed the bitter self-parody with a 'cool pretence that she is congratulating him on his sexual prowess [which] ironically deflates his vengeful achievement' (Paul Taylor, *The Independent*, 20 June 1991).

231 *Toledo . . . fox* different types of short swords (the latter inscribed with a wolf, commonly mistaken for a fox)

I ever thought a cutler should distinguish
The cause of my death rather than a doctor.
Search my wound deeper: tent it with the steel
That made it.   235

VITTORIA

O my greatest sin lay in my blood.
Now my blood pays for't.

FLAMINEO   Th'art a noble sister—
I love thee now. If woman do breed man
She ought to teach him manhood: fare thee well.
Know many glorious women that are famed   240
For masculine virtue have been vicious
Only a happier silence did betide them.
She hath no faults, who hath the art to hide them.

VITTORIA

My soul, like to a ship in a black storm,
Is driven I know not whither.

FLAMINEO   Then cast anchor.   245
'Prosperity doth bewitch men seeming clear,
But seas do laugh, show white, when rocks are near.
We cease to grieve, cease to be Fortune's slaves,
Nay cease to die by dying.' [To ZANCHE] Art thou gone?
[To VITTORIA] And thou so near the bottom? False report   250
Which says that women vie with the nine Muses
For nine tough durable lives. I do not look

---

232 *cutler* one who deals in knives and cutting utensils
234 *tent* i.e. use a tent or plug to search or clean my wound; with a pun on tend, care for
       (with a possible reference to miraculous cures effected by wounds)
234–5 ed. (one line in Q)
236–7 *blood . . . blood* Cf. I.ii.274. Usually interpreted as conventional penitence, however
       uncharacteristic: 'My greatest sin lay in my sexual passion; now my life-blood pays
       for it'. (An actor, of course, could deliver even this meaning ironically.) However,
       the first 'blood' could also mean simply 'high temper, mettle', so Vittoria maintains
       her spirited self-defence; it could also mean 'kindred, family', so Vittoria targets
       Flamineo.
238, 240 *woman; women* (woemen Q) The unusual spelling here may just indicate a pun:
       woman as 'woe-to-man'.
245 *I . . . whither* Sinners proverbially died not knowing where they were going.
246–7 Webster's source (Alexander's *Croesus* I.i.65–73) clarifies this image: 'Vaine foole,
       that thinkes soliditie to find / . . . The fome is whitest, where the Rock is neare / . . .
       The greatest danger oft doth least appeare'.
250–2 *False . . . lives* Proverbially, nine lives are attributed to women and *cats*, not Muses.

Who went before, nor who shall follow me;
No, at myself I will begin and end:
'While we look up to heaven we confound   255
Knowledge with knowledge'. O, I am in a mist.

VITTORIA

O happy they that never saw the court,
'Nor ever knew great man but by report'.

Dies

FLAMINEO

I recover like a spent taper for a flash,
And instantly go out.   260
Let all that belong to great men remember th'old wives'
tradition, to be like the lions i'th'Tower on Candlemas day, to
mourn if the sun shine for fear of the pitiful remainder of
winter to come.
'Tis well yet there's some goodness in my death,   265
My life was a black charnel. I have caught
An everlasting cold. I have lost my voice
Most irrecoverably. Farewell, glorious villains.
'This busy trade of life appears most vain,
Since rest breeds rest where all seek pain by pain.'   270
Let no harsh flattering bells resound my knell,
Strike thunder and strike loud to my farewell.   *Dies*

ENGLISH AMBASSADOR

[*Within*] This way, this way, break ope the doors, this way.

---

258   s.d. *Dies* ed. (Vittoria dies Q)
261   *wives'* ed. (wides Q)
261–4   *Let . . . come* Proverbially, 'If Candlemas day [2 February] be fair and bright, winter
        will have another flight'. Like the lions (kept in a small zoo in the Tower), the
        courtier who anticipates gloomy weather even in bright sunshine 'will keepe him in
        such humilitie and lowlynesse as Princes like of' (Pettie II.211).
266–8   *I . . . irrecoverably* another metatheatrical joke, since an actor with a long part like
        Flamineo's might well be in danger of losing his voice at the end of the play
267   *trade* habitual course of action; passage to and fro; profession practised as a means
        of livelihood
272   *Strike thunder* a prodigious sign associated with the fall of great men (cf. *The
        Revenger's Tragedy* V.iii.44: 'Duke's groans are thunder's watchwords'); also, of
        course, a theatrical directive (or a reference to the offstage pounding of the doors
        by the ambassadors: NCW V.vi.270 n.)

LODOVICO
    Ha, are we betrayed?
    Why then let's constantly die all together,   275
    And having finished this most noble deed,
    Defy the worst of fate, not fear to bleed.

    Enter AMBASSAD[ORS] *and* GIOVANNI [GUARDS *follow*]

ENGLISH AMBASSADOR
    Keep back the Prince – shoot, shoot–

    [GUARDS *shoot at conspirators*]

LODOVICO   O I am wounded.
    I fear I shall be ta'en.
GIOVANNI   You bloody villains,
    By what authority have you committed   280
    This massacre?
LODOVICO   By thine.
GIOVANNI   Mine?
LODOVICO   Yes, thy uncle,
    Which is a part of thee, enjoined us to't.
    Thou know'st me I am sure, I am Count Lodowick,
    And thy most noble uncle in disguise
    Was last night in thy court.
GIOVANNI   Ha!
GASPARO   Yes, that Moor   285
    Thy father chose his pensioner.
GIOVANNI   He turned murderer!
    Away with them to prison and to torture.
    All that have hands in this shall taste our justice,
    As I hope heaven.

---

275   *constantly* resolutely
277   s.d. ed. (following 1. 273 in Q)
281   *This . . . uncle* ed. (This . . . Mine? / LOD. Yes, Q)
285–6 ed. (Was . . . Ha!/Yes, . . . pentioner. Q)

LODOVICO   I do glory yet
That I can call this act mine own: for my part,   290
The rack, the gallows, and the torturing wheel
Shall be but sound sleeps to me. Here's my rest—
'I limbed this night-piece and it was my best'.

GIOVANNI

Remove the bodies. See, my honoured lord,
What use you ought make of their punishment.   295
'Let guilty men remember their black deeds
Do lean on crutches, made of slender reeds.'

                                        [*Exeunt*]

Instead of an Epilogue only this of Martial supplies me:
Haec fuerint nobis praemia si placui.
For the action of the play, 'twas generally well, and I dare   300
affirm, with the joint testimony of some of their own quality
(for the true imitation of life, without striving to make nature a
monster), the best that ever became them: whereof as I make a
general acknowledgement, so in particular I must remember
the well approved industry of my friend Master Perkins, and   305
confess the worth of his action did crown both the beginning
and end.

FINIS

---

292 *rest* peace of mind; final resolution; remaining hope
293 *limbed* limned (painted, portrayed) with a possible pun on 'limbed' as 'pulled limb
     from limb, dismembered' (though the *OED* records the earliest use of this verb in
     1674)
     night-piece painting representing a night-scene; tragic composition (used later by
     Webster himself to describe his elegy upon the death of Prince Henry (*A
     Monumental Column*, dedication))
295 *ought make* i.e. ought to make
299 *Haec . . . placui* 'These things will be our reward, if I have pleased' (Martial II, xci, 8).
301 *quality* profession
305 *Master Perkins* Richard Perkins was the leading player of Queen Anne's Men, well
     known for both his experience and his versatility; he probably played the part of
     Flamineo.